The LIBERATION
of WINIFRED BRYAN HORNER

The LIBERATION *of* WINIFRED BRYAN HORNER

Writer, Teacher, and Women's Rights Advocate

As told to

ELAINE J. LAWLESS

INDIANA UNIVERSITY PRESS

This book is a publication of

Indiana University Press
Office of Scholarly Publishing
Herman B Wells Library 350
1320 East 10th Street
Bloomington, Indiana 47405 USA

iupress.indiana.edu

The paper used in this publication
meets the minimum requirements of
the American National Standard for
Information Sciences—Permanence
of Paper for Printed Library
Materials, ANSI Z39.48–1992.

Manufactured in the
United States of America

Cataloging information is available
from the Library of Congress.

ISBN 978-0-253-03234-8 (cloth)
ISBN 978-0-253-03235-5 (paperback)
ISBN 978-0-253-03236-2 (ebook)

1 2 3 4 5   22 21 20 19 18 17

For Win,
And for all who loved her—
We recognize her absence as her presence among us.

Win Horner on her ninetieth birthday, surrounded by three of her grandchildren: Alexandria Horner, Leela Grace, and Ellie Grace, August 2012. *Photograph by Ron Gurulé. Courtesy of the Win Horner family.*

Ninety Years

Little sister, only girl
Grew up strong to face this world
With the fire in your eyes
Would it come as a surprise
All the lives that you would change
In your ninety years?

Chorus:
Ninety years of a life on fire
Blazing trails, walking on a wire
Ninety years lived with love
Fighting hard to rise above
You've showed us how to really live
For ninety years

From Missouri to Michigan
Edinburgh and back again
And every spring in a Texas town
We saw your students gather round
And all the walls you've broken down
In your ninety years

River days and city nights
All in bed in the morning light
From Washington to London town
You've taken us this world around
All the stories written down
In your ninety years

Written by Winifred Bryan Horner's granddaughters Leela and Ellie
Grace and sung with great love in her honor, in celebration of her
ninetieth birthday on August 31, 2012. Also sung at "A Celebration of
Win's Life," March 29, 2014. © Leela and Ellie Grace, 2013. Used with
permission.

CONTENTS

Writing Win's Life

For months, I have been spending my days sifting through the stacks of Win Horner's folders and boxes. They moved into my study immediately after her death in early February 2014, and they continue to dominate the small space in my home. I feel her presence here. The room has become a kind of makeshift altar dedicated to her life, a littered space with stacks of her papers, photographs, articles she wrote, articles written about her, her obituary (which she wrote herself), scraps of notes scattered on every surface, including the floor. Mostly I know what is in each stack, and am sometimes reminded by the color of a binder or a folder. There are leaning towers of old newspaper articles, carbon copies of letters, stories about the farm, all weathered to a dull, brittle brown. I have to be careful or they will crumble if I handle them, or, horrors, the date might fall off. Folders hold her many files, notes, and calendars—along with tucked-in photos of her children, grandchildren, her husband Dave, his dogs, and the farm. Win documented her life in all its complexity, all its messiness. Some days I just sit on the floor surrounded by this material proof of Win's life and wonder at the task before me. I sneeze when I open the folders; my fingers are black from the carbons of the many, many pages she typed on her old manual typewriter; I try to sort through everything and make some sense of a life well-lived and thoroughly documented.

This book is not a memoir in the conventional sense of that term. Win Horner did not write this book. Rather, Win agreed to orally relate her life story and stories to me for me to record. When we first began our

work together specifically for this book in October 2013, she made an
outline she wanted to follow. She told me she wanted to include these
aspects of her life: her childhood in St. Louis and at Water Oaks (their
summer cabin on the Meramec River in southern Missouri), her schooling at Mary Institute and Washington University, her marriage, her life
with Dave when he was in the military during World War II, her time as
a teacher at the University of Missouri, her time at Michigan getting her
PhD, her time at Texas Christian University as an endowed chair, and, finally, her retirement and her return to Columbia to live with Dave again.

Somehow, when we began, and even when I had all the transcriptions
in front of me to study and think about, I still thought perhaps this would
be a kind of proxy memoir—that is, I would relate to the reader Win's life
story as she told it to me. Certainly, our conversations did follow a kind
of chronological path from her childhood through the various segments
of her life to her final return home. But this initial assessment of what I
had in my hands about Win Horner's life was but the bare skeleton of
what I would discover as I trolled through the boxes, read the brittle papers, studied her dissertation, read her articles and stories, listened to her
voice, and watched her beloved face and gestures on video. Three years
it has taken me to formulate some of the salient features of Win Horner's
life and her art—the art of writing.

Win Horner believed in writing the way some people believe in religion. She did not love writing as some people love God, nor did she see
writing as an icon of adoration. Win believed in the power of words and
the power of writing the way some people believe in the power of religion. In fact, Win was not above quoting scripture to make her argument
for the power of language—"In the beginning was the Word"—which
should remind us that those uttered words were transformed into things
and beings. She was happiest, most content, when she was working,
which for Win meant when she was writing, transforming words into stories—artful depictions of life.

Combing through all of the folders, files, and boxes that litter my
study, I have come to understand Win better now than I ever did when
she was living. Perhaps the most important fact I have uncovered is that
there wasn't a period in Win's life after the age of ten or twelve when she
was not consistently writing. She did not just *want* to be a writer; she *was*

a writer. The subject matter of her writing was her life and all the people who shared her life with her. Although her husband and children knew she had written a great deal, there are surprises in her boxes—stories they had never read, a humorous "novel" of her time following Dave in the military, an essay on suicide, another on the value and challenges of a strong marriage.

Remarkably, even as a child, Win thought of herself as a writer. Tucked away in her many treasured boxes, I found her early diaries written at Water Oaks when she was twelve. Her mother had given her some new stenographer's notebooks and invited Win to begin writing down her thoughts during the long summer months. Apparently she also had an earlier diary, which she mentions in her book *Life Writing*: "I remember receiving a small diary when I was eight years old. The most fascinating things about it were the lock on the leather binding that held it shut and the tiny key that came with it. In the five lines provided for each day, I seldom went beyond the daily activities of getting up, eating, and going to school. As my entries became more and more repetitive, I became increasingly bored—in spite of the thrill of locking my diary each night and carefully hiding the key in my underwear drawer, the most private space I had." In describing the differences between diaries and memoir, she writes, "In their daily-ness, they [diaries] are embedded in the present without the long view. They lack the perspective that later experiences may give to an event." By the time Win was twelve, she had graduated from the methodical diary entries to her journals, which reveal a girl far beyond her years, precocious writing, and a budding talent. Her journals at twelve are far more than simply a daily record of the summer of 1934. In her entries, Win copied poems, kept lists of the books she was reading and from whom she had borrowed each one, and spent pages in deep philosophical thought about life and what she might experience as she grew up. She pondered religion, wrote about her special quiet times with her mother, and questioned what her elders had told her about God and eternal life.

Because there are few other diaries or personal journals in the boxes strewn about my study, I was convinced that Win did not continue keeping chronicles of her life after those summer journals. Yet, sitting on the sofa in Win's apartment at TigerPlace, a senior residence in Columbia,

with her youngest daughter, Beth, I marveled as she brought out irrefut-
able evidence to the contrary. Gingerly, she lifted notebook after notebook out of the boxes that had been brought to town from the river. As
she opened the covers and turned the swollen pages, I could smell the
mold and the tang of the river in these summer documents. I knew Win
had written in her diaries as a young girl; what I did not know was that
when Win spent the summers at the cabin with her children, years later,
she would bring her typewriter and would often spend her time writing. At the end of each day, Beth explained, their mother would arrange
all the children around the large table and give them the task of writing about their day—every single day everyone sat and wrote about their
day, together. While the children studiously filled their pages, Win would
write long entries in the official cabin journals, which now number in the
triple digits, all carefully dated and signed by Win or whoever was spending time at the cabin. "If you visited the cabin, you had to write about it,"
Beth told me.

Then, pushing the boxes of cabin journals aside, she made a space
in my lap for another example of how her mother had chronicled their
lives. These thick standard-sized scrapbooks often sported only one photograph per page, most often of some of the children pulling antics in
the river shallows, followed by paragraph upon paragraph of handwritten
narrative—the stories that went with the picture. Mere captions would
never do for her mother, Beth asserted. Pictures were only a conduit to a
story, a story Win fashioned on the rough, multicolored scrapbook pages,
her pen making deep grooves in the pulpy paper.

No matter what she was writing, Win had an uncanny sense of what
mattered in a story, recognizing how each story in its essence captured a
truth about herself, the world, or other people. Reading Win's stories, as
well as hearing her tell her favorite ones (even hearing her family relate
them to me now), has enabled me to see how these stories functioned
within her life and the life of her family. She had the ability to compose
her life as a story even while living it, identifying and reflecting on its
themes, the pivotal moments, and a pithy punchline that nailed the importance of the story to her life as a whole. She documented everything,
archiving the backstory, keeping the material evidence for the composi-
tions she created. When she would tell a story during our conversations,

she would often say, "Ah, *there's* a story," or, "Now, there's a good one. Have I told you that one before? Well, it bears repeating," noting for herself and me that she was about to share a story, one she had composed and often shared, one that held a truth that deserved our attention.

By telling her life through well-constructed stories complete with dialogue, description, and careful plotting, Win demonstrated her own understanding of the power of words and language in story to relate the larger narrative of her life. Through story, she transformed life. Her writing transformed life into art, testaments to her and her family's experiences, challenges, successes, and failures. Many of the stories she told or wrote became family stories repeated by her husband and often told by Beth, the professional storyteller in the family, who relies heavily on Win's stories for her repertoire.

Although Win claimed that she "quit" working when she came back to Columbia, she actually did not quit at all. She taught courses on memoir writing every semester for several years to adult learners, she was a member of several book groups, she played bridge with a group of friends, and she joined an investment club and learned a lot about finance and 401(k)s —information she loved to share with whoever would listen. She had lunch with friends from town and friends from the university; she worried about her family, especially her four children, now grown and facing their own private endeavors and demons; and she helped her beloved grandchildren in every way she could.

What Win meant when she would complain that she had come home and quit was that she had not come back to Columbia and continued to work—that is, she wasn't writing. For years she often lamented to me that she wanted to write her memoir, but for some reason she was not doing it. We talked about this a great deal, partly because both of us "suffered" from a kind of compulsion to write—we shared a true love of writing and the need for an ongoing writing project. Writing made us happy. And talking about writing made us happy. We each recognized the release from reality, from the mundane, and the loss of self that writing provided—and how time and other duties (like dirty dishes or ungraded papers) could be ignored when we were writing. We agreed in good spirits that losing oneself in the writing was a very special kind of high, leaving the here and now by expressing in words carefully chosen, in language deftly designed, whatever it was we wanted to say, hoping our efforts might compel someone else to read it. But even beyond thoughts of an audience, Win and I knew we shared the magic that happened when we could find the time to just sit still and write. Yet, as Win's health declined and she had to be tethered to her oxygen tank and the miles of plastic tubing that followed her around her apartment, she began to fear she might not ever get her memoir written.

After Win had been home for several years and become quite stressed over her failure to write, I mentioned the possibility of my recording her story for her. I told her I could use both audio and video to capture her life story. Then, I said, I would give her the printed transcriptions of her own words and she could edit them for her memoir. "Thanks, but no thanks," she flatly responded. "I want to write it myself. It's the writing, you know, that is what I want. I want to write it, don't you understand? And, there's a difference, a major difference, you know, in telling my story and writing my story." Of course, as an expert on rhetoric and writing, Win was absolutely right. There would be a difference, although I never thought one was superior to the other. In fact, as a folklorist, I was prepared to argue that her oral story could be just as interesting as her written story. Further, I knew that when Win told her stories, her expressions were vivid and enthralling, and that she had mastered the art of a well-developed, well-crafted story. While it was true that her writing could give her words a unique life on the page, and although I understood her reluctance to embark on a recording venture, I continued to suggest that she tell me her life story orally. At the very least, I argued, she would enjoy telling her stories to me while I recorded them for her. We could meet, have tea, coffee, or wine, and I would listen while she talked. She rejected my idea.

As more months passed, I noticed Win becoming more distressed about the fact that she was not writing. She seemed to be spinning her wheels, she told me, and it wasn't productive. She would talk about how difficult typing had become for her fingers, and she acknowledged that her health was failing. During her ninetieth year, her COPD had gotten worse, she had some heart issues, and she had to be on oxygen twenty-four seven.

Finally, in September 2013, about a year after she and Dave had moved themselves and a few of their most precious belongings into TigerPlace,

Win agreed to tell me her life story so that I could record it. Recently I found the following entry from my own journal, dated September 19, 2013: "My birthday gift arrived early this year. Wini has agreed to let me record her life story for her memoir, *and* she just gave me a box of her letters and writings with the thought that somehow I can make some sense of them and work toward a book about her life as an educator and female academic. Right now I feel blessed and thankful and honored and humbled. She could have given these to anyone, but, instead, she gave them to me! What a burden, what a joy. Good projects really *do* fall into your lap."

From October 10, 2013, until January 29, 2014, I drove over to Win and Dave's new *digs* (Win's word) once a week, usually on Wednesdays, to record her story. When I would arrive at their apartment through the screened porch and their private back door, Win would be waiting for me at the end of the long dining room table. She would be surrounded by yellow pads with handwritten notes she had made about the things she wanted to talk about for each session, mostly in chronological order. She always greeted me with broad smiles, kisses, hugs, and an eagerness to get started. She was delighted with the process once we got going, and she could not wait to get her hands on the transcriptions so that she could *whip them into shape* (also her words). That's what we were talking about up until late January 2014.

Win never saw the transcripts, but she left me with the gift of her stories told in her own words. The difficult task of shaping the focus and coming up with a good title have fallen to me. I never intended to do this work without her, but here I am, alone, preparing her story to share with you, her readers. Writing a book is not new for me, but writing the life of my friend and mentor is unlike anything I have ever attempted. I am reminded by other writers that it is never enough to write about someone because you loved them or think they were "special." To write someone's life, one must be able to somehow discern what her story means, and why someone else would want to read it and benefit from that reading. I am invited to develop a persona that will draw readers to Win's stories, to hear her as the storyteller of her own life, as I did. What I present here are Win's words and stories, largely unedited by me and interwoven with samples of her writing and articles about her life that she and her family provided for me. I think of Mitch Albom's book *Tuesdays with Morrie* as a kind of model for the book I have composed with Win's stories. Like Albom, I visited my older, dear friend to record her stories in the hope that I could share her extraordinary life with readers. In presenting Win's stories, I seek also to illuminate and honor my own relationship with her. In 1983, our lives intersected, creating bonds that lasted more than thirty years and never faltered. She trusted me with her stories, and for that I am forever grateful. I miss her every single day.

When Win agreed to tell me her life story orally in order for me to record it, she was pleased not to have to deal with her computer keyboard and the immensity of a book project at age ninety-one; instead she could think about how to frame the story of her life. As a writer and a teacher of writing, Win knew about the importance of defining moments, illuminating stories, and using humor to help shape her life narrative. I definitely saw Win perk up when we agreed to tell her life story together—her eyes sparkled and she smiled more. As we worked, she shared her thoughts about the purpose of her book:

In a world where women were nonpersons, I have written and taught my way through the demands of family and friends, warding off the barbs of some of my colleagues, avoiding the quicksand of departmental politics and gossip to reach the academic pinnacle of an endowed professorship. It is from my vantage point of professor of English emerita, and Lillian Radford Chair of Rhetoric and Composition emerita, that I speculate on how I got from there to here. I want to tell this story because from my present vantage point it seems unbelievable as I look back. My younger friends raise their eyebrows in disbelief when I tell them that as a tenured member of the department I was told that if I attended department meetings there would be trouble. That is the story I want to tell.

It is my honor, with this book, to help Win tell her story.

The LIBERATION
of WINIFRED BRYAN HORNER

Meeting Win

I FIRST MET WIN HORNER during my on-campus interview visit to the University of Missouri (MU) in Columbia in early 1983. I was thirty-six and Win was sixty-one. At the requisite interview dinner, I was admittedly overwhelmed to meet such a large gathering of English professors, all male but one. Before I could remove my coat, a man quickly approached me, greeted me generously, and promptly kissed my hand. Father Barth, collar and all, was the chair of the English Department, and a Jesuit priest. I am sure my cheeks were bright red, as I was not at all prepared for this peculiar gesture in this setting.

Within seconds, surely noticing my discomfort, the only woman present made a direct path to my frozen position at the entrance to the room. Win Horner was smiling broadly as she took my coat. She leaned into my ear and whispered, *sotto voce*, "My dear, let me take that. So, how far along are you?" I was shocked that she would ask me this totally inappropriate question during an interview dinner, just seconds after the chair had kissed my hand. I was, indeed, five months pregnant, but trying to hide it behind a flowing A-line dress bought just for this occasion in two colors, red and blue. Noting my dismay, Win confided, "We'll talk about this later. No worries!" Big smile. She took my arm and introduced me to everyone else in the room, telling me a bit about each one as we circled the table, acting as though she had known me for years. Dressed in a straight black skirt that fell just below her knees, stylish pumps, a crisp tailored blouse with an antique cameo at the neck, and a red blazer, Win handled the situation with expert finesse, finally bringing me to a chair next to her own at the far end of the table. By this time, I could breathe again. I was completely entranced with this self-assured woman, her welcoming smile, and her generous manner. As we sat down at the table, Win assured me, "Now, don't worry. This will be our secret. I will drive you home, and we can talk more then."

Throughout the meal, I was struck by the fact that Win was quite boldly holding up the conversation at our end of the table, often diffusing ignorant questions, such as, "And what religion are you and your husband?" This group had obviously not gotten the memo on appropriate questions to ask at an interview. As the evening wore on, Win was the one to detect that I was fading, even though I had declined the wine. Being jet-lagged and pregnant did not help at all. I did notice that Win eagerly downed a couple of glasses of red wine. Toward the end of the evening, she asked the host if he had any scotch, which gave me a bit of a pause. But she never missed a beat. She could definitely hold both her liquor and her place at the table.

Of course, Win Horner was also a fabulous driver, even with several drinks under her wide, fashionable belt. Around ten o'clock, she delivered me to the hotel near campus where I was staying. We sat in the car for several minutes that cold night, talking about the department, the town, and the campus. Win was amazingly kind and generous to me; she told me that my interview lecture on southern Pentecostals had been fabulous, noting that the "old farts" liked my work because deep down they were all *very* religious. She said this with a twist of her mouth that suggested more than a bit of irony. Several had attended seminary, she told me, but "couldn't hack it," so they married and became college professors instead of clergy, except for Father Barth, of course. They all loved Byron and Keats, the Romantics, the Victorians, and they protected their literary periods with a vengeance. I had applied for an open position in folklore studies, but Win acknowledged that most of them had no idea what folklore studies or "ethnographic research" actually entailed, and they probably did not care. That I studied religious groups would probably suffice, she explained. That night, Win assured me that I could count on her for support if I got the job offer. She must have felt cautious in her encouragement for me to come to Missouri, knowing the players and the stakes so well. In the end, I accepted the position, as well as Win's pledge of support. I did not know then what she definitely knew—that I would sorely need it in the years to come.

When I first met Win on that fateful night, I assumed her to be a long-standing senior faculty member of the English Department. She was poised, self-assured, and meticulously professional. She obviously knew all the other faculty members well, and they seemed to accept her presence at the dinner I attended. Certainly I noticed that no other women were present. Later I would learn that there were, in fact, two other female faculty members in this department—one about my age but who never, in twenty years, gave me so much as the time of day, and another, Mary Lago, older than Win by ten years, who would return from England the following year and join Win in befriending and supporting me. That said, it was clear to me from my first visit that the men ran this department. But what exactly that meant would take me years to understand. I would not say Win Horner "paved the way" for me so much as she stood alongside me every step of the way. When Win made me a copy of the key to the library carrel she shared with Mary, I found handwritten posters in the tiny cubicle: "Elaine, Publish, Publish, Publish, and Keep Your Mouth Shut, Love, Wini," and "Elaine, Don't Let the Bastards Get You Down, Love, Wini." Her support was essential to my success. Over the years, my stories fed her stories and vice versa. Although we were a generation apart, our stories of frustration were peopled by the very same characters. Our bonds ran deep.

Over the next thirty years, as her friend and colleague, I would hear Win's stories in detail, one carefully crafted narrative after another, in a variety of settings. It took many years for me to grasp the struggle she had endured to get to where and who she wanted to be.

When Win left MU in 1985, two years after I arrived, to take the Lillian Radford Endowed Chair at Texas Christian University in Fort Worth, Texas, our friendship remained steadfast. Win took seriously her commitment to mentoring me as I faced challenges similar to her own in terms of gaining tenure and promotions in the English Department. Win would come to Columbia on a regular basis to be with Dave, her husband, who stayed in Columbia to run their farm when she moved to Fort

Worth. Every time she was in town, I would get a phone call: "Elaine! I'm here. Can you come over for a glass of wine? I want to know everything you are doing. Can you come at three o'clock today?" With delight and no hesitation, I would drop everything and go see Win. Over a late afternoon drink, or two, we would catch up, talk about our research and writing, and share stories. My love for Win Horner, and her stories, eventually led us to this joint project.

The basic facts of Winifred Bryan Horner's life are deceptively simple. Born in 1922, Win (alternately referred to as Winifred, her full name; Win, her shortened name; or Wini, by friends and family) attended elementary schools in St. Louis, Missouri. She graduated from high school at Mary Institute in St. Louis in 1939, and graduated from Washington University, also in St. Louis, in 1943. She married her childhood friend and sweetheart, David Horner, only a few weeks later. During World War II, Win claimed she moved seventeen times within the United States to follow Dave wherever he was stationed. After the war, in 1946, she and Dave moved to a farm in central Missouri, where their four children were born. In 1960 and '61, Win took courses at the University of Missouri, and in 1961 she was awarded an MA in English, while simultaneously serving as an instructor in the English Department (1960–1975). She also served as chair of Lower Division Studies intermittently from 1974 to 1980. In 1973, Win left Missouri temporarily to pursue a PhD at the University of Michigan, which she received in 1975. By 1982, Win had finally achieved the rank of (full) professor in the English Department at MU. In 1985, she left MU to accept an endowed chair in rhetoric at Texas Christian University (TCU), where she remained until 1996, when she retired at age seventy-four and resumed living with Dave in Columbia, Missouri. She died on February 4, 2014, at the age of ninety-one.

From this brief outline, it may not be apparent how unusual her life and career actually were. Close attention to the dates of her career accomplishments reveals the details that are significant. Win got her MA when she was thirty-nine years old, while her four children were still at home. Following that milestone, she taught at the University of Missouri with an MA for nearly twenty years while directing the composition program in the English Department and living on the farm with Dave and their children. In 1975, when Win was fifty, she went to the University of Michigan to get her PhD, reluctantly leaving her husband at home to care for their son, who was still in high school in Columbia. Despite completing her PhD, Win was not awarded the rank of full professor until she was sixty years old. She was sixty-two when she was offered the endowed chair at TCU. Eager to continue her career beyond Missouri, she and Dave agreed to a commuter marriage. Dave would stay in Columbia to care for his beloved farm and beagles, while Win took off for Texas. During this time she mentored countless graduate students and published nine groundbreaking works in her field.

With such additional information, the implied simplicity of Win's short biography has taken on unexpected nuances that beg for illumination: Why did it take her so long to go back to school and get her MA? Why did it take nearly fifteen years before she went to Michigan to get her PhD? Why did she have such difficulty getting promotions in the English Department where she had worked for so many years? What does the offer of the endowed chair at TCU tell us about Win's career? When I began to record her life story, Win Horner, then ninety-one years old, knew she had lived an unusual life and was proud of her successes, but she was also acutely aware of the many barriers she had faced, all of them gendered.

Throughout her life, Win Horner advocated that women could do and be anything they desired, yet she was cognizant of the social and cultural mores of the era she lived in—mores that for many women stood in the way of accomplishment. By 2014, Win had lived long enough to recognize that things were changing for women in terms of their educational and professional opportunities, yet she was also attuned to the reality that even with these advancements, women were rarely named the CEOs of companies, the presidents of universities, or the chairs of departments. She became acutely aware that the national conversation on "the woman question" had really not changed all that much since the nineteenth century. Inequality between the genders is still evidenced in wage disparities, promotion statistics, household responsibilities, the balancing of mothering and careers, and reproductive rights. She was passionate about women's rights and worked for Hillary Clinton's 2008 bid for the presidency. She would have been proud beyond words to see Clinton receive the Democratic nomination in July 2016, and she would have been crushed to see the difficulties a woman running for president faced. For women to have equal footing in all matters, she would say, they need to have the same standing in society in every way. Only when it is no longer unusual for women to be doctors, lawyers, astronauts, priests, professors, mayors, senators, and presidents, and when they are paid the same wages as men in the same ranks, Win would predict, will the subordination of women and the diminishing of women's roles in society cease. Win would also say that it took her quite a long time to recognize just how devalued women and their work are, and how her own interactions with the world were determined by the fact that she was a woman. Only when she was offered an endowed chair at TCU was she able to reap the rewards of a life struggling against the system. She had earned her seat at the head of the table, not because of her gender but because of her determination and intelligence. When she was able to relax into her new role, she excelled, publishing works that transformed her discipline, while nurturing a new generation of rhetoric students and scholars.

At the age of twenty, Win knew exactly what the cultural expectations were for her when she married David Horner. Only weeks from her undergraduate days at Washington University, Win got caught up in the strained fever of World War II. The boys were going off to war, and the girls were marrying them before they left town. Whirlwind weddings caught them all by surprise. The young men looked dashing in their new uniforms; the young women glowed under their tulle veils and shared a wedding dress with a long train. It did not occur to her, then, to resist the duty of being a good wife and a potential mother. Although Win never said she looked forward to these aspects of her life, she did remark on many occasions that she felt this responsibility heavily as a woman. She knew that wifely devotion and dedicated motherhood were the name of the game, and at first she felt comfortable with these expectations. In truth, like so many young women, she had not yet examined what they meant for her near and distant future. She told me multiple times, "I bought the whole thing."

But Win's life held many challenges and surprises—both for her and for her family. For a woman born in 1922, her career path was uncommon.

She was a highly educated young woman with a college degree. She mar-ried an equally well-educated young man she had known all her life and embarked on what she totally expected to be a "normal" marriage and life on a midwestern farm. Gradually, Win began to see their admittedly unrealistic plans unravel.

After the war, as her husband looked for a farm to buy, Win remained in St. Louis, surrounded by her classy wedding presents, living first with her own parents, then with Dave's. "The first was miserable," she told me, "the second was worse." While her girlfriends in the city were buying fan-cy clothes and finding new apartment furnishings, Win was often in bed recovering from a miscarriage. Later, at their farm, she continued to try to "hold" a pregnancy, but lost one baby after another while she despaired at the realities of the farm. A dedicated city girl—one who loved noth-ing more than the busyness of the streets, the restaurants, and her high-heeled shoes—Win could hardly believe she was living in houses without plumbing, electricity, a washing machine, or a refrigerator, where their drinking water came from a frog-infested cistern in the ground. Never one to whine, Win tried to make do. She still believed her duty was to stand by her husband, support his dream, and "produce four children." For several years, she continued to endure disappointing pregnancies, until, in 1949, she finally gave birth to their first child, daughter Win. It took several more pregnancies and miscarriages to finally result in her "requisite four," accomplished at a high price to both her body and her mind. Finally successful birthing children, Win was less successful in becoming the dutiful farm wife. To anyone who asked, she would admit that she hated the farm. Hated, hated, hated it. She struggled with her depression for years, recognizing that she would never be happy as a farm wife.

Up to this point in her story, Win's journey was similar to those of many postwar brides in the 1940s. My own mother married in 1941, lived in St. Louis while my father was overseas during the war, and followed him to a similar hardscrabble farm in southern Missouri in 1946, where I and my three brothers were born. But unlike Win Horner, my mother was not well-educated, was not encouraged by her family to excel, and could not fathom a life different from the one she had with my father on the farm. Her story is more historically typical. In many ways, this comparison of women's lives following World War II makes Win's atypical story especially dramatic and worthy of attention.

Even as a child, Win had known she wanted to be a writer, yet her journey to find her place in the world as a writer, a teacher, and a scholar was a long and arduous one. Her liberation came in fits and spurts. She had to reject the farm life she detested without rejecting her husband, whom she adored and respected, and her children, so long in coming. Before it was fashionable, Win located ways to divert her energies from the demands of a traditional marriage and motherhood in order to follow her own dream. To be sure, Win's "liberation" came not in a rejection of her role as wife and mother, but rather in her desire to "have it all"—her marriage, her children, her writing, and her career. But, as she would repeat often, she just couldn't have it "all at the same time."

Win's love of writing had begun when she was a preteen child. In her early journals, penned at the family summer home near the Meramec River, Win wrote about her life: reading with her mother, the dark and stormy nights in the primitive cabins, and her romps in the woods with her brothers and the Horner boys. In college she found venues for her literary imagination by editing the student journal and writing radio spots for a listening public fearful of a new global crisis. Following her new husband around the country during the war gave her new fodder for her writerly efforts. Alone much of the time, she filled her days and long nights writing a novel-length, comedic memoir that made light of Dave's assignments and her frustrating attempts to find living quarters for them in strange towns and temporary jobs for herself to help pay the bills. Dave says now that he had no idea Win was sitting at her manual typewriter night after night composing a hilarious account of their days during the war.

Dave completed his college hours when he got out of the military, and began to look for a farm to buy. This was Dave's dream: they would buy land and run a successful farm where they would raise their family in country bliss. No one in either of their families had ever been a farmer, and to this day no one knows where Dave got this idea (not even Dave).

But it was not a passing whim, as Win discovered. Dave was serious about pursuing his dream of running a farm, and Win thought she could, and should, follow his plan for their married life. So she packed up all their wedding gifts and followed him to a farm in Huntsdale, Missouri, in late 1946.

By the time Win was in her late thirties and had finally delivered three of her four children, her desperation on the farm had resulted in a deep depression, which (luckily) motivated her to begin writing about their life on the farm. She would write whenever she could fit it into her very busy life between animal care, harvesting, egg production, and wiping noses. Writing became her work, her passion, and her salvation. During the next fifteen years, she wrote hundreds of stories of her family's experiences on the farm, some of which were accepted for publication in small magazines of the time. But that kind of writing was not Win's goal—she wanted to write pieces that would find national recognition. Finally, in 1958, she published an article on the failure of the family farm in the *Saturday Evening Post*. Ironically, the article that got her a modicum of both local and national renown was sympathetic to the plight of the small farmer. Her picture was in the local *Columbia Tribune*, and the *Post* sent a photographer out to do a piece on this new writer and her family. She got a letter from the White House, and Senator Stuart Symington from Missouri read her article into the Congressional Record. The attention to her article was filled with sympathy for her and her husband who were trying to make it on a small family farm. Win captivated her audience, but she was not seeking their sympathy; she was looking for proof that she could write well. The publication of this article convinced her that she could actually be a writer—it set the stage for her to leave the farm, go over to the university, and change the course of her life. In an abbreviated list of accomplishments I found in her papers, Win includes the date of this publication alongside her other major life events: birth, graduation, marriage, Huntsdale Farm, *Saturday Evening Post* article, MA, PhD, endowed chair.

Recognizing that she had to make a radical move while still living on the farm was a serious complication for Win's new life plan. But leave she did, and basically she never looked back. Off she went in the family car, stopping to put on tire chains for the icy back roads into town, hoping to find a professor who had drunkenly invited her to come teach freshman composition at the university. She found him, and "the rest is history," she would exclaim. The next twenty years were complicated, frustrating, and rewarding all at the same time. Win fought a lot of battles and felt she had to scratch her way to the top of the university hierarchy without any assistance. Many years later, when she accepted the endowed chair at TCU, she felt she could thumb her nose at all those who had found her single-minded determination abrasive and disruptive. Once she found herself exactly where she felt she belonged, Win thrived. She was the happiest she had ever been. She also insisted that Dave Horner was her strongest supporter and ally, helping to carry her through the most difficult of times. In the end, he shared her success like a badge of honor.

Win Horner had never really considered whether or not she was a feminist. In fact, when we discussed how we became feminists, she wondered if that was a term women took for themselves when she was in school. "Let's look it up in the OED!" she exclaimed, something she often suggested. (As a linguist, Win loved the derivation of words and she loved the OED.) By 1982, she admitted she was definitely a feminist and delighted in "causing trouble" along with her colleague and senior faculty member, Mary Lago. In the fall of 1985, when she moved to Texas, she surprised herself by announcing to her first class that she was a feminist and they better know that going in. Stating this, however, did not mean that Win was devoted to any ideological rhetoric or particular political stance save the right of women to have the same opportunities as men. For Win, it meant she had found her path and followed it as she could. Her liberation from social norms never meant that Win wanted to be liberated from her marriage and her children. She was not refusing to be a good wife and mother, but she was modeling how to be a different kind of wife and mother, one who trusted her own instincts and followed her own dreams, no matter what it took to get there. Fortunately, as her husband recognized what was making Win miserable, he stepped up and helped her get the kind of support she needed to succeed. As I sat with Dave in his small residential apartment after Win's death, he would shake his head and tears would fill his eyes as he told me that he just wished he had noticed how miserable she was early on. After reading the manuscript of this book, he told me, "I knew Win, but not nearly as well before reading this book as I do now. I wish I had realized much earlier just how miserable Win was on the farm. I could have helped her a lot more than I did. That would be my greatest regret."

When Win moved to Texas and began her new position at TCU, she reveled in her role as the first endowed chair in rhetoric. She was asked by the provost there to "put TCU on the map," which she took as her mission, one at which she excelled. She took on many graduate students, mentored them, and took great care in introducing them to the people they needed to know to get the very best jobs on the market. Her former students are now the leaders in rhetoric and composition throughout the country, and all of them sing the praises of their teacher and mentor.

As I worked on this book, many of her former students spoke with me or wrote to me about her mentoring style. She was always attentive to their concerns and generous with her advice. She did not suffer fools, however, and expected women, especially, to pay attention to the world around them and help themselves in whatever ways were available to them. Three of her former students—Nancy Myers, Sue Hum, and Kristie Fleckenstein—paid the following homage to Win in the *Peitho* journal's memorial tribute to her and her work.

> It is our experience of this robust mentorship and the gentle face of gendered networks—ones that create who we are and empower us to believe that anything is possible—we wish to emphasize in this short list of Winnerisms. These are one-liners that kept us on track in the profession that we pass on regularly to our graduate students and that we hope will help others too.

> **From Win to You:**
> - All ideas are meant to be shared.
> - A good dissertation is a done dissertation.
> - Your graduate school classmates are your future community in your discipline.
> - Professors should always ask what graduate students are working on: ask their ideas.
> - Quit flagellating yourself and get on with your writing.
> - You can always take your publications with you to a new position.
> - You've got to stand up for yourself because no one will give you anything unless you do.

Certainly, over the years, I heard Win say exactly these same things to me or to other women she was mentoring. I have even passed some of them along to my own graduate students.

After extending Win's tenure as the endowed chair to thirteen years, TCU was ready to pass the prestigious position to a new professor. Thinking it might be time to return to Columbia and be with her husband, Win stepped down. I was delighted when she returned to Columbia, where we continued our late afternoons of talk, storytelling, and glasses of wine as we had done for nearly fifteen years.

Those talks eventually led to our collaboration on this book. And once we had set the date for our first interview, she began to dig into her many boxes and files, searching for documents that would guide her back to the beginning.

1

Barefoot Girl Running with the Boys

Lately I've had some of the strangest feelings that I can't explain at
all. I want to know more than I know now. I want to learn about the
strange things beyond. I'm impatient, and it seems strange to live in a
world where one knows no more than the life that you are living now.

—Winifred Bryan, age twelve

WEDNESDAY, OCTOBER 10, 2013. THIS is the first day of our planned
sessions to record Win's life stories. When I arrive at Win and Dave's
apartment at TigerPlace—the retirement residence where they recently moved following some problematic health issues for Win that taxed
Dave's ability to care for her—Win sits at the end of the table surrounded
by sheets of handwritten pages and a yellow legal pad next to her elbow.
She has obviously been writing down dates and things she wanted to be
sure to tell me today. Her handwriting is labored and shaky at times, but
her notes help her to stay *on track,* she tells me with a big smile.

Win waves goodbye to Dave as she reaches up her arms to hug me.
Dave tells me hello and goodbye, announcing that he is off to the farm,
leaving us "to it" as he goes out the door, grateful to be able to be outdoors
where he is happiest. Win does not stand in greeting, so I bend down,
careful not to squeeze her thin bones too tightly or dislodge the oxygen
tubing on her nose. I gently kiss her on the cheek. *That's how you spread
germs, you know,* she mutters as she kisses me right back. *You're not even
supposed to shake hands anymore. Spreads germs. Bunch of nonsense.*

She is being silly; her smile is bright, and she chuckles as I put my jacket over a chair and set up the recorder between us on the table. *You want water?* she asks. *Coffee? Get whatever you need; it's on the counter.* I pull out the recorder and a bottle of water I have brought with me, cracking open a new journal I have bought just for this purpose. Even though I am recording her story, I realize there will be dates and specifics that I might need to jot down in order to keep her story straight in my mind. People tell their stories differently. Some are methodically chronological in their telling; others jump around from story to story. I have no idea how Win will want to tell her tale, but I am definitely excited to begin. Evidently, so is she.

I had worried about Win's stamina for these long recording sessions. I realized the "ka-thump" of her oxygen tank behind her would provide the background to all of our conversations. It never missed a beat. I was confident this would go well; after all, Win and I were great friends and enjoyed each other's company. We had met like this for years. It helped that I knew most, if not all, of the people she would be talking about—people I had also come to know well over the past thirty years. My assumption that Win's stories would revolve around her career as a university professor was somehow both true and not true. While her joy in her academic work was the centerpiece of her life, she definitely planned to put this story into the context of the times and the expectations that she had to struggle against.

Win Horner lived her life as both the subject of her story and the witness to that story. She knew she was capable, smart, even "special," as her mother insisted. She thought of herself as a writer, perhaps even an academic, before she probably could articulate this desire. Her independent childhood and early years as "one of the boys" in her family had not prepared her for the surprises she encountered on the journey that lay before her as a young woman eager to get started. Although she was not yet aware of the world's opinion of her gender, luckily her mother had instilled in her a love for the written word, and the boys had taught her how to swim, dive, challenge, and compete. These skills would serve her well in the years to come. The one thing she knew to do as she set out was to write it all down. Her pen was in lockstep with her feet.

Once Win is certain that Dave has left in his truck, she prepares to begin her story. The day is warm for October, and we leave the door open to the screen so we can hear the birds in the trees outside the porch. She asks me if I am ready. I am, and she begins to talk.

I find it odd now to think about my childhood as one of privilege, yet in many ways it was. Born in 1922 in St. Louis, the only girl of four children, to a blue-collar family could have been pretty rough. Yet, because my father worked with the St. Louis Transportation Department, he always had a steady income, and my mother was a seamstress. We came from well-educated, although not rich, stock, and somehow our parents ran with a more wealthy crowd in the city. My father had many friends, most of whom had more money than we did. My father's connections resulted in four men investing their collective savings into a plot of rough land two hours south of St. Louis on the Meramec River for the sole purpose of providing a summer escape from the urban heat for their wives and children. The men were young and eager to find a way to enjoy the river.

I remember going down to what we dubbed Water Oaks on weekends, while the fathers built a series of primitive cabins all along the river's edge. The families became very tight-knit. The mothers loved spending time together along the water's edge, smoking and drinking their gin and vodka, gossiping and being lazy. They allowed all the children free rein in the woods and in the rather languid water. As soon as the cabins could keep the rain off our heads, the fathers went back to the city during the week and the mothers and all us children remained at the cabins. There was no plumbing or electricity, but that made the summers all that more exciting. I think there were about six boys—and me, the only girl!

I need to make it clear that we were not rich. But we were privileged to have the kind of life we did. I was privileged in having the mother and father that I did. And I was privileged to have my brothers. When we lived in St. Louis, our fathers worked hard at their jobs, and our mothers took care of the children and the household duties. Now, I find it rather amazing that my father, Dave's father, and a few other men managed to buy that rough acreage south of Columbia and St. Louis on the Meramec River, during the Depression. You have to understand these families had known each other in St. Louis for generations. Their grandfathers had known each other in

school; the grandmothers were all friends. And they were all highly educated families. They all put their money together and bought five hundred,
or was it three hundred acres, right on the river, with each family getting
about sixty acres. It was scruffy land that was pretty much useless for
farming or anything else, so they got it on the cheap. But for them to be able
to buy this land in the midst of the Depression was quite a big deal.

Part of the reason the fathers could buy this land was because they were
able to keep their jobs during the Depression. All the men in our families
were engineers of one kind or another. Once the land was purchased, the
men went down there together and built three cabins, rough buildings
without the need for insulation or any extras. I would say the cabins were
simple. The living areas were up a flight of outside stairs and the kitchen
was on the first floor. Each cabin had a big covered porch, and each one had
a kitchen, a pantry, and a large living and dining area. Each had a couple
of bedrooms and there were extra cots everywhere for guests and for new
family members. My brothers all slept on the porch, even though it often
rained on them, or, rather, the wind would drive the rain onto the porch,
and they would have to sleep on the sofa and the floors. I slept in a small
alcove next to my parents' bed. My mother hung this long burlap curtain
between their bed and my small cot. I remember being quite curious about
the various shadows that would play out on that curtain and the noises I
would hear from my parents' bed whenever my father came down to Water
Oaks on the weekends. I found all that rather amusing. Other nights it was
completely silent, although I could easily hear my mother's gentle breathing
when she was sound asleep, or I knew when she was reading late into the
night because she kept her lamp lit. I always tried to fall asleep before she
blew out her lantern, because then it was so very dark out there.

Years later, I found out that one of the reasons that motivated Dave's
father to urge all the fathers to buy this land away from the city was that
Dave's grandmother had a Down syndrome child, a girl, who of course eventually became a young woman. For years they used to take her to Maine for
the summers when her father was still alive. But when he died, they wanted
a summer place closer to St. Louis where they could take her, so that's one
of the reasons they bought the place. Actually, we rarely saw her. I think the
grandmother would take this child, woman, down to the water's edge during the morning hours and let her play in the sand and shallow water, but

by the time all of us kids slapped into the water, she was back at the cabin "resting."

So, we were doubly privileged to be able to leave the city all summer, every summer, and head for Water Oaks. The day after school let out, my mother would pack the touring car for the entire summer. Once we got to Water Oaks, we did not go off the place for three months. As children, we roamed the land, on our own, all summer. We climbed trees, jumped over rotten logs, followed trails out through the dense undergrowth, chased rabbits, and flew into the river at all our favorite diving spots. We would collapse on the pebbly "beach" when we simply ran out of steam. Of course, while living this way every summer, we never gave it a thought.

Our mothers came with us, leaving their homes in the city and their husbands to fend for themselves. They did not watch over us much. Rather, they would sit in the end of a boat, smoking and talking, for hours on end. They barely looked up even at the sound of screaming or crying, knowing the older kids had the sense to get them involved if absolutely necessary. Otherwise, they chatted quietly amongst themselves, about what I do not know. Sometimes I would hear one of them mention their husband's name, or a new product one of them had tried, or they might share the names of reliable maids in the city.

It never occurred to me that I was more like the mothers than the brothers or the fathers. By that I mean that in our summer lives gender did not matter for me at all. When I was young I never even thought of myself as different from the boys. Before we left for Water Oaks the barber would come to the house, and Mother would instruct him to give us all short summer bob cuts, identical. And she brought to the cabin bags of shirts, shorts, socks, and shoes in various sizes and shapes. We would wake up in the mornings, one after the other, and grab something semi-clean that might or might not fit very well and head for breakfast. Our mother never really noted what each of us had chosen to wear; she did not care. Her back would greet us as we entered the large kitchen/dining room area, the sizzle of bacon inviting us to sit while all the smells in the kitchen made us salivate like puppies.

We didn't talk much until we had eaten our scrambled eggs and bacon, drunk our milk and juice, and swiped our dripping mouths with the backs of our hands, wiping our fingers on our shorts for good measure as we headed for the door as a unit. Our mother yelled behind us as the screen door slapped shut, "Stay together; stay within shouting distance; come if I call you; wear shoes in the woods." Her voice faded as we skipped across the gravel driveway, met the other kids, and roamed the nearby woods first, still a bit slow and sleepy, knowing it was too early to hit the water when the dew was still on the grass. We slipped into the undergrowth, watching for snakes, following the sounds of the elusive pileated woodpecker, the one Dave's dad had told us was quite rare. We recognized the bird's distinctive hammer and call and struck out, single file, to see if we could spot the one we'd adopted as our "Pecker." It never failed to amuse us to say "Pecker." We all knew we ought not use this word while in earshot of our mothers. But the boys swaggered just slightly as they repeated the word under their breath: "Here, Pecker, here, Pecker. Where are you, Pecker?" Frankly, I found their humor slightly dumb. I'd seen all their "peckers" at one time or another, and I just didn't get that they were such a big deal.

I think I did feel a wee bit of envy when I realized that among all the children traipsing through the woods every summer, I did not sport a "pecker" when I needed to pee. I was totally dismayed that taking time to piss in the woods meant exposing all my privates, front and back, and lowering my backside toward the tickling grasses in order to squat and urinate, while the boys merely turned toward a tree and wrote their names boldly in a hot yellow stream on the bark. Or, I felt left out when they all stood in a line and arched their "peckers" toward a selected mark to see who could piss the furthest. I could not participate in these boys-only capers. More often than not, I would leave them to their contests and strike out ahead of them up the ridge, hoping to make a discovery that might top their pecker prowess.

Some days, my foray ahead of the boys was highly successful. I remember finding a dead turkey once. We circled around that bird for a long time, gently prodding it with our toed shoes, perhaps afraid it really wasn't dead. We tried to figure out how the bird had died. We found no blood, no evidence of a gunshot wound or an arrow, but it was fresh, untouched somehow by the buzzards or underbrush animals, ants, and maggots that could locate carrion seemingly the moment a heart stopped beating. We didn't dare try to pick up the turkey and somehow hoist it back to the cabins, having agreed this was not a gift our mothers would appreciate. So, we proceeded to pluck all the best feathers, still shiny and smooth. These we would take home with us at lunchtime.

In the backyard between the cabins, we would add our feathers to our summer altar. We didn't call it that, of course, but, in a way, it really was a ritualized accumulation of each summer's escapades and discoveries, our findings, which could tell the tale of any given Water Oaks summer—feathers, bones, exotic flowers wilted beyond recognition, rocks, fossils, wasp nests, bird nests, and snake skins, tributes to our fearlessness. Our mothers paid scant attention to our growing archive of natural history, but it was our pride and joy. Early on in our Water Oaks summers, we had constructed a kind of haphazard museum-display kind of structure out of abandoned planks of wood and shoved it under the broad eaves of our outdoor storage shed, which mostly kept it out of the wind and rain and viable at least for the length of one full summer. We were always discouraged when we returned the following year and found it in disarray, pondering together who or what had ravaged our collection while we were gone. Had wolves come to reclaim bones—or Indians? Had birds flown low to recapture their loved ones' feathers? Had the snake skins slithered off the shelves and returned to the earth? Of course, we never discovered the answers to these questions. Soon enough we were clearing out the remnants of last summer's treasures and preparing for the new ones to come. Off into the woods we would tramp, eager to locate even better specimens than the year before.

I always felt a great sense of satisfaction as the collection grew. Whenever I was alone, which wasn't actually very often, I would make up stories in my head about each of the artifacts and elaborately connect them in a narrative of my own making. My internal narrative would grow as the shelves accumulated more items. I doubt the boys shared this storied pastime, but I never asked them, nor did I share my own stories with them, fearing they might find a way to make fun of my growing imagination. Somehow, I recognized my ability to narrate the summer through our varied objects as a singular talent, one I owned but the boys did not, something I owned that no one else knew about. I loved the stories I made up on the spot and elaborated on them at night as I tried to fall asleep with the purr of night noises as the background music to my tales—crickets, cicadas, frogs, birds, and sometimes coyotes traveling close by, or a panther's call, which our mother said gave her the creeps because it sounded so much like a woman screaming. I never wrote down my imagined tales, but I wish I had. They were full of intrigue and fabulous characters, tied together by a special narra-

tive voice I polished to a shine. I imagined this narrative voice as being very sophisticated and stylish, something akin to both Jane Austen and the Grimm Brothers combined. But then, my memories may be tricking me on this. While I know I did write elaborate stories in my head all summer long, how good they actually were can never be revealed. Perhaps it's better that way. I can remember them as splendid tales woven by my own (superior) brain, the early precursors to a life of writing and a love of language. Either way, my brain was very active during these hot, humid summer days; it would spin tales that really never ended but rather slipped into my unconscious. They are still in there, somewhere; there's just too much other stuff in there as well, relegating them to a misty area I can almost access but never actually retrieve, something like a dream. I also remember that when it was raining, I would often sit at the end of the big kitchen table and play with cards. I would line up the king, queen, jack, and ace, and for hours, I would make up stories about the queen, the king, and the jack. For hours! I don't know what these stories were, either, but I was very busy making them up in my head.

Another thing. My brothers and Dave's brothers would always be building new tree houses, endless tree houses. Part of the fun was finding just the right tree, with limbs that could cradle the rough boards in a semilevel position for a tree house that could support as many as seven or more children at one time. These were tree house mansions! We eventually built one that was pretty incredible. It had a roof and at least one side. Sometimes we would go up there to read or just have long conversations. Later, when the boys were older and they would bring their girlfriends, they would take the girls up to the tree house and talk and sing for hours. The other boys would climb up onto the roof of our cabin to join in the singing, and our parents would all sit on their porches and sing with us. It was really idyllic. It really was.

When we grew weary of roaming the woods, we would head for the river, picking off ticks as we cruised along. By ten or eleven, we were hot, sticky, tired, and ready for the absolutely shocking first moment of hitting the cold water in the river. Within only a few minutes, the water felt silky smooth and not cold at all, but the first immersion of the day would always take our breath away. The highlight of this moment was the sheer intensity of jumping from a state of hot to a state of cold so harsh our teeth would chatter. "Exhilarating" is barely sufficient for this slap-in-the-face moment. We lived for this jolt.

Over the years, we had established several favorite sites for the ritual of the first dive into the water. Each location had its own special draw. All of them offered an extra thrill to the shock of the cold water because all of them resided on the ridge high above the river. But we were not stupid children; we knew the thrill could swiftly turn into a disaster if we flew off the ridge into shallow water or into a deep pool with hidden sharp rocks. Every year, we did a formal assessment of the river during our first few days there, determining where the river had changed during the winter, where new dangers lurked, checking the shallows, changes in rock beds, noting how we needed to modify our diving patterns to match the water's depth and making notes about where the hidden rocks were. Sometimes the older boys talked through the changes, I think so the younger kids would hear the older boys' cautions and remember where and how to dive safely.

Next, we would dutifully check the ropes we had tied to tree limbs that hung far over the river, some with old tires securely tied to the end. We had other favorite sites as well. One was a horizontal tree limb that hung far over the river, nearly to the far side over a stretch of narrow water. Brave children could take this challenge, stepping carefully along its wide, flat sur-face. Doing this took clear thinking and expertise. We had to train our toes (without shoes) to dig into the bark for grip as there were no other limbs to serve as handholds on this particular tree. I loved the thrill of climbing up onto this living plank, totally trusting my toes and my slight body to make it to the end before gracefully diving into the brace of the first splash and coming up screaming from the cold. It was hilarious when one of the boys would "choose" not to dive in off the tree limb. We would tease him merci-lessly, calling out, "chicken," "wimp," "sissy," "girl." Even "pussy" sometimes came out of some of the brothers' mouths. They were hardest on their closest kin. I joined in on the egging, although I remember being confused about the taunts of "girl" or "pussy." Those gave me pause, and I never yelled them out. I was a girl, yet I was usually the first to fearlessly cross the danger-ous limb and the first to hit the water. Apparently the boys saw no prob-lem with their language use and its gendered impropriety. I doubt it ever crossed their minds that their words had anything to do with me. I don't think they even thought of me as a girl. I was just one of the summer gang *and I looked and behaved identically to them on all visible fronts. And, most importantly, I was an equal with them in all our adventures. Superior, even, in some respects, which I suppose contributed to their lack of a gendered identification for me.*

My wonderful older brothers actually helped make me competitive all my life. Down at the river we swam and swam, and they would spend the summers trying to dunk me, that is, hold me under the water. Then they would pull me up by my hair—I didn't have much hair—and see if I was alive. If I was okay, they'd dunk me again. Their attention to me varied between harassing me and challenging me in all their games. Except for Dave. He quietly watched over me even from our earliest years.

Some of the boys were born engineers and were always building something new for us to all do together. At home in the city, my oldest brother would build elaborate highway systems in the dirt. He was a great inventor of games. Luckily our backyard was basically just a flat dirt area. Our mother would never allow us to play in other children's backyards, but she would be happy if other children visited in ours. We were all delighted with the highway systems he built in the dirt, adding tunnels and overpasses with shoeboxes and clothespins, anything he could get his hands on. They were really elaborate, and we had a few little cars we could push around the streets and roadways in the dirt.

On the river, they would create similar kinds of games on the sandbars that existed all up and down the river. Sometimes our parents would walk a ways with us to discover a new sandbar. They would sit on the bank while we cavorted, running up and down those sandbars, sliding into the water on our backsides. Some of the sandbars were as large as this room, and they sloped down to the river just perfectly, so my brother would bring a tennis ball and make long paths in the sand. We would build all kinds of curves and tunnels in the sand, and then we would send the tennis ball down the paths into the water, where it would politely wait for us to fetch it and do it again and again. It was wonderful, and everyone got fascinated with it, including our parents.

At Water Oaks, the engineer fathers would encourage the engineer sons to build dams. We were always trying to dam various parts of the river where it snaked around rocks and broken tree limbs. But every time we would build what we thought was an excellent dam, it would wash away.

But that never deterred us—we built dam after dam, and sometimes when the fathers visited on the weekends, they would help us with our dams and encourage us by making suggestions for a successful dam. That was good, because then we'd build more dams. And by damming the water, we could create these little pools. We captured tadpoles and put them into these little pools, where they always died. We were content to do these activities all afternoon during the summers.

Eventually, each family bought a flat-bottomed boat, which added all kinds of new activities. We could paddle down the river, up the river, and be occupied for hours. And, one year, I remember my brother built a super high dive. I find it amazing now that none of us ever got hurt during all these escapades. I was the only one to break my nose diving into the water. That wasn't so good, and it wasn't funny. It was never properly fixed, and it never really bothered me until now. That's why I'm having so much trouble now with the oxygen tanks. My nose is crooked from that river dive, so I cannot breathe in hard enough to use the portable oxygen tank. Now I pretty much have to use the larger tank all the time, which is a pain in the butt to carry around in the car, to lunch, or to book group.

At this point, Win gestures to the oxygen tank nearby and gives it a jerk with her right hand as she grimaces to mark her ongoing frustration.

We were always challenging each other to contests. We had various games connected to prizes, or what we would call "coups and grand coups." Like all kids, we would divide ourselves into various Indian tribes, and the "coups" then would be some of the large feathers in our collection for certain feats. Once, I was told that if I would walk up to the mailbox, in the dark, by myself, I would get a grand coup. Well, one night I did it—actually I ran most of the way, but I did it, in the dark. My mother never knew I was even gone, but I got that big feather! I was the bravest of the younger children. And I always wanted to be the best!

I often tell the story that when we were five and six, somewhere in there, my mother gave me a new autograph book and it was passed around our large families and everyone wrote something in my new book. Did I already tell you this story? Oh, well, it's a great story. Okay. My birthday falls on August 31, so it always occurred over the Labor Day weekend, when we would all be at Water Oaks for a long weekend. That was a big thing at Water Oaks. All the families would gather and cook and it was a big holiday.

The place was hopping with families. So it was very nice for me because it was also my birthday! Everybody would gather at our cabin or Dave's family's cabin and celebrate my birthday. This always made me feel very special. When I was about five, my mother gave me this autograph book for my birthday. And everyone wrote in it. I still have it. And I will never forget that Dave wrote in my little book, "I just want Wini to be happy." I was a bit taken aback, not quite knowing how to respond to this, but I stuttered, "Well, okay, thank you," and went about reading all the other notes that had been written in my book.

Now, everyone, including me, thought Dave had written this in my little book because earlier in the day I had been hollering for the other kids from one of the boats to hurry up. And I yelled, "Hey, yous!" And everybody laughed, kids and parents, all of them laughed at what I had said. Someone yelled out, "Did you hear what Wini said? 'Hey, yous!'" They thought it was hysterical. Really, they thought it was terrible for me to say that, so they all had witty things to say about it in my autograph book. "Who says 'yous'?" they all exclaimed. And I cried because I was so embarrassed and hurt. Now, Dave had only known older brothers in his house, so he says he had never seen anyone cry. He said the real reason that he wrote that in my book was because he had seen me cry and it had upset him. I was his buddy and they had all made me cry. He was six and I was five. So he wrote, "I just want Wini to be happy" in my little book. But really, I think it was more than that.

Win leans around to see if Dave is in their bedroom next door to where we are doing her interview, asking, *Is Dave in there? In the bedroom?* Assuring herself that he has gone, she continues.

Actually, I think there was more to what he wrote than that, because when I was sixteen, we had another party. Either I received a new autograph book that year, or we had located the one I got when I was five, but either way, on my sixteenth birthday, down at Water Oaks, we passed around my autograph book again, and Dave wrote the same thing in my book: "I just want Wini to be happy." And I think it has been like that all our lives. All our lives, Dave really wanted me to be happy. But he never wanted to be responsible for anybody else's happiness. Interesting. I was sixteen when Dave first kissed me. After all those years of being buddies, he kissed me, and we've been together ever since. In fact, we were never not together.

That's how I knew I'd made the right choice in a husband, because he always noticed if I was happy or not, and he always supported me in whatever I wanted to do.

Anyway, back to Water Oaks. Once we were in the water, we spent hours splashing about, swimming our various eclectic swimming styles learned from previous summers in the water and copying what the older boys knew how to do. It occurred to no one in those days that we ought to have swimming lessons. We just jumped in and swam, awkwardly at first, but effortlessly with each summer's river time. Our laughter and squeals, screams and taunts echoed out over the hills and floated above the heads of our mothers sitting and smoking near the water's edge. When they got hot, each of them in turn would rise elegantly in her bathing suit (our mother's was a stark white against her browned skin) and plunge into the pools of clear water to cool themselves. Then they would gracefully walk back to the other mothers and continue their conversation. They never toweled off, preferring to let their skin remain wet and cool as the water evaporated off their creamy skin. We thought our lounging summer mothers were beautiful. They were totally ours for the summer, but they also pretty much ignored us, a kind of summer truce that created the basis for our independent lives. They were there to watch over us, we knew that. But their watchful eyes were shaded in the summer glare, their conversations drifting lazily along the shimmering water as they relaxed totally, free from their busy city lives and the demands on their time there, especially the demands of their husbands. Here they moved slowly, languid, their wardrobe and their bodies, like our own, loose and easy.

I do recall that the winter before our first summer at Water Oaks, when the cabins were ready for us, my mother went to the YMCA during the winter and learned how to swim. She figured she should learn how to swim if she and all her children would be on the river during the summers. Oh, and she also learned to drive—well, sort of. Her driving would be like, gas, brake, gas, brake, like, chirp, chirp, sharp and jerky, but I do think she could have gotten us somewhere in an emergency. We always came down in several cars and then the fathers would take two or three of them back to the city during the week and leave one for the mothers for just such an emergency.

Our mother loved Water Oaks. She loved being there all summer. She had spent her high school years with her grandmother on a sort of farm, where they had a big garden and canned vegetables and wove things, stuff like that. So she loved that outdoor kind of life. I remember one year she had us picking all the berries down at Water Oaks, and she made some jelly on this funny little stove we had down there. She loved it.

One of our favorite games was to quietly flip over the canoe and dive below it, coming up under the wooden frame where there was sufficient air to sustain us while hidden from sight. Slowly, we would maneuver the canoe across the water, getting closer and closer to where our mothers sat. At first, they would notice and comment on the silence as the squeals, screams, and other child noises ceased. One of the mothers might say, "Where are the kids?" Another might say, "I don't know. I can't hear them." Gradually, without worry, the mothers would listen more carefully, trying to locate their children's voices as distinguished from the other noises in the trees, the bird calls, the waterfalls, the crickets. Then we might hear a more concerned mother's voice calling our names: "Wini? Dave? Where are you?" We could barely keep from laughing as we held our place beneath the boat, all seven of us, silent, holding our breath to keep from giggling or snorting and giving ourselves away. We never tired of this game to scare our mothers into actually noticing us. Eventually, we could surmise that all the mothers were standing up, yelling our names, and cursing a bit because their afternoon interlude had been interrupted by absent children.

Eventually one of us couldn't hang on any longer and would tip the canoe or make a noise to let the mothers know where we were. The jig was up. We'd flip the canoe with one swift stroke and scream, "Surprise! Here we are!" We never tired of this game. Now I realize the mothers were in on the game all along—certainly after the first time we pulled this prank on them. They played to our needs, our desire to have their full attention, if only for a moment. Their exasperated responses to our trick always pleased us, and we happily obliged when they sat back down and instructed us to "go play," or "get lost." The game confirmed our need to know they were actually watching over us and paying attention, acknowledging our desire to be noticed, laughed at, released again to our own private world of play.

I think our mothers knew and cherished the privilege Water Oaks provided, but children just move into a landscape as instructed and become one with it. For months in the summer we had woods and animals and water and dark, starry nights. And we took all that for granted. We grumbled because the cabins were rough, the beds were uncomfortable army cots, because there was no plumbing or electricity. Our elegant three-holer out-house stood what seemed like miles from the cabins, so we reluctantly peed in the night jars (with lids) our mothers placed in the pantry. Even creeping through the cabin in the night could be an experience in terror. There were no nightlights or light from streetlamps down here. Our bare feet would slip quietly on the wood floors as shadows crossed our path from cot to pot. Creaks in the floorboard would startle us and the night noises, snores, and grunts of our brothers and mothers would cause us to try and wait out ev-ery urge to pee. But then we would brace up our courage and slip as silently as possible toward the pantry, smelling the night jar even before we arrived at the pantry door. We tried not to let the door announce our primal urg-es, but invariably the rusted hinges would betray our nighttime activity and creak far too loudly. I hated the smell of pee and poop in the night jar and had I the courage, I would have much preferred to head outside for the outhouse. But the potential dangers outside always outweighed the lesser dangers of making it to the pantry. So I often held my breath and clenched my nose shut with my fingers when I removed the metal lid of the night jar. Then, of course, I had to let go of my fingers in order to pull down my pant-ies. Once again, I found myself wishing for a tidy pecker so I would not have to crouch over the cold pot and pee. I tried not to actually sit down, but that inevitably went awry and I ended up with wet panties or, worse, a pissed nightgown that I would have to exchange before crawling back into my cot.

Now I wonder if our mothers delighted in the lack of plumbing or elec-tricity. Surely their duties in the kitchen without water, including emptying the night jar, were not enhanced by the depravity of the cabins. But I never heard my mother complain or offer any desire to be back in the city. I did often hear her say how much she treasured this time in the quiet woods, away from the traffic and the crush of the city. At night, she would light a lamp and gather us around her on the sprawling secondhand sofa and read Dickens to us. I can hardly read Dickens anymore, he's so slow and plodding, but then having her read to us was a delight. She kept a dictionary down there for us to look up words we didn't know. She mostly knew all the words in Dickens, but she taught us to love to read and how to learn about the words and the language. And we all did! There in the silence of the cabin, surrounded only by the muted night noises, she would pull Dickens off a shelf and she would read it to us until we could hardly keep our eyes open. Can you believe that? She read Dickens to us in the summers in the cabin before we slipped off to bed.

I loved those evenings. My memories of her voice reading to us are good memories, cozy and safe. She loved to read, and she instilled in each of us a love for books. I remember one time we had a big thunderstorm, with lots of lightning and thunder, so we had to all stay indoors. My mother offered us twenty-five cents, a quarter, which was a big deal at that time, for the best story we could write about the storm. So we all took the challenge and we spent hours writing about the storm. And she told us they were all so good, she gave us each a quarter! Can you believe that? I think we all learned to love to read at Water Oaks. We had an enforced one hour of quiet time after lunch, and if we couldn't sleep, we would read books.

And there were other special times with my mother that I remember from those summers. Every night she and I would walk alone together up the road to the mailbox to collect the mail. In the summers it would stay light, even in the woods, until well past eight, even nine. It was about a half mile up from our dirt road on the main road, and as we walked, my mother would teach me French. I have no idea why she knew and loved the French language so much, but she did. And she chose this opportunity to teach it to me. Years later, I was able to test out of the French classes in college because of my knowledge of French—knowledge freely given to me on our long walks in the twilight up to the mailbox in the summers. And sometimes in the mail would come a big box of books from the library near our home in St. Louis. There we belonged to the St. Louis Mercantile Library, and my mother had persuaded them to send us books throughout the summer. Then our fathers would take them back and deliver them to the library on their return trips. It was things like that I know we took for granted.

I do remember coveting my mother's swimsuit—a "bathing suit," she called it—as I got older. As kids, we had no swimsuits. That was a ridiculous idea. We simply jumped from water to land seamlessly, our clothes drying or soaking up water depending on our mood, the day, and our games. But when I began to sprout breasts, I noticed the boys' glances when my wet tee shirts accentuated my nipples and the ridges that made circles on my skin. At times the boys would giggle and point at my chest asserting itself. Other times their faces would turn bright red and they would turn away, bothered somehow both by my emerging breasts and by their own reactions to my sudden difference. One summer, our emerging sexuality led me to notice when their peckers would bulge beneath their wet shorts and, in turn, I would point and giggle, or turn away in surprised embarrassment. I think this was the summer I turned thirteen. Dave and his brothers were fourteen, fifteen, and sixteen by then. Even though I thought our mothers were oblivious to our lives and verbal exchanges, the following year a one-piece girl's swimsuit miraculously appeared in my summer bag of clothing. It was royal blue, and I guess after that we all had to admit Wini was no longer just "one of the boys."

On the weekends, our fathers would join us at the cabins. Generally the fathers worked Monday-to-Friday jobs in the city. Our father was an engineer and he luckily kept his job throughout the Depression. He did not make a lot of money, but he had a steady income. On Friday evenings after work, our fathers would meet up with each other and drive down together to Water Oaks. They would bring groceries, booze, and newspapers for the mothers to read. Their arrival was always an exciting time; we waited impatiently to see the dust of the cars as they headed down toward the cabins. Our mothers cooked more for dinner on the weekends, but only for Friday and Saturday nights, because by late Sunday afternoon, the fathers would be gathering up their belongings and would head back to the city. Sunday nights always seemed especially quiet after all the noise of male voices and big shoes clomping on the wood floors, the smell of cigarettes and cigars heavy in the cabin, more food smells, more laughter. Our mothers seemed glad to see them come and happy to see them leave.

I remember the year our fathers decided to create an elaborate pipeline from the spring into the cabins. Why they didn't just route river water to the cabins is beyond me. But several of them were engineers, so this should not have been a difficult task for them. I do remember that they would often be gone for hours working on the pipeline. One day we got curious and the pack of children went in search of the fathers. We found them drunk as skunks sitting on tree stumps deep in the woods. They weren't working on the pipeline, they were boozing it in the woods, telling jokes and bullshit stories to entertain each other. Later, in the city, the men would laugh about their escapades at Water Oaks with the beer. But their operation did actually work, because they put a pump on it. And the pump would pump the *water up the hill from this spring to a tank. And Dave and his brothers would get into this tank, and their chore was to take the frogs out. So this was our water supply. Then from there at the top cabin, it went downhill through miles of galvanized pipe to the different cabins.*

Oh, I almost forgot. We were always singing together at Water Oaks. We were a singing family. We would sit up late in the night, especially when the fathers were there, and sing for hours—college songs, old hymns, popular songs our mother knew all the words to, and silly songs that made the children laugh. One of my brothers was very into music and he would coordinate our singing. He would make little instruments for us, like with toilet paper and a comb. Did you ever do that? And he would make other instruments, even a crude violin, so that we had a sort of orchestra. And I would play the violin. It was great fun. Some of our children still sing. We were all singing families. We loved to sing. That must have been something if someone heard us singing at the cabins in the night. But the singing bug missed Dave and me. We never sang except at Water Oaks, still don't. But we loved it then and the memories of singing together are some of the best.

I think it was sad when several of the boys turned seventeen and eighteen, graduated from school, took summer jobs, and began to stay in the city with the fathers. Because we were the youngest, Dave and I stayed the longest at Water Oaks. We did that until I was about sixteen.

I remember one night when my mother and I spent some time down there toward the end of the summer, just my mother and me. And I remember one night sitting outside, and it was a beautiful night, the stars, you know, there were always so many stars down there. We were sitting out there and just getting this kind of high. And I remember thinking—I was sixteen—I would think, "Wow, I can do anything in the world." And I remember that moment, just thrilled with being alive and being with my mother.

Another thing that was important was that I loved school. You know, everybody else loves summer vacation. Well, so did I, but in the fall I could hardly wait to get back to school. And I bought my notebooks, and I wrote poetry. All of that. I mean, I loved school. I loved learning. And I was always bound and determined to be number one. And I know, later when we were on the farm, this was much later, my mother said, "I always thought you were sort of special." You see, she was very disappointed in some of the choices I was making. "I always thought you were special," I remember her saying that to me, and I think she always did think I was special. And I think I was special, too, but I shouldn't have ended up on the farm. That was her point.

Win's stories about her summers at Water Oaks paint an idyllic picture, while her writing from this period of her life gives us deeper insights into what she was thinking and feeling. Much of what she wrote was typical girl diary entries, while other sections of writing reveal a young mind much older than her years. Although Win did not talk to me about the journals she kept at Water Oaks as a young girl, I found them in some of the boxes I have in my study. Sharing what Win wrote during those summers adds an enchanting dimension to her stories as well as some surprising depth. In 1934, when she was barely twelve, Win already took her writerly task quite seriously:

BOOK ONE

Winifred Bryan
Born August 31, 1922
Daughter of
Mr. and Mrs. W. E. Bryan
Baptized and Confirmed
in the Episcopalian Church.
Born in St. Louis, Mo.
Winter Home
5915 DeGiverville,
St. Louis, Mo.
Summer Home
Water Oaks
R.R. #1, Box 15
Steeleville, MO

I am going to write a diary that it may be published when I die.

I dedicate this book to my parents to whom I owe my education.

WLB

August 15, 1934—5:00 PM

I am writing the first sentence in my diary.

Mother said it might be a good idea to write in my diary now and not by lamplight tonight.

This morning the boys left for camp. Everything was up in the air. The boys laid all their things out on the bed except for a few that were coming in the wash. Mr. Nixon was late, but when he did come Mother unpacked the wash and helped the boys pack. In less than no time they were off, and Mother and I certainly felt very lonely when the car went up the road. To appease my loneliness Mother allowed me to cook lunch. We had peas as our main dish and I learned how to prepare canned peas. I also did the dishes while Mom straightened the things upstairs, but they were not as much fun as preparing the meal, but it was all part of the job.

Tomorrow I am going to the old schoolhouse with the Nixons. There isn't much more to say except I'm very lonely. Goodnight.

There are pages and pages of handwritten journal entries during the summers of 1934 and 1935, but I can find no other records of her Water Oak summers. In this one diary, Win writes about her mother reading literature to her, and it is possible to see Win's love of language emerging. She describes the rainstorm as "coming down in sheets and torrents." Of her best friend, she writes, "Barbara and I are going to have a club and it will be very mysterious. We haven't decided on a fit name as yet, but we will." Her language seems beyond her years, as she tries out various styles of writing in her diary: "This morning Mary Alice and I went for a delightful little stroll, and came home with an uplifted spirit and a pair of wet feet. The day was wet and over-cast and the drizzling rain lent a misty atmosphere to the air. The weeds were all studded with Natures Diamonds which transferred to our heavy shoes as we brushed past. The mud was thick all along the road, but all of it, the mud, the rain, and the weeds each added their touch toward making that walk beautiful to me."

A day later, her entry takes a more philosophical turn when she ponders life and death and the role of religion. Her entry on July 2, 1935, reveals the depths of young Win's thinking. Her words expose many of the issues she would take to her grave nearly a century later.

I'm beginning to feel the meaning of that old saying, "Life is complicated." It certainly is. Lately I've had some of the strangest feelings that I can't explain at all. I want to know more than I know now. I want to learn about the strange things beyond. I'm impatient, and it seems strange to live in a world where one knows no more than the life that you are living now. I'm uncertain whether you really live eternally, or if that's just religion. How can I have faith when I have no foundation to build my religion on? How can I, or why should I, believe history? Yet look at the multitudes of faithful believers in God and Jesus Christ. The bible was supposedly written thousands of years back by the apostles of Christ, but how can I believe what my father or my mother say. Scientists dig out theories and call them facts, and I am called upon to believe them and—shall I?

No, I will find out for myself. Is this narrow mindedness? I'm afraid so, but here I am wandering into unknown realms. I have made a surprising discovery today. There is no-one who has entire control of himself. Perhaps you can keep yourself from willful sin, but who is the person who can love God when there is no love in their heart? I find my entire life is governed and ruled by obstinate moods. The new moods I have experienced of late I can-not describe. They are mainly ones of uncertainty. I do not know whether to love the world or hate it, to be good or bad, and I usually lapse from this uncomfortable state into any other mood. I feel that if I could control this period I could control most of my pettish, stubborn feelings.

What are the moods? There is the Religious Mood, Mood of Indifference, Ambitous [sic] Mood, and Mood of Resignation.

Among these, the first and third are more desirable, while the forth [sic] tends to make an inferiority complex.

I don't know what mood I'm having right now. I think it's ambition. Right now the bugs are eating me up, so I'll go inside now.

During their time at Water Oaks, Win read voraciously, as did her mother. She borrowed books from neighbors and kept meticulous records of who owned which book, so that she could return them when she finished. She adored this time with her mother; together they built many summer memories that could take them through the long winters in St. Louis.

August 16, 1934—8:00 PM

Last night it rained and Mom and I had to get up and put down all of the shutters. This happened at about 11:00 PM. At four I awoke again and the wind, rain and lightning combined finally persuaded us to repare [sic] to the bed inside. But when we were in there we found matters no better for in spite of the roof over-head a light shower was being sprinkled on the bed. We remedied this with an old rain-coat covering the damp portion of the bed. It was a steady rain all morning. In the afternoon it looked clearer so Mother and I visited the Walkers. Our dog, Lad, and the chickens did not get on very well, but in spite of the fact that I had to stand over him all day armed with a switch we had a grand time.

When we went home it was nearly dark and I rode part way on Marcia's horse.

Tonight when I went to get the milk I got pretty scared but I just whistled and thought about Lad which made me laugh and forget my silly fears.

I'll close now. Goodnight.

The Summer of 1935

Part One: Our Arrival [the history of Water Oaks]

Towards the first of the year 1935 and near the end of the first semester at school the novelty of classes and report cards, had well worn off and all the senses not dulled by school were alive and eagerly looking forward to the summer at Water Oaks.

When I was only three years old [1925] my father, Mr. Horner, an old school friend of mother's, Mr. Toensfeldt, a fraternity brother to Dad and Mr. Wormen (I don't know what our connections with Mr. Wormen are, but he's a good friend of their ours now.) clubbed together and bought three hundred acres of land. At Mrs. Horner's idea we built little cottages on this property where I have spent every summer since I was three years old. Today I have more feeling toward that little place than any other I know. When I grow up, for I'm only thirteen now, I shall say that I spent the happy days of my childhood there, but right now I'm rolling around in lazy contentment finding my youth very enjoyable.

I was also very eager to get back to the country as the result of a letter which arrived in February that read something to the effect of the following:

Dear Winifred,

I have a riddle for you to guess.
It's something
1. Brown and white
2. Very roly poly and mischievous
3. Has four legs—
And it's for you—

With Love,
Rosalie Walker

P.S. It's a little puppy. Write soon and tell me what to name it.

I was so excited that I refused to do any home-work that night and was occupied with the dictionary eagerly scanning Christian Names for Men (to name the dog) in the back of the volume. Week after week flew by and my spirits rose higher and higher and my grades went lower and lower, until it was time to leave for Water Oaks.

Win loved to talk about her childhood, particularly about the many years her family spent on the Meramec River at Water Oaks. In addition to the families who founded the Water Oaks compound, there were other families nearby with whom they socialized. Some of these families obviously had girls Win came to know over the years. But largely Win spent her summers playing with a group of five or six boys—her brothers and the Horner boys. These were formative years for Win in terms of how she thought about herself. To hear her tell it, she was no different from those boys, at least not for many years. Neither she nor they considered her gender to be different from theirs. They got the same summer haircuts and wore the same clothes. Although the differences in their anatomy gradually became of bemused interest, as when Win envied their "peckers" when urinating in the woods, she never lost the grounding she got there of equality and fairness based solely on talent and grit. In most things she could keep up with the boys, and in many ways she could best them. And she never let them forget it. She was strong, loud, brave, and determined. She confesses she was confused when the boys would call out words like "chicken," "wimp," "sissy," "girl," and even "pussy," to whichever of the kids wavered before plunging into the cold river from their favorite diving spots. Win attributed Dave's reluctance to join in the name-calling to his "having figured something out a long time before the others did." At this point in her story, she did not say exactly what Dave had figured out, but her perception of him as different and perhaps more astute than the other children would stay with her for a lifetime.

One of the major themes in Win's stories about her own life has to do with her steady relationship with David Horner. Having met as children, they grew up together nearly as siblings within the tight-knit group of families that were bonded in St. Louis and took their bonds to the Meramec River every summer. Both Win and Dave held to the idea that they were profoundly linked early on and were meant to be together throughout their long lives. What Dave wrote in her little book became the evidence that her decision to marry him was a good one. No matter where Win's journey took her, Dave was there by her side, encouraging her and making it possible for her to be successful in any way that he could. "I just want Wini to be happy" has become the epigraph for her tremendous devotion to this man for nearly a century.

Although life threw Win many curveballs in the years following her childhood and schooling, she held dear her sense of belonging and equality with boys and men. When gender inequality did rear its ugly head, she was not prepared. While the years spent in the company of the boys, competing with and challenging them, set the stage for her eventual success, she was depressed when she learned how her gender might limit her in the eyes of men. Until she began teaching at Missouri, she had never thought of herself as much different, and certainly not "less than," because she was a woman. Embedded in her account of her childhood summers at Water Oaks, we can hear several of Win's most frequently told stories—how their families managed to buy the land there, how "the mothers" spent their summers on the river while "the fathers" continued to work in the city and visit on weekends, and how all the children learned to love books and reading, far from the libraries and electric lights. This love of reading, writing, and learning, fostered in Win at a young age by her mother, would be one of the qualities that would guide her throughout the rest of her life.

2

Loving School and Being Popular

In the city where we lived, I can remember going to sleep to
the sound of the click of high heels walking along the sidewalks at
night.... I loved it all, the sounds of the city as I fell asleep.
I felt completely safe.

—Win Horner, on growing up in St. Louis

HAVING FALLEN IN LOVE WITH writing and books as a young child,
Win could not wait to begin school. She had fond memories of going to
school in St. Louis in the 1920s and later to college. She recalled how safe
she felt in St. Louis walking to elementary school, even after she was es-
corted by a policeman when a man exposed himself to her in the alley
behind her house. Her mother was angered by the incident, but Win was
unbothered—after all, she had seen it all before running free with her
brothers and friends at Water Oaks. Telling these stories about her youth-
ful days gave Win great pleasure. As a child she exhibited a matter-of-fact
approach to life and a lack of concern with breaking a few cultural taboos
that would later serve her well in her adult life.

Although they were not rich, all the members of Win's extended family were well educated, as were the parents of the other families that sum-
mered at Water Oaks. Ensuring that their children had a quality education was very important to Win's parents. It was understood, Win says,
that all the children would go to college. It was not discussed; it was assumed. Although Win's mother attended college for a year, she always
regretted that she had dropped out to get married, and she let Win know

she hoped Win would not follow that same path. A determined woman who wanted Win to have the very best schooling possible, Win's mother somehow managed to get her only daughter enrolled on scholarship in the most prestigious girls' school in St. Louis, Mary Institute. Win could not have been happier, and she later credited the school and her teachers there with her continued love for books and writing. She loved the classes, the books, the assignments, the notebooks, the pens, the paper, the poetry, and her friends. Few of her brothers, and not even her childhood friend and future husband, Dave, shared her love for schooling. Perhaps she loved school so much because she excelled at it, or perhaps she excelled at it because she loved it so much. Whatever the reason, Win was encouraged by her successes in school. She was highly competitive and always wanted to be the best in any class. When she wasn't the very best student, she found ways to improve her status, sometimes by getting the number one student to tutor her. In this way, she learned new skills that she quickly put to use in order to be number one again.

Mary Institute was a feeder school for girls to attend Washington University. At Wash U., as locals refer to the university, Win's life took a different turn, and, as she would say, "Here was a story!" Win's interest in being the best in the class became complicated by the fact that she also wanted to be the most popular girl in the class. As her popularity grew, Win would say, her grades faltered. Instead of studying for her exams, Win would plot how to get a dance partner for each of the important university dances. She became a careful flirt, setting her sights on the most popular boys in order to enhance her status as most popular girl. First one, then another, fell to her whims, and she danced off to the events on the arm of first one boy, then another. Win would laugh, however, when she admitted she had absolutely no interest in any of these boys. Already she had given her heart to Dave Horner, but that did not stop her from having a delightful time in college. That is, until her parents discovered how significantly her grades had dropped.

As she told these stories, Win's facial expressions were priceless. She could laugh at her own antics and feign distress when her father discovered her new approach to schooling. Mouth open wide, eyes bright, head cocked to the side, Win would let her face tell the story of her parents' dismay. But her laughter revealed that Win was having a great time, just a lovely time, both in school and in the recounting of how popular she became.

In the city where we lived, I can remember going to sleep to the sound of the click of high heels walking along the sidewalks at night. We lived on a street that went between two very busy streets with buses and streetcars running late into the night. We lived right on DeGiverville. Delmar and De-Baliviere are two really busy streets now, but this was before DeBaliviere got so busy. I loved it all, the sounds of the city as I fell asleep. I felt completely safe.

We lived in a pretty simple house. There was a point at which all of my mother and father's friends moved out to the county—that's what people do in St. Louis when they make it, they "move to the county," still do. But somehow my father lost some investments overnight, and the money he had put away for a house in the county disappeared. So when our friends' families left for the county, we stayed in the city. Our house was small but comfortable. It had one bathroom for our entire family—our mother and father, three boys, and me. So in those days, you did not use the bathroom to powder your nose. You went to the bathroom to go to the toilet and to take baths.

I remember great times sitting on my potty in the bathroom while my father shaved. We had lovely conversations. He would be standing there in his "altogether," as my mother would put it, and I thought nothing of it. Usually my mother and I made use of the bathroom first, and then the men of the family took over. We knew what shared space meant. The house was small, compact. We had very few closets, and they were tiny. But then, we didn't have that many clothes. I had two pairs of shoes, and that was very luxurious. And I had white-ribbed stockings held up with garters for Sunday, and brown ones for everyday.

When I was quite young, I went to a school that was only about three or four doors from us; my brothers went to a different school. The other students at this school were all from the same area—many lived in a bunch of apartments that had been built all around us. We were lucky because we owned a house. I recall my mother letting me walk to school by myself. I used to bang out the back door into the alley and walk down that narrow dark space toward the school. One day there was a man there, and he exposed himself to me. It didn't bother me that much. I had three older broth-

ers and a dad, so I thought, what's the big deal? I've seen that. I'd seen them all at one time or another. But I told my mother and she became very upset. I don't know how she arranged for it, but after the guy exposed himself to me, a policeman would come from the corner every morning and walk me down this little alley to school. That was so lovely; I felt very special.

It probably was not such a great neighborhood. I heard at one point that some of the Italian Mafia families lived near our neighborhood. There was this one little girl who had a white bunny fur coat. I thought it was just gorgeous, but my mother thought it was so tacky. Mom didn't go out and get to know the neighbors that much, I remember. At home, she was very vocal about the kinds of things we might tell her about the kids at school and their parents. She was quite protective. But as I got a bit older, my mother did allow me to ride on the streetcar with a girlfriend every Saturday. We felt so grown-up. We would go down to Grand Boulevard, have lunch sitting at the counter in Walgreens, and then we'd go to the movie. That was all very exciting.

I loved school, and I did really well in every class. I was always the smartest one in the class, until one year there was a person who was smarter than me. That upset me. I told her I wanted to hire her to tutor me, thinking I could learn what she knew and be the smartest one again. I got her to tutor me, but I actually learned there wasn't very much she could teach me. Maybe we were both smart for a while, I don't actually remember. The stakes were pretty high. At the end of the year in elementary school, the teachers would line up about six students who would get "double promoted." That meant we would be allowed to skip a grade. I always got double promoted, and as a result I graduated from high school really, really young. Actually it probably wasn't such a good practice. I don't think they do that anymore. I graduated from high school when I was barely sixteen, because I'd been double promoted a couple of times.

When I was going into the sixth grade, my mother somehow figured out a way for me to enter Mary Institute in St. Louis, a private school for the smartest and most elite girls. I am still not quite sure how she did that. My brothers went to Soldan High School in St. Louis, which was really a very good school. That was a story! My mother had actually talked to the principal about sending me there as well. But he cautioned against sending me there, telling my mother, "Well, I don't know if that's such a good idea *for a little girl. A lot of our students are from 'broken homes.'" He meant, of course, that some of the students had divorced parents. So my parents shook their heads and decided that it was not good for their little girl to go to a school with students who might have divorced parents. Good grief. But that was a lucky thing for me, because that's when my mother scrounged around and somehow got a half scholarship for me at Mary Institute. All my friends in the neighborhood told me, "They're so snobbish. You won't like it." But they were wrong. I loved, loved, loved it.*

All during my childhood, my mother was wonderful about allowing us to bring our friends over to our home on Sundays. We would all get up early, and she would make her wonderful version of cinnamon toast and cereal. Then we all went to church. When we came home, in the afternoons, my father and brothers would gather around the radio and listen to the New York Philharmonic. My mother was in the kitchen cooking up a storm. Sunday night each of us invited a friend over for dinner, which meant there was always a big group of people for Sunday night supper. That made for a wonderful mixture of male, female, youngsters of all ages. After a large dinner, we would mostly play games. We played clapping games and charades and things like that, all of us. Or we would sing. We'd get together, after dinner, and our father would lead us in singing. It was wonderful. We sang fraternity songs, old college songs and hymns. We sang and we sang.

My mother always had help around the house. She always had a laundress who would come on Monday and do the wash in the basement. On Tuesdays, Mother would iron. At least once a week, a cleaning woman came to help clean the house. I've never really thought about that, but that was quite privileged, although I am pretty certain we paid them pennies. They were the people who couldn't find any other work. They did cleaning and washing for those who could afford to pay for help. Also, we usually had a high school student who would come in from the country, live with us, and go to high school. I never thought of these girls as maids. They were considered family. This was the way my parents helped other families who had less than we did. I remember one girl that my mother was very, very fond of. They helped her all the way through college. She was a wonderful person and stayed close to our family for years.

As I remember it now, our mother had quite a lot to do keeping up with four children, all the wash, cooking, everything, even with help. I remem-

ber, too, that if the laundress, or the boy helper, or whatever, didn't arrive on Monday morning promptly, my father was sent down to find them. My mother was like that. Things were to be done properly and on time. We had to have everything washed on Monday. There were clotheslines strung all over the basement, where we had big boilers and water heating on a little stove. It was quite a job! It was a big job. All of her helpers, I think, were black women, but the cleaning woman was not. She was white, and her husband was a handyman. One night my mother paid her to babysit all us kids. Our parents didn't go out very much. But I remember this one time, the cleaning lady babysat us, and we talked her into taking us to a movie. Whoa. Boy, my mother, was furious. She fired her on the spot and didn't ever have her babysit anymore. My mother thought she was a bit "shifty," if you know what I mean. But she was very fond of her husband, the handyman, and I recall him coming around quite often to help with things at the house. I loved it, all those people coming in and out of our house, taking care of things. But then I never thought anything about that. Most of my friends at Mary Institute had maids, real maids, who did everything, even cooked the family meals. We never had a maid like that, but then, my mother was never in the basement helping launder the clothes with the laundress, either. She always had a schedule of what she needed to get done. She was always very busy. On Monday, she would gather up the laundry and send it downstairs. Tuesdays, I remember all that laundry piled up on the tables, and she was folding it and putting it away and mending. Everything was mended, you know, with a darning needle. We don't have such a thing anymore. Now we just throw it away, but then we all had darned socks. She would darn our socks with a darning egg. She spent Tuesdays sewing and mending—mending socks, mending everything, sewing on buttons, things like that. And she sewed, for us and for other people. All her life, she loved to sew. She made all of my clothes and her own as well. She could get lost doing that, in her own world. She was actually very creative. I remember she had an old pedal sewing machine that my father put a motor on for her.

My mother was not a socialite. In fact, she rarely visited with other women or left the house. In many ways she was actually way ahead of her time. How can I explain this? She was not a recluse. She avoided women's groups because she saw them as frivolous. She didn't belong to any women's groups or meet with her own friends. But she was progressive. She taught *me to always sign my own name, Winifred Bryan Horner, never Mrs. David Horner. She would tell me, "You are a person, not just someone attached to somebody else." She taught me that. And she always told me I was special. I always believed that, too, that I was special. I think that helped me through the years when I was really struggling.*

It's really strange the things one remembers. Even at Mary Institute, the girls were obsessed with boys and all things sexual. I remember one girl there who told me a dirty joke, but before she told me the joke she was explaining to all the girls how she had been experimenting with putting toothpaste on her clitoris. She showed us how to do that. I didn't think it was very exciting. It just kind of stung. But one day she told us, or perhaps just me, a dirty joke, and I told it to someone else at school and all hell broke loose. The teacher got me out in the hall and sat me on the bench. She wanted me to tell her the dirty joke. "What was the dirty joke?" she insisted. Oh, God, I was so embarrassed. I can remember it to this day, because I certainly did not want to repeat that joke to the teacher! I can't remember all of it, but it was something about a boy who told a girl, "I have a banana," and the little girl said, "Well, I have a fruit basket," or something like that. And the little boy said, "Could I put my banana in your fruit basket?" Can you believe that joke could cause all that trouble? Terrible, just terrible! Ha ha! Thinking about that incident later in life, I decided that this female teacher, to my mind, had a little bit of a prurient interest in this joke. Did you know that in those days, the St. Louis teachers were not allowed to be married? So, I decided later she might have been interested a bit in a little dirty joke, I'm not sure. At any rate, she finally got the joke out of me, and then we went down to the principal's office. Oh, I was embarrassed! And that high school student disappeared. We never saw her again. All that seemed a bit harsh for an adolescent dirty joke.

At Mary Institute, I met many of my long-term girlfriends—girls who, like me, went on to Washington University. We were sorority sisters. Both my family and Dave's family had been very instrumental in the support of Washington University. I think at one point Dave's grandfather was the chancellor at Washington University. We had a long heritage with Mary Institute. It was the preparatory girls' school for Washington University— Dave's mother went there; my mother went there. It was a serious school.

By the time I went there, it was the debutante school and all that, but I loved it, and I learned a great deal.

Not so much when I went to Washington University. By then I was ready to be a party girl, but there was a problem. I was on scholarship—that was the only way my father could afford to send me to Washington University—and my bad behavior got me into a lot of trouble with my father.

It was really funny—well, not so funny, actually—because at Wash U., I was bound and determined to be popular. I wanted to be the smartest in every class, of course, but I also wanted to be the most popular. And if I couldn't be the most popular, then I at least wanted to be very popular—the best, always the best—the smartest, and the most popular, which ended up being quite a difficult thing to pull off. It took a lot of work on my part to be popular. The studies always came easy for me, but I ended up spending a lot of time learning how to be popular. I studied the people that were popular. I researched it. I looked at them, and noticed they always seemed to be just so happy. So I was bound and determined to learn how to be that! I remember one of the things I learned was that to be popular, you could always tell a guy something like this: "You are so deep." Oh, man, that was wonderful to tell some guy he was deep. And the other line was, "I just don't understand you." Oh, that was good. We all wanted to be misunderstood, and the guys really wanted to appear "mysterious."

And guess what? I was popular. I did it! The rather strange part of this was that Dave and I already knew that we would probably be together forever. Sometime when we were children, we had made this determination. So all my work to be popular at the university was a bit off the point. Yet I worked terribly hard to go to all the dances on the arm of the most popular boys. I would scout it all out. I figured out which guy I would work on. He sat next to me in the history class. I worked on him all semester, and I finally got there. However, in the process, my history notes didn't fare so well. And, are you ready for this? I lost my scholarship! I was very, very popular, but I lost my scholarship. And my poor father was clearly not happy with me, for good reason. He was supporting me at Washington University—perhaps he paid probably a hundred dollars a semester tuition for me—but I had one brother at Purdue, and another one at the University of Chicago. All at once! I think my mother must have been a very good economizer. She did a lot with a little. But I had not noticed any of this.

I felt successful because at Washington University, I was a BMOC, you know, "big man on campus"—well, actually, I was BWOC, since I was a woman. And I was the first woman editor of the magazine. I was this and I was that. My successes were legion. But in the process, I lost my scholarship, and I was not invited to join Phi Beta Kappa. And the axe fell. Either I get my grades back up, or my father was going to pull me out of the university.

All of our families had gone to Washington University, so there was a tradition there. In those days, the professors knew our families. It was just amazing. I remember having this very well-known, highly regarded history professor. And the first day of the first class, he said, "I would like to see these students at the front of the class after class," and he ran off a list of names. The list included me. So, here were about twenty of us, staying after class. And he looked at us and said, "I have had your parents or your brothers or sisters in my class before, and I expect you to do well." That was it. Imagine! Can you imagine that? There was lots of pressure to do well, but I wanted to be popular. Much to my chagrin, he actually kept track of us. He was not impressed at all that I was popular.

And I made it into the sorority, the one I was supposed to get into. It was considered the best, of course. And they were my good friends for a long time. But during my senior year, I had had it. I didn't like it anymore. I didn't like the blackballing thing. Blackballing was the way we voted on who got in and who didn't. We would pass around a box, and we each had a marble, a white one and a black one. Well, you could put in a black one to vote someone down, and that was blackballing a person, so they couldn't get in. No explanation or telling who did it. They just didn't get in. It was not good. I just think that whole thing is wrong. It's just like voting on tenure at the university. People say things you cannot defend, and the vote is secret. It's not fair. Since then, I have not wanted to belong to groups that were exclusive. Later I would remember my mother saying she never wanted to be a member of a club that chose its members.

Once my Greek professor actually called my home. I lived at home, you understand. So my mother came to the phone. And I could hear only silence as she listened to my professor complain about my poor performance in his class. Finally I heard my mother say loud and clear, "Well then, flunk her. Fail her! And by the way, she's really not such a nice girl." She meant if I wasn't doing my work but only wanting to be popular. In the end, he was still trying to help me. I was faint with relief, and the night before the final, I spent the whole night trying to learn Greek. He thought I was such a nice young lady, but now I wonder about that!

Even though Win delighted in telling me she was a bit of a renegade in college, some of her papers suggest otherwise. It seems Win, the young woman, and Win, the older woman telling this story years later, wanted to paint a picture of a party girl with a new date every night. Yet it is hard to imagine her juggling all these young men, keeping them at bay when she had already settled on David Horner as her husband. But it is equally hard to imagine that Win wasn't serious when she claimed to be a big woman on campus. Luckily I found a folder marked "Wash U" in the stacks of folders in my study. I pulled it out. The pages were dark brown and brittle, and the date was March 22, 1942. I had unearthed a letter to a professor, the chairman of the board of student publications, at Washington University. This would have been Win's third year; she was a junior. She typed her letter of application:

> Dear Chairman:
>
> Once again this year, I am putting in my bid for the editorship of our school literary magazine, The Eliot. In my three years' work on the magazine in the positions of managing editor and member of the Literary Board, I have gained a great deal of experience. This experience, I believe, has been of value to me for I have become thoroughly acquainted not only with the mechanics of The Eliot but also with the problems of organization. In this letter I am outlining the solutions which I have worked out to these problems. . . . There is much room for improvement. In lurking around the office for the past three years, I have been thinking about several plans which might ameliorate the condition.

Win's single-spaced, typed, five-page letter outlines in great detail how she will improve the offices, proficiency, and financial situation of *The Eliot*. Her networking skills are evidenced by her suggestion that the staff have regular meetings with everyone on the campus interested in writing. She does not mince words, including some to the professor to whom she has addressed the letter: "It would be wise to have the faculty advisor present at as many of the meetings as he is able to attend." Win already knows how face-to-face conversations about the goals of the magazine with the staff and others interested in writing will improve the journal itself. She suggests inviting "all of the advanced composition and journalism classes, and a member of their class would be chosen as The Eliot representative." Included in Win's long letter are suggestions for specialized editors, a "Make-up" editor to lay out the magazine, a literary editor, managing editor, feature editor, copy editor, and photography editor. She proposes a kind of round-robin system for reading and voting on magazine submissions, and a regularly scheduled date for publication that is hard and fast. To that end, Win outlines a full year's suggested schedule, including a Freshman Issue, a Winter issue, an Exam Issue, a Valentine Issue, and a Senior Issue. She includes a photograph she feels is appropriate for the cover of the magazine. And she suggests that each issue feature a "popular student nightspot" that could tie in with advertisements, which would relieve the magazine of some of its financial burden. She suggests "News from the Front," to link the magazine to the politics of the times (this was 1942, after all), and she recommends that the editors write reviews of current movies, plays, and books. "This would give the members of the staff a chance to try their hand at reviews, which is a very important type of writing," she says. Finally, Win has another suggestion: "No fraternity politics, this is of paramount importance."

To put herself forward for the job of literary editor, Win tells the chair,

In my three years at Washington, I have had published over 70,000 words in the three campus publications. I am very much interested in writing and am at present writing two radio programs a week for KFUO. I will be a senior at the college . . . and incidentally, being a girl, am in no immediate danger of being drafted.

In this application there is one point which I would like to make absolutely clear. In the event that I received this appointment, I would abandon all of my other extra-curricular activities. . . . I feel that it is the job of the editor to see that all of the members of the staff are doing their work promptly and well. The plan which I have outlined here seems to me to be very practicable and it is the result of three years' experience on the staff as well as a great deal of thought. I sincerely believe that if given the opportunity I could put these ideas into actual form and make The Eliot something more than a proverbial "pain in the neck." Thank you very much for your consideration in this matter.

Sincerely yours,
Winifred Bryan

In Win's handwriting, at the top of page 1 of this letter, I find these words: "Received Appointment, April 8, 1942." I think that despite Win's being set on presenting herself as a party girl, her commitment to writing and to the writing opportunities for Wash U. students, including herself, is evident in this letter. She promises to abandon all other "extra-curricular" activities and devote herself to the literary magazine. Her suggestions to the publication's advisor also hold the promise of a diversified writing agenda, including student stories, plays, and poems, while also calling for book, movie, and play reviews, because "that is a kind of writing students should learn how to do." Already Win is looking beyond the sanctified space of literature in the pages of the "literary" magazine. She plans to invite the composition and journalism teachers and students to join the ranks of the magazine. Not even Win knew she was advocating for good writing in every aspect of university life, both in the classroom and beyond, as early as 1942. Many years later, she would identify this as "writing across the curriculum" in her position as director of the composition program at Missouri. But the seeds had been sown at Washington University, and Win was already on a roll. She argued well for this unpaid editorial position her senior year at the university, and undoubtedly she did become BWOC, a position she certainly held with aplomb. I can just see her striding across campus with a new lilt to her step, shoulders back, a smile on her face.

In the folder with her application letter, Win also included carbon copies of four articles she wrote for the KFUO radio station spots she mentions in her letter. Penned during the Depression years, when Win was in college, these are imaginary accounts of car trips to interesting towns in the region. They are dated in her hand: "KFUO, Saturday, 4/4/42; 4/11/42; 4/18/42; and 4/25/42; all aired at 4/15 P.M." The imaginary accounts are of drives to Ste. Genevieve, Hannibal, St. Louis,

and St. Charles, Missouri, respectively. She begins the first of these traveling excursions to Ste. Genevieve this way:

With the rubber priority, most of us are confined pretty much to
our homes these days. A joy ride through the state is now a thing
of the past and our voyages must be confined to rides to the end of
the streetcar line on a Sunday pass. However, with the first days
of spring, that fever of adventure comes once again. So sit back in
your chair and come with me while we take a trip through the rolling Missouri countryside.

This afternoon our tour takes us to the picturesque town of Ste.
Genevieve on the sunny banks of the Mississippi in southeastern
Missouri. We approach the town by way of the State Highway from
the north; our modern vehicle traversing the same road which was
laid down as the royal route between Ste. Genevieve and St. Louis
by the King of Spain when that illustrious monarch held sway over
this land. And before that time, the highway was used as a path
by the Indians who roamed the Missouri hillsides. What a pageant
lies before our eyes as we imagine the scores of travelers who have
faced this same sun and whose feet have tread the same ground.
First, the redskinned Indian, marking his way by the sun, hunting
game and walking stealthily to avoid any chance enemy lurking
by the way. Then the early French and Spanish pioneers traveling
over the road in covered wagons facing the glare of the hot sun.
After them the early traders transporting goods between the cities.
And, then, the lonesome cry of the train whistle bringing a world of
industry and machinery in its wake. This is the road which we are
traveling now. What dreams, what sorrows, what hopes have been
cherished along this way.

Win's detailed account of this "trip" takes the listener into the town as
though traveling on specific roads. She describes the breathtaking views
from the impressive hills in this part of Missouri, and she talks about
the limestone quarries and the "three large lime-kilns belching clouds
of smoke." She describes in detail the narrow streets, the older houses
built in the 1790s by the wealthy residents, and the rows of tiny houses
probably home to the factory workers. She writes about the church on the

hill and Du Bourg Place, the town's public square, the Louisiana Academy Building, organized in 1806 as a free school for the children of poor whites and Indians, the historic home of Senator Lewis F. Linn, and that of Dr. Benjamin Shaw, one of the earliest physicians in Missouri. Win writes of the respected family name of Valle and the various Valle homes in the town, and she tells of the tradition of La Guignolee, in which, on New Year's Eve, the Valle family opened their doors and fed the whole town, rich and poor alike. What she then describes, without naming it, is the modified version of this tradition, known elsewhere as "mumming," where town residents travel house-to-house singing in exchange for food. Win closes that afternoon's radio show with the following:

The inhabitants of quiet Ste. Genevieve are making their way towards their homes in the waning light of the evening. Do you see that old woman walking down the street? Her head is slightly stooped and she walks slowly in the dimming light. In her arms she carries a bundle of groceries and nods occasionally at the passerby who respectfully tips his hat. She winds slowly down the street, past the old houses dreaming at her from out of the legends of the past. She passes the small church lifting its spires in the clear cool night air. She pauses but for a moment and then moves on and is lost in the darkening shadows of the oncoming night. The streets are deserted now. One by one lights appear in the windows. It is with deep regret that we turn our backs on the quietness and calm of old Sainte Genevieve, and make our way home once again.

In similar fashion, Win describes a trip to Hannibal, the home of Mark Twain. In another, she walks the streets of St. Charles, pointing out the sights in this historic town to her listeners all over the city. And she brings them all home with her account of downtown St. Louis, her own hometown.

This afternoon our tour takes us into the heart of our own city of St. Louis. We walk to the nearest corner and board a street-car which takes us into the downtown section. Yes, I know what you are thinking! "Isn't this silly? Why, I go downtown every day. Why in the world should I trot around down there on a beautiful afternoon like this?" I know you've all seen the office buildings and the department stores, and of course, you haven't missed the Plaza. But, have you ever been through the old Cathedral or fingered through the musty files which are still on the Judge's desk in the old courthouse? You haven't? Well, come with me. You have a lot to learn about your own city.

Win writes that the first settlers to the area now known as St. Louis were a group of monks who founded the Jesuit mission of St. Francis Xavier and worked with the Indian tribes of Kaskaskians and Tamaroans in an effort to form a stable settlement, which lasted only three years. She tells of Pierre Laclede Liguest, who brought the fur trade to the city and suggested they name the city after Louis IX, the Crusader king of France. By 1768, Laclede's fur business helped make the city a center for trade, and in 1803, the Louisiana Purchase made it the "crossroads of the continent." Win relates the story of the famous Dred Scott case, which took place in the Old Courthouse in downtown St. Louis. She further notes that "Louise Minor, a pioneer woman suffragist, sued for the right to vote." She concludes this travelogue with her typical goodbye:

The afternoon is coming to an end and we board our street-car to get home again before dark. We quickly pass through the old part of St. Louis, the tiny group of historic houses near the waterfront, and once again we step into the modern world of speed and noise. How strange and incongruous it seems! The tiny Cathedral crouched in between office buildings and noisy busy streets, and the Old Court House—now only a refuge for bums, old and out of use, tribute to the men who built them and above all, a living memorial to the men who founded the modern, prosperous city of St. Louis.

It is important to remember that when she wrote these radio stories Win Horner was still a teenager. During a time when she was apparently doing poorly in some of her classes, applying for the editorship of the literary magazine, and flirting with all the most popular boys in her classes, Win was also busy *writing*. Long before the internet and the quick facts available today on Wikipedia, Win must have spent long hours in the library gathering the information for these radio spots. Her style is captivating. She takes her listeners on day trips to towns they already probably know fairly well but tells them stories of interest they may or may not have heard. Win's sense of humor is already in evidence, and her sense of plot and action, her ability to bring her listeners along for the ride, are clearly being honed.

Apparently Win ended her college career at Washington University in high style. She had loved every minute of her time there and she had met both her goals—to write and to become popular. Her ability to juggle all the varied aspects of her personality and her interests had already taken hold. She was an organizer; she loved to take on leadership roles; she understood the importance of working well with others; she loved to socialize and tell stories; and she was energetic, witty, and fun to be around. All of these characteristics should have enabled Win to succeed, but her accomplishments and the strong support of her family had, as she put it, *not prepared* her for the obstacles that lay ahead. It would take thirty years before she could find her way again to the person and the writer she thought she would become as she completed her college education at the age of twenty.

Recently Dave Horner described the year 1943 to me as "fast and furious." In February of that year, he and Win had a formal engagement party in St. Louis. In early June, Win graduated from Washington University. Whatever plans, hopes, and dreams the young Winifred Bryan had at that moment were put on hold, for with World War II underway, she and Dave Horner did what all their friends were doing—they quickly got married. Their wedding took place on June 15, and by July, Win had packed her first tidy trunk of essentials and struck out to live as close as she could to her new husband as he traveled with the army.

And, as Win would say, "therein lies another story."

3

Funny War Bride

War or no war, pay or no pay, we're going to get married, come hell or fury. But, hell and fury never really came. They just sent small deputies, representative samples of their talent into our lives.

—Win Horner, *Bag and Baggage*

AFTER HER TIME AT WASHINGTON University, the story of young Winifred Bryan takes a sharp turn. Like so many people of her generation, she and Dave Horner prepared to meet the reality of the war by getting married. The "boys" were leaving the country to "go fight," and the girls wanted a proper wedding. Win and Dave got caught up in the frenzy. Today Win is ready to talk about this phase of her life. *What a time it was,* she repeats several times, pausing to shake her head, remembering the beginning of the war and the start of her marriage. Then she begins to speak.

We basically got married because everyone else was getting married, although Dave still says we got married so we could have sex. Ha! Which I guess was true on one level.

So, let's start with the wedding. I need to say that this was during the time when I was still completely doing the "traditional track." It was a most traditional wedding. I still have the veil that my mother made—it was put over our face and then it was lifted, you know, like this, once we were announced "man and wife"—not husband and wife, but man and wife—so Dave could kiss me. Now, in the tradition in which I grew up, the wedding gifts were not practical things. They were china and silver. And that's what we got for wedding presents. Really, really practical for the farm—ha! Well, not so much, really, helpful, for where we were headed. Although I did not realize this at the time.

For our wedding, we got all this beautiful stuff. In St. Louis among our crowd, the tradition was that you displayed your wedding presents in a room in your house. So we did this in my parents' house. And then you had a tea and everybody came and looked at your wedding presents, and compared their wedding presents with your wedding presents. There were no real surprises because it was all the expected china and silver. All the practical things like sheets and towels, that part was supplied by the bride's family. And I had—are you ready for this? I had a hope chest! Yes, I did! In my hope chest, I had embroidered napkins. I had tablecloths, pure linen. That was about the extent of my trousseau. My mother and I made those, a lot of them. I embroidered for years, it seemed, for what I did not know at the time.

Our wedding, that is, the ceremony, was very traditional, you know, the vows and all of that. One thing I need to explain to you, which may seem as traditional as everything else, was that I was a virgin. Really! Now, who could believe this? That I was a virgin? Most of my friends were into heavy petting, and I was, too. This is very funny, because these activities were a bit curtailed for me because I was very flat chested. Unfortunately, I still am! So I always had my bras stuffed with stockings and other things. We didn't have nice pads in those days, so all that stuffing really did reduce the possibilities for successful petting. Indeed, it kept me covered and a bit safe. Our wedding was pretty important. We got married, and pretty quick, I was no longer a virgin. We had our honeymoon down at the family cabin, down at Water Oaks, because we couldn't afford anything else. We had no electricity and no running water, but we didn't care because we spent most of our time in bed!

Actually, I think I need to go back just a little bit, before the wedding. Dave had left Washington University for the University of Illinois. He knew he would be drafted, so he signed up for the military. But he was enrolled in the agriculture courses with the understanding that he could complete his university degree, then start his army training in meteorology. But two months later, he was called up much earlier than he expected. He was lucky, *though, because all through the war, he stayed in this country and he never had to become a foot soldier. My family insisted that I graduate before getting married, but even then we married against our family's wishes. They thought we were much too young. Which, indeed, we were! And we had no money. But that did not seem to matter to us.*

Then we began the constant moving from one base to another. I went everywhere Dave went. I think his first post was in Michigan. By that time, I had developed a painful urinary tract infection. This is a great story! Ha! You will love this. I thought the pain and discomfort were just symptoms of normal marriage and sex. I thought that was the standard thing, but it did make me wonder, "Was this the great thing the poets write about?" For it really was not so pleasant. In Michigan, when Dave was in the military, we did have some friends, particularly this friendly older couple who lived next door. In my misery, I explained my problems to the woman. She laughed at me, but she also told me what to do. "I think you have an infection," she said. "This is not just what sex feels like normally. I think you need to see the doctor." So I saw the doctor, and I got an antibiotic. And then life looked up, and marriage and sex took on a new meaning for me. Much better, I told her later. Dave was, of course, delighted. During his meteorology training, Dave was allowed twenty-four hours a week at home with me. And, of course, those we spent mostly in bed.

Win laughs at this story in her delightful way, shrugging her shoulders and opening her mouth wide in mock embarrassment.

During the war years, Win followed Dave to every military base where he was assigned, often to the chagrin of the officers in his regiments. War wives were not encouraged to follow the men in uniform because it distracted them and used up all their military pay for the meager living quarters the wives could find in the nearby towns. But Win and Dave were determined to live together as much as possible. During these years of traveling all over the country, Win wrote her first lengthy piece, which she called a novel. She titled it *Bag and Baggage: The Sad Saga of an Army Wife, the Girl He Didn't Leave Behind Him.* The manuscript proudly bears the author's name: Winifred Bryan Horner, 706 West Prescott, Salina, Kansas. It runs 176 typed pages and describes in detail what Win's life was like following Dave from base to base—from descriptions of how she walked the pavement until her feet were sore seeking lodging for them in every post town, to the inadequate bus systems, their meager financial situation, the various jobs she took to help them make ends meet, and how she longed to be "domestic." At this time, Win was only in her early twenties, but she was already honing her literary skills as well as her wit and sense of humor.

What follows are some of my favorite excerpts from this hilarious account of a young married woman dutifully following her new husband off to his military appointments.

Chapter One: "Off We Went"

In following my husband from camp to camp during the past eight months, I have aged considerably in thought and appearance, but I had no idea how extensive this physical deterioration was until the egg woman mistook me for my husband's mother. I was busy in the kitchen trying to prepare a meatless dinner in our two pans when Dave came back and said with just the hint of a smile that the egg woman was at the door. "She said she wanted to see my mother, and I suppose she meant you." Picking up my crutches, I rose from my wheelchair and brushing the wisps of gray hair back from my wrinkled forehead, I limped to the door. The incident was passed off with profuse apologies on the part of the egg woman and feeble attempts at laughing about it on my part. But the whole thing had an unmistakable air of tragedy. To be taken for the mother of your twenty-two-year-old husband at the age of twenty-one is one of those unfortunate moments in life!

Your shoulders are bound to stoop a bit when they've borne the weight of several suitcases and a trunk, and a few white hairs just may creep in when at twelve o'clock at night in some strange army town you still haven't found a place to sleep. As a matter of fact, I don't have any white hair, and I don't use crutches yet, but if our Army perambulations keep on at their present rate, people will begin to mistake me for my husband's grandmother!

Dave's and my marriage could hardly be called a war marriage in the usual sense of the word, since our courtship extended over some twenty years. For the first fifteen years of our life, we were able to knock each other about and managed to become thoroughly aware of each other's faults and the few isolated virtues which we possessed at the time. Dave did not even realize that I was of the female gender until some years later he asked me why I wore a piece of net at the top of my swimming suit. We pondered on this fact for a few minutes and then posed the question to our wiser elders, who said something vague about our knowing later. For the most part, during the early years, I was nothing more to Dave than a little squirt who could be batted around at pleasure.

In the course of time, when I was 16 and Dave 17, we arrived at the dating stage with Dave standing back to allow me to go through doors first and with me looking soulfully into his eyes realizing with true feminine instinct that here was a male who must be flattered and attracted. Dave grew to the height of six feet, and I began to wear tops to my swimming suits for more obvious reasons, although I never excelled in that category all my life.

In June of 1943, I ambled up the aisle in a borrowed dress to the tune of "Here Comes the Bride." I was a little scared about the wedding, but all the way up the aisle, I had to support my father who was considerably worse off than I. My part in the affair, however, was nothing compared to Dave's. In accordance with the gruesome custom of our time, he had to stand in full view of the assembled congregation the whole time that my attendants and I slowly sauntered down the aisle.

Dave was already in the Army when we were married. In fact, he had been wearing the GI khaki for three and a half months. He enlisted at Chanute Field in the Army Air Corps Reserve in October, 1942, and was told at that time that he would not be called until he had finished school some eleven months later. In spite of this rosy promise, the Army, under circumstances beyond their control, called him to active duty in February of the next year. It came as a shock for we'd become engaged four days before. Plans for our wedding were knocked awry. We'd have to wait until after the war, I thought. Grim thought! Yet, how could we live on a cadet's pay of seventy-five dollars a month? For four months we muddled that and other little items over and in June came to the conclusion of our day. War or no war, pay or no pay, we're going to get married, come hell or fury. But, hell and fury never really came. They just sent small deputies, representative samples of their talent into our lives.

While I was finishing school, Dave was taking his basic training at Boca Raton, Florida. He arrived with some thousand other cadets and for a few weeks the army was at a complete loss as to just what to do with all of the new recruits. The basic training lasted for three and a half weeks, and at the end of that time with seven hundred other cadets, he was sent to the Meteorology Training School at Grand Rapids, Michigan. This course covered thirty-three weeks and was divided into three terms of eleven weeks each. Between each of these periods, the cadets were given a seven-day furlough.

It was during Dave's first furlough that I re-entered the picture to complicate his life and bewilder the army. On June 15, we were married, and I subsequently accompanied my new husband to Grand Rapids where I lived in an apartment, and Dave went back to his barracks. At that point, Dave still had twenty-two weeks of his training ahead of him, and as for me, little did I know what I had ahead of me! It wasn't exactly an ideal existence for a newly married couple with so little time to ourselves, but we managed until, in September, the school was moved to Chanute Field in Illinois. I, and about two hundred other cadet wives, took up our residence in the already overcrowded town of Champaign. It was there on November 29 that Dave received his commission and a pair of second lieutenant bars. Naturally, we were both eager to know where he would be sent, but we didn't find out until two days before graduation. At a big assembly, the commanding officer read off the cadets' names and the posts to which they would be assigned. The army tried to station the new officers at posts fairly close to their homes. Dave got Salina, Kansas, which is about six hundred miles from St. Louis, the army's idea of being "close to home."

After a ten-day leave, we made our way to Salina, rather sadly prepared for whatever fate awaited us there. In spite of the way everyone shook his head when we inquired about apartments, we managed to find a fairly respectable one after three weeks. Dave's hours became easier, and he was home every night for dinner. We even had enough time to have a healthy argument now and again.

A few years ago, all a bride had to know was how to cook and sew a straight seam, but the war bride has to know how to find an apartment, how to cook in any kind of a kitchen, how to get train reservations, how to conduct herself under the eagle eye of an MP, and how to make ends meet when half your income goes for rent. During the past eight months, I have managed to learn a few of these things the hard way, so, if broken dishes and wrinkled clothes don't turn your stomach, I refer you to the following pages wherein is detailed the ridiculous fate of one army wife who just didn't know any better.

Chapter Two: "Our Old Kit Bag"

My first real introduction to my new role in life was on my wedding day. The traditional bride spends the day beauty napping or in other equally lady-like pursuits—but not the war bride. Her wedding day is occupied with packing the "old kit bag." On this day of days, I had been trying to jam all of my clothes, our household belongings, and a chosen few of our wedding presents into my all too inadequate trunk. As a matter of fact, I was the only person in the house calm enough to do the job. My mother was no help, since she was inclined to get sentimental over the whole process while my father and brothers, in honor of the occasion, were toasting the bride downstairs.

The bride, in the meantime, was sweating away upstairs trying to pack. After everyone else had left for the church, my father and I were balanced on the trunk trying to get it to close—he in his tux and I in my wedding gown. It stubbornly refused and when it finally succumbed only after Dad and I had jumped up and down on it for a few minutes, it closed on my train. Then the question arose as to whether I should drag the trunk down the aisle with me, or whether I had better leave the trunk as well as my veil at home. Since my father didn't like either of these suggestions, we opened the trunk and after a few more acrobatics on its already battered lid, succeeded in shutting it.

In the rest of this chapter, Win describes the travails of packing and unpacking all their worldly possessions when Dave's orders moved them to a new place, sometimes weeks or months after setting up house in one unfortunate apartment after another. Win recounts how she failed to master the task of repacking, as more things seemed to accumulate with each move.

Chapter 3: "The Filthy Lucre"

Faced with the problem of trying to recover from our last cross country move, and saving something for the next, we came to the unhappy conclusion that our children would just have to work their way through college. We figured it would be character building anyway. So, we busied ourselves with the more imminent task of making our running expenses meet. A second lieutenant's pay sounds like a small gold mine, but in this day and age it's nothing more than a drop in the bucket. Just as you are beginning to get nicely settled and the tangled finances are beginning to straighten themselves out, your husband's orders come through and he is transferred to California.

When Dave and I started out, we didn't have money, but we had a lot of security. We are young and possess a certain amount of respect and fondness for each other. I have perfect faith in his ability to make a million dollars and he has perfect faith in my ability to cook, although that is sometimes misplaced, and in my ability to find an apartment. If you think it's easy to make a million dollars, it's nothing compared to the task of finding an apartment in an army town. And, so, we started out with our love in our pocket, our youth in the bank, and our unlimited confidence in each other, and we've never been poor.

After Dave's meteorology training was completed, he was assigned to his first airbase, the Smokey Hill Air Force Base near Salina, Kansas. The assignment was given out in typical military confusion. From the 720 cadets who were graduating, it came as good news when it was announced that all the assignments were domestic. None of them went overseas. It came as further good news when a young captain in charge announced that "trades" were acceptable, because people got assigned anywhere around the country. So, they all began to scramble up to the microphone. And this one young guy from New York said, "Here's a hundred dollars for anything east of the Mississippi." He wanted to get back to New York. Here were all these cadets, grabbing the microphone, trying to make trades. And then one kid grabbed the microphone and pleaded in a strong Brooklyn accent, "I'll trade Nebraska, for anything east of the Mississippi."

In the meantime, the secretarial pool had been typing the original orders and had completed the letters A through H. So, then it was announced that only trades from I through Z would go through, which meant Dave's original assignment to Salina, Kansas, went through. And that's how we went to Salina, Kansas. Now during the war, there was no construction. So it was very difficult to get any place to live. We went to Salina, and we traveled with just one trunk, which had our china and our bedding, but none of our silver!

Our first apartment after we got married, Dave had gotten it ahead of time, was a master bedroom in an old mansion. And the bathroom was half the size of the apartment with a spacious tub. It was a wonderful little apartment. The bed came down out of the wall. And I cooked dinner. The guys were incarcerated except for 24 hours on Saturday night. So I took a job. And I cooked dinner for two other cadets' wives. And I got 60 cents apiece from them to cook for them, which helped.

And, then, Dave had to go and graduate. And we were assigned to go somewhere else. I'm thinking we went back to Salina. Our orders were all messed up, as I described. But, when we landed in Salina, Dave was supposedly available 24 hours one day a week. That was very nice, because he had graduated. He was now a lieutenant, a second lieutenant.

I, in the meantime, once again spent my time looking for a place to live. First of all, we were in a little hotel, but you could not stay at the hotel more than four days. You had to get out, because they needed the rooms. So I started looking. And I still looked pretty nice, you know? So I went to the housing facility, and the lady there said, "There's this real nice family willing to rent to a couple, but they want to pick out who stays with them." So, it was clear, they didn't want just anybody. I went there to meet this lady, and, of course, I got it for Dave and me.

Dave loved it. It was a really nice family, and it was a lovely room. But by now, I was into domesticity, you know? I wanted to start being a wife and have my own house. So, eventually, I found this other place. It was one room at the back of a house. And the address was 820 Highland Rear. That really upset our family. They said, "What kind of a place is 820 Highland Rear?" But I didn't care. It was private and it was ours. It had a bathroom, and we had a hot plate. That was enough for me. I fixed breakfast, and I would rinse the dishes in the shower after Dave had taken his shower and left. I would wash them in the shower! And I was so happy. I would darn socks. I was domestic. And we ate dinner at the officers' club every night, which I loved.

Then, finally, we found a little house. Oh! I was so excited. It had a bedroom with a real bed in it. And it had a kitchen. And it had a living room and a little dining area. Oh, it was just heaven. And I got so domestic you could hardly stand it.

Dave came home from the office one evening and he said, "And what did you do today?"

And I said, quite proudly, "I ironed your underwear."

And Dave looked at me and said, "You ironed my underwear?"

And I said, "Yes. I ironed all your underwear. And I fixed dinner."

And Dave said to me, "Win, I thank you for all you did today, but tomorrow why don't you get out of the apartment or read a book, and we'll talk about that when I get home. I really don't think you need to ever iron my underwear again."

And then I knew I had married the right man.

Actually, I spent a great deal of my time drinking coffee with my "fellow" officers' wives, who also lived in these little dollhouses. I wasted my time, but I was enjoying the coffee. We would start as soon as our husbands went to work. We would meet and drink coffee. We'd try to get back when they came home from work. And we talked about nothing, absolutely nothing. None of us were doing anything.

After a look at the financial situation of Cadet and Mrs. David A. Horner, it becomes apparent that since the Cadet part was worth only seventy-five dollars per month, the Mrs. found herself obliged to venture into the business world and earn a little "where-with-all." At that time, I did not see myself as a career girl at heart, and as a matter of fact, domesticity was much more in my line. I'd take a plain apron in lieu of a white collar any day of the week, but there comes a time in the life of every soldier's wife when she isn't allowed to choose her course of action. So, with a tear in my eye, and a catch in my throat, I bid a fond farewell to my little kitchen and plunged into my pursuit of the old "do-re-me."

For a time, I had a job at a bank. During the course of that first job in the bank, I managed to sadden the heart of my employer, lower the office morale, and greatly improve my shorthand and typing at their expense. After the first few weeks, I was given a desk in the vault and there behind locked doors, I was assigned the task of keeping up the bankbooks. I found it very difficult to concentrate on the work at hand, while carts laden with packages of ten dollar bills rolled back and forth beside my desk. No matter how hard I tried to balance the figures before me, I would find myself considering the possibilities of walking away with several thousand dollars in my purse. It looked so easy, and during the course of each day I would figure out two or three foolproof methods of robbing the bank. Only my early memories of Dick Tracy and his lesson that "Crime Doesn't

Pay" held me back. So, I watched the carts roll by and did nothing more than gaze sadly at them and wistfully finger a few bills.

After that, the job at the bank became more interesting and less dangerous. My smarts and education came in very handy. The bank officers, all men, were on the first floor. On the second floor was a pool of secretaries. And in charge of us at a desk was this woman who always wore a hat. All of us typed all day long, mostly typing names on war bonds and things like that, which was very tedious. But every once in a while, one of the officers downstairs, one of the men, would call for one of the "girls"—we were not "girls" but that is how they referred to us—to take a letter down. Oh, that was very important, when that happened.

So, finally one day I was called. Now, I had taken shorthand, but I wasn't very good at it. So I went down there, took my little notebook, and the officer dictated this letter. I took it all down very dutifully, but in the end I couldn't read my shorthand! Basically, I memorized what he had said. So, I went back to my typewriter, real quick, and wrote a really good letter—better than his letter, I might add. I fixed it up for him, correcting his grammar and making it sound much better. So, I became very much sought after, because I wrote these brilliant letters for them that made them look so good. Because I was a good writer! Already, I was a writer. I just memorized what they said, then I would get right up there to my typewriter and write it out with a few embellishments. I became much sought after, which made me quite proud, and I thought I had "arrived" at the bank. Mostly they called for me to type their letters.

Unfortunately, Dave was transferred after three months. They moved these cadets everywhere. And then we went back to Chanute Field for him to finish his training there. When we got there, we didn't have a place to stay, but our family had some friends there and they took us in. We had one room in a house that was very friendly. And I took another job. This time I worked in an office where there was one young captain who came in every once in a while. He was in charge, and there were four "girls," working there.

Number One girl did most of the work. She really ran the office. And this captain would come in every so often and say hello in between his golf games. Ha! He was never around.

But here, I got a different job and I loved it—a job which my friends had gotten for me. So, they didn't know what to expect when I arrived. Earlier I had honed my shorthand skills and typing skills, and I still looked pretty good! This job was quite different. Here I worked in the lab. And I loved it, because I took notes during autopsies. It seemed I had a really strong stomach, so the doctor would do the autopsy, and I would take notes. I did very well at that, too, because I had had four years of Latin and one year of Greek, although I had not excelled in either one. But I knew how to spell the medical terms, sometimes with the help of a little dictionary. But he was quite impressed, and my desk was in the lab. And they used to let me run the samples. I would go up and collect the sample. I didn't actually "take" the sample, I just collected it and I brought it back to the lab. They would make a slide of the red blood cells, and then I would sit there with little clickers and count the red blood cells. Click, Click, Click, like that. Then, they would get a little slide of the white blood cells, and we would do the same thing. So this office was clicking all the time. Click, click, click, click, click, click. And I was running around taking samples back and forth. I actually enjoyed it. It gave me a chance to walk around the hospital, get to know the patients. It was a wonderful job. I loved it.

Then, for three months, in Champaign, I was employed in a hospital as secretary to the pathologist. From stenographer to secretary was a considerable promotion and from bank dictation to medical dictation was quite a leap in spite of the fact that my salary remained the same. My employer and I got along fine since he had a weakness for secretaries with pretty legs, and mine aren't considered so bad in some circles. After I had settled down and rearranged the supplies on my desk two or three times on my first morning, the doctor came in and said that he wanted to do the "surgicals." I took my shorthand book and followed him into his office having no idea what was in store for me, but expecting the worst.

There before my eyes were arranged all the odd pieces of anatomy that had been removed from various patients during the last few days. They ran predominately to appendices and pieces of the female anatomy which one doesn't mention in polite company. Then the doctor proceeded to remove these gory objects from their bottles and measure and describe them in minute detail. "The specimen consists of," and then would follow a weird description with appropriate adjectives like "gray-yellow, smooth, and glistening." At first I was too embarrassed and too busy trying to get the peculiar medical terms down in my notebook to look around much, but after I got used to it, I found myself studying some unfortunate woman's erstwhile fallopian tube just as intently as he did. As a matter of fact, it was all very enlightening although the medical terms were a bit bewildering at first.

All this time, my education was continuing by leaps and bounds. You can't work around a hospital where ovaries are used as decorations in your office and not begin to learn a great deal about the birds and the bees. Every day I was learning something new about my anatomy and everyone else's. These pieces of information I would faithfully relate in full to my husband. The day I discovered fallopian tubes, I asked Dave if he knew about such things. He said that, of course, he did. I proceeded then to get very angry and asked him why he had never told me about them. He looked at me for a minute and then said quite calmly, "Well, Win, to tell you the truth, your fallopian tubes just never came up in the conversation before."

Just like everything else, the army has its own peculiar brand of bus, the "carry-all." My first acquaintance with this phenomenal variety of transportation was at the Air Base in Salina. To begin with, they are nothing more than glorified trucks with a bench of sorts running around the inside. For a roof, you have the great out-of-doors, unless you are willing to consider the little piece of canvas a roof, but it actually does nothing to ward off the elements. These buses, manned by harassed-looking females, circle the field at irregular intervals, never pausing in their course. They proceed at a regular pace of about twenty miles an hour and slow down to a conservative ten at the corners so that people can get on and off.

Naturally, I realized that these inventions of evil were designed for soldiers and not for me, but Dave, who considers me imbued with strange powers, was firmly convinced I could ride on them. I was introduced to them with very little ceremony one pleasant day when my husband suddenly jumped aboard one and called for me to follow. I was a little taken aback by this strange procedure, but since association with the army has taught me to take these little things in my stride, I just looked wonderingly at my husband who was riding off in a whirl of dust. From his shouts, I finally concluded that I was to follow his example, and, picking up my heels, I went in pursuit with my skirts flying indecently. The passing soldiers looked on smilingly at the sight of the strange female bearing down on the truck full of soldiers, but I was in no mood to consider the effect I was producing. My one idea was to reach the fast disappearing "carry-all," which was bearing my spouse away from me. Egged on by the be-khakied passengers, I finally reached its wobbly posterior. Grabbing the floor-boards, I clung for dear life to the hands which were stretched out to me, and then collapsing completely, I hung in that undignified position for another block or so. The "carry-all," in the meantime, with the usual military abandon was proceeding merrily along at its breakneck speed, completely ignorant of the corpse it was dragging along.

Getting off was even worse. We circled the field three times. I was trying to get up enough courage to make the break. Dave was trying to be helpful, and our other companions came along for the ride and to see the show. There is only one way to get off of a moving vehicle, and any other method results in disaster. Being of the uninitiated, my attempt ended in just that. My mistake was in thinking that getting off a moving "carry-all" had some relation to jumping in the water, so I just couldn't help closing my eyes and holding my nose. When I opened my eyes, I was still clutching my proboscis, while the rest of me was scattered at random over the ground. I landed at a startled corporal's feet, who crossed himself and muttered a prayer when I descended upon him. Dave arrived at this juncture and stooped down to pick up the pieces. At least the soldiers in the disappearing "carry-all" appreciated the whole affair. They knew they hadn't ridden around the field three times for nothing.

In various ways, the army illustrated its disregard for the cadet wives and the privacy we all craved with our husbands. Often, we would get either one, two, or three hours together, which never gave Dave time to come "home" to our apartment. In those circumstances, I would take the bus out to the base or the small town closest to the base. As I look back on it now, it seems that ninety percent of our time off was spent in searching for an inconspicuous place to exchange a goodnight kiss. So little time was spent in the actual process, but so much time and effort was consumed in figuring out ways and means. Other couples seemed content to display their affections in public, but Dave and I were never comfortable kissing for an audience. So, much of our time was spent trying to find a tiny shop entrance or the backside of a shed where we might end our short time with a passionate kiss. Rarely did we actually achieve anything satisfying for either of us.

During our conversation on this particular Wednesday, Win added some thoughts to her written memoir of army life that seem fitting to include here.

When Dave was transferred to Kansas City, he was an adjutant. It was a step up. He'd risen in rank. The adjutant is the person who does the work for the colonel. And one of his jobs was to alert the colonel's wife when her husband was coming home. Win smiles at me with mischief in her eyes. *Dave failed to do that one night and, boy, he got cussed out by the colonel's wife. I took a job typing address labels on a linotype machine, which was about the most boring thing in the world. But my typing skills increased, and then my jobs became more and more boring. But with Dave's salary as a second lieutenant and my jobs, our savings increased to five thousand dollars. Man, we thought we were rich!*

One last thing about Kansas City. Dave was adjutant and the colonel was tired of the war, he said, so he said to Dave, "Just write your orders where you want to go." So Dave wrote his orders for St. Louis. And that's how we came back to St. Louis for a while.

At the end of Win's army memoir, there is a kind of afterword titled "After the War," which explores Win and Dave's dreams for their future farm.

On more than one occasion, our landlady had made the remark that she had never as yet encountered a soldier's wife who emptied her wastebaskets. This she attributed to sloppy housekeeping, and although I never really thought about it before, I realized immediately that this bulging receptacle was not due to any lack of good housekeeping on our part. As a matter of fact, the Horner wastebaskets are religiously emptied twice each day—by me in the morning and by my unwilling spouse in the evening. But, in spite of everything we do, the wastebasket continues to look like an overstuffed trash heap, occupying one unsightly corner of our room.

The item which occupies a large portion of the wastebasket has to do with all the postwar plans that most GIs spend nine-tenths of their time thinking about and the other one-tenth putting down on paper. I'm convinced that the present paper shortage is largely due to the amount of papyrus which is consumed in this past-time. Naturally, these plans run considerably to houses—beautiful, expensive postwar mansions which are the dream of many soldiers and their principal incentive for buying war bonds. Every soldier has his own idea of the perfect home but one thing they all agree on is that these future homes will be built with the idea of settling down and spending a life-time there. The foundations go deep into the ground and the thick walls are designed with an idea of permanence.

I suppose permanence is the dream of every soldier and, particularly, his wife. Sometimes in the long summer evenings when Dave and I are fairly well settled in our home of the moment, and there is no new move in sight, we settle back in our chairs and start talking. These conversations inevitably begin with the phrase, "after the war." Then, Dave takes out his pipe and I stretch out on the couch and as the shadows lengthen, we lose ourselves in the dream of the days after the war. We discuss our home of the future and if a paper and pencil are at hand we draw a few floor plans, being very careful to include the bay windows that Dave loves and the open fireplaces that I love. After our house is drawn, Dave starts talking about the horses he is going to raise, and I dream about the family dinners I will cook. When we've gone over the whole thing for at least the tenth time, we sigh a bit and go to bed, but somehow or other the hope that there will be a time when the war will be nothing more than a chapter in the books makes the next day seem more worthwhile.

After one of these evenings, our wastebasket is filled to the brim with all manner of papers. First of all, there will be the reams of floor plans. We always start out with the bathroom whose real merits we have learned to appreciate in our travels. Then, there is a large dining room with lots of windows and a comfortable living room with a huge open fireplace. In back of the dining room is a kitchen opening into the laundry room. Adjoining the living room, there will be a small study for Dave where he can retire in peace when our ten children begin to get on his nerves. Upstairs there is the second bathroom, as when we feel particularly wealthy we put in an extra one for good measure. Our bedroom occupies most of the second floor and has three exposures. What little floor space is left by this time is divided into bedrooms for the children and a little sewing room for me. Variations on this theme are sketched lightly on some ten or twelve sheets of paper with a view of the exterior from all angles.

Buried under our computations about how we will live while Dave completes his degree, comes a series of sheets covered with what to the untutored eye appear to be nothing more than scrawls. At first, even I was confused by these unintelligible lines, but now I recognize them as Dave's hog sheds. While I dream about my ideal kitchen, Dave spends his time mapping out cow barns and hog sheds. After the war, we are going to buy a farm with whatever money we have managed to save. The house which we planned is to be a farm house and my ideal kitchen is to be a workroom for the butter and egg end of the farm. All of our plans for the future begin and end with this in mind. Dave's hog sheds may look like just any old hog sheds, but they are not. The automatic feeders in each stall and the sanitary chemical doormat may look like scrawls, but to one in the know, these plans are deluxe as far as hog sheds go, which isn't very far at that.

As for the days after the war, I dream about the trunk up in the attic which will stay in the attic from year to year gathering dust. For the most part, it would just sit there with our other wartime articles of luggage and rot. In an old box in the corner of the attic there would be Dave's uniform all packed away in mothballs disintegrating from disuse. Downstairs we would be eating a big steak swimming in butter, and I would be swinging my nylon stockings seductively at Dave. (There's something about the knee wrinkles in rayon hose that just isn't enticing!) We'd be staring at four walls twelve months out of the year—the same old lovable walls. We'd be living near the same city, going to the same grocery store, week after week. And after the first ten years or so even the butcher would consider us one of his permanent customers.

Maybe every once in a while, we'd get just a little bored with our new life and we'd think of the first years we were married. Then, we would sit down in front of the fireplace, and I would get out my sewing while Dave filled his pipe and we would remember our army life. I'd forget how tiresome all those apartments were and how hard it was to find them. Then, I'd sigh a bit and say, "Remember when we were first married—wasn't it wonderful?" And Dave would take a draw on his pipe, and watching the smoke curl in the air, he would lean back in his chair and say, "I guess we just didn't realize it then, but it sure was fun."

Despite these carefully made plans, Dave and Win's fanciful dreams would falter in the years to come. Certainly Dave got what he wanted—a working farm in the Midwest—but he could not have anticipated the difficulties they would encounter actually trying to survive financially on a small family farm. And his wife, the city girl who wanted to be a writer, was in for a big shock. The task of actually finding a farm they could afford and moving to an isolated farmhouse without running water would push Win to her limits.

4

Washing Diapers in Cistern Water on a Missouri Farm

The first I knew the Post wanted to publish my article was when a photographer showed up at the farm.... I thought I was the cat's meow. That was so great. I loved it all.

—Win Horner, upon her first major publication

THE DESCRIPTIONS OF WIN AND Dave sitting at the small table in their rented apartment in Kansas as Dave completed his military time are sweet and innocent, but their imagined life on a farm was hardly realistic. Of course, neither of them knew that at the time. Both of them could hear the brook just down the hill from the house, and the birds, and imagine how wonderful the fresh air and the night sky would be miles away from the city. More than once in our conversations, Win would exclaim, *How did two well-educated city kids get this yearning for a farm? Especially Dave. Where did that deep desire to have a farm, to work the soil, to raise cattle and hogs—where did that come from?*

But try as she might, Win could not locate any person or incident in Dave's young life that might have set the stage for his longing for a farm. But his desire ran deep and guided him throughout his life. To this day, Dave owns a large farm and drives out every single day to check his cows and calves, walk the fences, and talk with his hired hand. Even after he and Win moved into town and the children attended the Columbia public schools, after he had accepted a full-time position as meteorologist

with the National Weather Service, and even during all the years he was
a county commissioner of Boone County and served on hospital boards
and with Planned Parenthood, Dave kept his farm and his dogs. Some of
the saddest moments in his life before Win's death were the days his dogs
ran off or were killed in the road by careless drivers. Win knew all of this
about Dave and she tried her best to be a loving, supportive wife. She also
wanted Dave to be happy, but the next fifteen years on hardscrabble Missouri farms found Win miserable and depressed with four small children
and her own dreams evaporating.

*Now, Dave had long dreamed of owning a farm. And my desire was to
marry Dave and live happily ever after. I shared his dream. At least that's
what I thought then. I was still into that traditional way of thinking about
things, you know, "follow your man." I thought my life on the farm would
resemble something like* Gone with the Wind, *you know? I would stand
on a high hill with a leghorn hat and ribbons down the back, in a dress—I
can see the dress where it flapped around my ankles. It had a big skirt and
a bow, a velvet bow. And I would have servants running hither and thither
and yon. Yes, servants! Oh, absolutely. Why not? I can remember writing
once that the only thing that ever flipped around my ankles were blue jeans,
rubber boots, chickens, and children. Of course, Dave had a much clearer
conception of what was in store for us, but somehow he didn't mention
those particulars to me. We never talked about it much on our dates before
marriage. As a matter of fact, we didn't spend much time talking at all. We
just sort of mooned over each other, and, well, we won't go into all that now.
At any rate, we didn't go to the farm with our eyes closed totally, but just
like puppies, they were just barely open and not very far.*

*When Dave and I were married he was in the army and the idea of a farm
still seemed far away. I thought of it still as on a hilltop and with lovely
candlelight all over the place. Oddly enough, it wasn't such a jar when we
finally bought our first farm, and I settled into the routine of farm living.
Maybe it was that after three years of living out of the trunk and finally
being able to spread over one hundred and twenty acres made the difference—at first. We actually did live on a very hilly farm, and what with
gardening, painting the house, canning, washing the thirty-six parts of the
separator twice a day, believe me, I didn't spend any time standing around
on the hilltops, certainly not in a dress and bonnet. Then, when the children*

began arriving, I discovered that a farm is really the best place in the world to raise four youngsters. It just wasn't the best place for me.

Anyway, I digress. When the war was actually over, we started looking for land with our five thousand dollars, but Dave wanted to finish his schooling first. He had a year left, and his father gave him a thousand dollars to finish that year. So we were rich! We thought.

But when we went to look at land near the University of Illinois, well, you could not touch land there with five thousand dollars. So we shifted our interest to near the University of Missouri and farms near there. And Dave's father, hoping to cure his son, insisted he get an agricultural engineering degree, which did not bother Dave in the least. We were still in la-la land at that time. We used to sit in St. Louis and read these land ads, all about babbling brooks and rolling hills. Oh, we thought, this is for us. And finally we, or rather Dave, bought a farm with a babbling brook.

By this time I had embarked on my next project, which was to produce four children. Dave was looking for a farm, while I was busy trying to get pregnant, but instead I was having miscarriages. I had a lot of miscarriages during that time. He was looking for a farm and I was intent on producing babies. And that was okay. I let him go ahead and do his thing while I tried to do mine. I looked at some of the ones he'd made offers on, but this one seemed okay, the one that he finally found.

That began our years at Huntsdale. Dave's mother had a blue convertible, but she wasn't driving anymore. So Dave and I, we moved to this hardscrabble farm with our blue convertible. He bought about two hundred or three hundred acres maybe, and the house was there. But the house was nothing special. It had a standard living room, dining room, kitchen, two bedrooms with a bathroom in between. Except there was no bathroom there. I mean, there was nothing in the bathroom, no plumbing. It was just a room. And there was nothing in the kitchen either. It was just a room. It didn't have running water. It was cistern water. So you know what a cistern is? A cistern is basically collecting water off the roof. It comes down and goes into a hole in the ground.

At first we just had the cistern. And we tried to dig a well, but you have to dig way down. We needed that water source because it never stops, while the cistern can go empty. Anyway, we finally located a toilet and stuff like that. And we lucked into some kitchen cabinets. In fact, the day we moved from St. Louis, a neighbor of Dave's parents was redoing their kitchen, so we took their old cabinets with us. We just put those on the truck. And my father, bless his heart, put in the cabinets in our new house. But we still had no water supply except this hole in the ground called a cistern. And that was adequate for two people with not much plumbing. And I mean, no dishwashers, no refrigerator, none of those things. And we were so excited when we got our plumbing running that we burned down our outhouse. Well, our neighbors, they thought this was a little impulsive and not such a good idea. And as it turned out, they were right!

One day we cleaned out the cistern. And what we found in there was amazing—bones, trash, old cans. God knows what all was down there. But we had that all taken out, so we had a clean cistern. And we got our water by lowering a bucket on the end of a rope and pulling it up. We drank it straight out of the cistern. And we never had a sick day, not a one. No, it didn't hurt us.

I remember the moving day when the truckers came out from St. Louis with our stuff. I had two barrels, and in these two barrels were my wedding gifts, my sets of china and silver. These movers, guys from St. Louis, they said, "Ah, this is beautiful out here! Oh, man, I wish I lived here! Oh, you're so lucky!" Well, then it got dark, and they were a bit freaked. And they said, "Let's get out of here." They could hardly wait to get out of there, because the roads were not very good and there were no lights anywhere.

But soon enough, we had electricity. They had just gotten electricity in that neighborhood. And it was interesting. The first thing we bought was— what do you think? A refrigerator. We didn't have washers and dryers then. They were not made, the automatic ones. Anyway, we moved in. We got the cistern cleaned, and that was adequate for a while. We pulled up the water with a bucket. And we got along.

And then we discovered that house was infested with fleas! I remember that so well. I remember sometimes I would go back to St. Louis to visit—at that time we had, you know, we still wore these stockings—and the fleas would get under my stockings. Sometimes I'd be at a dinner party or something and get a bite, and I'd be sitting there just scratching away. Hated that. Terrible.

So we had a friend who worked for Monsanto. He said, "I'll give you something that will get rid of your fleas!" We were excited. Well, it was something called DDT. We'd never heard of it, so we were eager to try it. "Give it to us," we said. So we took it back down to the farm, and Dave mixed it up with water. And he stirred it, the bucket, with his arm. He did notice his arm tingled for a week or two after that. But it really did get rid of the fleas in the barn and in the house. So we didn't have any fleas anymore. But, you know, now we know that wasn't such a good idea. In fact, I had gotten pregnant before we left St. Louis, but at the farm I had another miscarriage. I think I had three more miscarriages. So I was not doing very well with my project to produce four kids. That was the normal number. We had to produce four kids. All my sisters-in-law had produced four kids. My family was a little smarter. They'd produced three each. But I had to keep up with the others. Anyway, that was my project, getting pregnant.

After Dave finished his degree, he got into farming full-time. And I tried to help as I could, but not out in the field. I tried to milk the cow. And that upset the cow so badly that—that wasn't so smart. I was trying to milk the cow, genuinely trying, but I just couldn't do it. On the other hand, I really got into the community. And the community was very tolerant of us in our little blue convertible. It was a terrible time to be farming. Many of them had lost their farms. And in fact, the one we bought, the people had lost that farm to us, had been reduced to living down the hill. But that woman was wonderful to me. I'll tell you, she helped me.

The big event of the year was the PTA. That was the big social event. Well, I didn't have any kids, but the PTA had a pie supper. So she came up to the house and she said, "I want to help you with the pie supper." She said, "I thought you might feel as out of place with the pie supper as I feel when I go to St. Louis." So she showed me how to decorate my pie thing. And she said, "Now, they will try to bid you up, but Dave has to buy it. Dave has to buy your pie." It was a tradition, see? Whoever buys your pie, you eat pie with them. So she clued us into all that. That was sweet. Wasn't it?

We discovered pretty quickly that life on the farm was very difficult. It was hard to make any money at it. We tried all these different ways to make money. At one time, we had chickens. I had like twenty chickens that I needed to dress. Cut up. De-feather. All that. So, this woman, she came up to help me. And one of the regrets of my life was, she sat there and showed me how to do it. Helped me do it. We dressed at least twenty chickens, and I didn't think to give her a single one. You know we all have regrets. That's *just one of mine. Anyway, she was wonderful, and at that time, I did not know that she had given up this farm and house and had to live down the hill. I didn't know that then.*

At Huntsdale, we really dove into the community, organized it, really. There was an old schoolhouse, so we got some money together and renovated it, redid it, as a meeting place and a theater. Then we started a 4-H Club, and even though we had no kids yet, Dave and I were—we were the codirectors. The whole thing thrived—Throve? Thrived, thrive, throve? Whatever. Anyway, we won prizes. And Dave was in charge of the cattle thing, and I was in charge of sewing. So these young girls made these beautiful dresses. Once, I got too close to one of the girls' dresses—I was smoking my cigarette, and I burned a hole in it. That was bad.

But I knew a lot about sewing. My mother was a real sewer. I knew enough to help these girls. And then we did this play! It was "Aunt Samantha Rules the Roost." It was the kind of play that high schools would get for their freshmen. They had done these plays years back, and they were very successful. I could not imagine that anybody would come to see this play. Dave's role was the grocery boy, and mine was the maid. They were minor roles. But we rehearsed and rehearsed and had a lot of fun. Oh, man! So we got to know the community that way. It was really fun.

Well, here it came the night of the play. And I thought, nobody's going to come. I couldn't believe it! It was standing room only! For one night? By popular demand we had to play it again the next night. And I became famous. I went to the grocery store in Columbia and people would say, "Oh, that play! It was wonderful!" I couldn't imagine this being successful. Well, the next night we ran it again, we again had a sold-out crowd! So by popular demand, we ran it one day the following week.

Anyway, the play was wonderful. My neighbors were wonderful. I used to go over and borrow cigarettes from my neighbor across the road. But by this time I was trying to quit smoking, because they thought maybe it had something to do with my miscarriages. But this guy, he rolled his own. So I would say, "Clint, can you roll me one? Can you give me a cigarette?" And he'd go like this. Win pantomimes rolling a cigarette. He'd lick it and hand it to me. That's right. Lick it and hand it to me.

Even with all that, I became pregnant again, and it looked as though I might even have this baby. So somebody did throw a shower for me. And I sat and listened during the shower—I was like six or seven months pregnant—and they were talking all about the horrors of childbirth! It was awful. Really, awful.

It was interesting because we lived on a gravel road. And we were very excited because we were going to get a new, better gravel road. So, in September or October, they worked all summer, grading it down to the mud, getting ready for the gravel. And then they left for the winter. So we were on a mud road all winter while I was pregnant. But I had a nice neighbor down the road from me, and I would go down and drink coffee with her. And it looked like I was going to have this baby. And by golly, I did. And that was our daughter, Win, Winifred. Took a while, too. I was married in '43, and I think it was seven years before she was born.

I went to the hospital in Columbia, and I'd been saying I was going to have a natural birth. Well, I got about halfway through, and they put the ether on me. And when they did that, I kicked the doctor! The nurse said, "I saw a Japanese woman do that one time, too." Well, you know, they put you up like this in the stirrups, and they strap you down. Anyway, so then I had a baby. And now I had a real project. Oh, man! I was into having this baby and taking care of this baby, and having another one. So then, soon enough, I achieved two.

In the meantime, we were trying hard to make money. So we embarked on a number of projects. First of all, we decided we would produce eggs. We built an egg house, that is, we built a henhouse. And you know, at this time there were incentives, this was the government trying to get farmers thinking of ways to make money. So we built this henhouse, and we produced eggs. Lots of eggs, which we then sold. But in those days, you did not wash eggs as you wash eggs now—you know, to get the little bit of shit off? We did not wash them, we had to sand them! So we sanded eggs, by the hour. Well, it was such a dumb job—to sand eggs! Hours and hours of sanding eggs. And I had this two-year-old running around. And you would sand some eggs and then I'd put them in the containers, which Dave then took and sold. And one morning she was going around and around, and she sat right in the middle of our clean eggs. What a mess! But we had good friends who would come out to help, and we would all sit around and sand eggs.

But it didn't make much money. So we tried something else. We decided we would raise sheep. So we raised sheep. And sheep have wool, and then *they have lambs. Lambing season was very eventful. And we always had an orphan lamb or two that they would bring in. That always happened in the middle of winter, and Dave would bring them in and put them in the oven. And we singed a couple of them that way. Then Dave started putting them in bed with me. I was taking a nap trying to hold another baby, I think. So he would slip a lamb in with me, and that was a little better. They didn't get singed that way. It seems like we always had one of these orphan lambs around that we were feeding with a bottle. But the sheep didn't seem to make much money either.*

During this time, I managed to type out several articles and I sent them off for publication to magazines, you know, like parenting magazines. As long as I could write, I felt I was doing something worthwhile. I have a few here in folders for you to read. See what you think.

Together we leafed through the brittle pages and talked about her essays on family life on the farm. In her October 1958 *Ladies Home Journal* article "I'm Fed Up with Family Togetherness," she humorously notes that going to a movie advertised as "for the whole family" with the children never worked out well when they went with four children in tow. The moviegoers would include "Win, who took a book in case she didn't like the movie. Richard who took five guns and a bow and arrow in case we saw any Indians. Beth, who took "Tear Bell" with 23 diapers, and little David who took the Sears catalogue to sit on and the cracker box (large economy size) in case we got hungry." In this article, Win concludes, whenever she and Dave try to do things with the children, more often than not "the result is a revolting mixture of moronic grown-ups trying to be children and frustrated children forced to act like adults." Win decides, "[T]he real fallacy in 'togetherness' is that children and adults differ widely in their basic interests. Take our own family. The children's favorite topics of conversation are giants, parents, bathroom frolics, and chigger bites (in season and out). Dave and I, on the other hand, like to talk about people, books, farming and the children."

To solve this problem, Win rearranges their living quarters so that the children have a room to themselves complete with plastic curtains on the windows, sturdy upholstery and a linoleum floor, where the children can "be children," while she and Dave sit quietly reading in a room with sturdy rocking chairs with needle-point cushions, soft rugs, and a low radio. The children are welcome to visit in the living room, but they must sit quietly, something that is, thankfully, not often of interest to the active children. The parents in this family regime also enforce a new dinner etiquette, requiring all conversation to "be of interest to everyone at the table." This means no one can introduce a discussion about the "length and consistency of a caterpillar's intestines," while eating.

As Win reads portions of her article to me, she chuckles with delight at her own depiction of her children arguing about which ones have "bosoms" (or are those chigger bites?) or whether the hole in Dave's ear goes out the other side.

I don't think it actually hurt them any to be asked to behave in a more civilized manner when in the living room or when we had guests. It was definitely more strict when we were growing up, the difference was that our parents did not realize we also needed a place where we could be "just kids."

But this was the kind of thing I was writing at that time. I just loved the writing itself, and getting something published was really magical for me. It was encouraging that several magazines wanted to publish my family stories because that made me think I could actually write. They rarely paid me any money. I think at the most I made $100 on one story. Those were really hard times for both Dave and me. Neither one of us was making money. Dave rarely got too discouraged, but I was miserable. We kept trying different things to succeed on the farm, and I kept writing my articles.

At any rate, the third thing we tried on the farm to make money on was tobacco. Oh, therein lies a story! We raised tobacco. And we were convinced, "Here's where our money is." And so we raised a tobacco crop. And if you raise a tobacco crop, you had to have a tobacco barn. And you hang it in the barn. Hang it in the barn, until it dries. Until it comes "in case," which means it's damp enough to work with. You dry it out first, but then it has to get damp enough to work with, then you tie it in "hands." When it comes in case, you immediately have to take it down and pack it.

Of course, it came in case on Christmas Day! I thought, we can't be in the barn on Christmas Day! But oh yes, you can! With our neighbors' help we all did it. We'd go first to one farm and then another. We went around and we took all our tobacco down. Then I think we had one day special for Christmas. That might have been the Christmas when we invited twelve guests for dinner after we did the tobacco. After we had all worked together, we invited them all to our house. I still had a penchant for candlelight although Dave can't stand it—he says he likes to see his food, silly man. Later I decided that candlelight with four children is too much of a fire hazard. The only time I remember that Dave willingly ate by candlelight was that night. I had boiled the country ham eight hours, and baked it for six, and sliced it and fried it. But as I was putting it on the platter to serve, I discovered hundreds of tiny worms swimming in the gravy. Seeing that, Dave served another round of martinis—straight gin this time—while I strained and restrained the gravy. I wish I had a recording of Dave's voice that night as he helped me serve the guests. "Candlelight—there's nothing like a dinner by candlelight—yes, sir, I love to eat by candlelight." I love to tell that story. The one time he agreed to candlelight.

But I digress.

After that comes stripping the tobacco. That's where you tie it into hands. I worked with our neighbors across the road, and then they came over to our stripping shed, which was a corner of the tobacco barn with a stove in it. I wasn't allowed to tie it into hands. You had to be very experienced to do that. So the man from across the road tied it into hands. We would take it somehow and pile it into bunches ready for him to tie into hands. That was hard work. Every morning at nine o'clock, I would go out to the stripping shed and work with my neighbors for eight hours a day. It was really kind of fun. Actually, I think maybe this was even before I had Win.

I remember one time when we stripped the tobacco. One day the woman said, "Well, where would you rather be?" And I said, without hesitation, "I'd rather be in a clean office with heat." And she said, "Oh, well, then." And I looked at her and I thought, I don't think she can really do that, you know, do or think of doing something different. That was a kind of a breakthrough in my thinking, that I could do something else. It hadn't occurred to me. I'm a little stupid sometimes.

Win looks directly at me and shakes her head, indicating her own frustration with the position she had been in on the farm and how long it took her to try to find a way out.

So we accumulated this tobacco crop and we put it on our rickety old truck. We were going to go to Weston and sell it so we took it to Kansas City where Dave's very wealthy uncle lived. We spent the night with them, and their chauffeur took their Cadillac out of the garage and put our tobacco crop in the garage to keep it safe. We had a wonderful dinner with them, and their cook fixed a wonderful breakfast the next morning. Win looks over her glasses at me for emphasis. *Yes, their cook! Anyway, we took off the next morning to Weston. And we got three hundred and fifty dollars for our tobacco crop! It did pay for the gas, because gas was cheap. But that tobacco crop didn't make money for us.*

I actually cannot remember exactly which year this was. I think I'm getting some of this a little mixed up. Memory's a little like that, you know. I mean, it comes in and then you remember another story.

At any rate, we both knew this farm wasn't working out for us. We decided we could not afford to own our farm and buy the necessary machinery to run it. So Dave decided the thing to do was to rent. So we sold our farm at Huntsdale. The only person who was really happy to see us go was the schoolteacher! She had two years of college, and Dave and I each had four. She was quite critical of us trying to farm. She had said, "They're not going to be here long." And she was right. Only thing, she was proud of being right. But I liked being with my neighbors, with people. That was the part I liked. I'm a people person.

Pretty quickly, we found this rental place, and it had a little house on it. And it had plumbing! Oh, man! So at that point, I think I had put in a washer and a dryer, too. But these people were extraordinarily difficult to work with. We lived a stone's throw from a milk barn, but we did not have screens on the house. When we asked for screens, "No!" was their response. "Nobody has screens." We didn't need screens apparently.

Well, at that point I had achieved two babies, and we were only there a year. Then we decided we better go back to owning. Well, maybe we were there two years. And while we were there, I joined a sewing club, which was kind of fun, because we had this one member that traveled all the time, and she would always come home with some new drink concoction. We would meet at her house occasionally, and she had a pool in her backyard. Really it was just a little kind of tub in the ground. So one night we had banana daiquiris, and we decided we'd all go swimming in the pool with no clothes on. So our sewing club was kind of fun. Also during this time, I decided to go back to the church, the Episcopal Church. And it's really interesting, because many of our lifelong friends came from that period of our lives. We really made friends there.

After that farm, we moved again, to the farm that Dave still has. It's three miles south of Columbia, contiguous to the university farm. I should mention that by then I had more children. After several miscarriages, I think I had achieved three children. We thought maybe that was enough. But then I got pregnant again. I remember going to the doctor and saying, "I want to tell you, I am depressed." And I was depressed. I was clinically depressed! I used to sit in a chair—this goes back, even after the first miscarriages, I think. I used to sit in a chair and I would dream I was dying. And I would sit there for hours. Over the years, occasionally, the doctor would come see me. And he would come into my room. Dave came in a little bit, too, but mostly the doctor, and I would tell him, "I'm really depressed." You know what he said? He said, "I would be depressed too." Oh, that really helped!

At this, Win laughs awkwardly and shrugs her shoulders.

While I was pregnant, I wrote another story. I was trying to write about how difficult it was not having any money. The children wanted a horse, but we simply did not have the money for a horse. I had a lot of fun writing about how we did, in the end, get a horse. Most of the articles I wrote during the years on the farm were about life on the farm, about the children, and about Dave. I wrote what I knew, what we were living. Here's part of a story I wrote that puts a different spin on things. I really did try to appreciate what we had, even though I was miserable. Let me read this to you.

When Dave and I were married, it hardly ruffled our families' relationship except that the wedding was a good excuse for a gathering of old friends. Dave's and my presence was incidental and unimportant, really. When I married Dave, I became a farmer's wife and acquired a mother-in-law who loves me in spite of having observed me through the unlovely stages of growing up. Dave acquired a brood of children who always slam doors and love the farm. They think living on the farm is the finest thing in the world. Our children have 17 cousins that live in St. Louis and among them they have 17 bathrooms, five station wagons, and only three dogs, two cats, one hamster and one lonesome goldfish. Our children have two bathrooms, one in the house and one in the yard, a pick-up truck and two tractors, 72 cows, three beagle hounds, two cats, two goats, 12 sheep, one guinea hen and a 300-acre back yard. As far as they are concerned we are rolling in wealth, and when the roof doesn't leak, and my washing machine works, and the sun goes down in a blaze of color over the front pasture, I know in my heart that they are right.

Win hands me the folder so I can read this story myself. I notice right away that in pencil, Win has marked through this last line and replaced it with "I can't help admitting maybe they are right." The first writing was apparently too strong. Win was never actually sure the farm was all that glorious, no matter how she might dress it up. Her stories of living on the farm walk a fine line between loving the land and the freedom it provides for her children and her utter desperation at having to live there. She claims she does not love the dirt, the manure, the grass, and the animals. She longs for concrete, carbon monoxide, noise, and busy streets. Yet, without fail, Win acknowledges the warmth of the people in the community, the way they come to her assistance, whether sanding eggs or tying the tobacco into hands on Christmas Day. She marvels at their gracious cooperative spirit, the selfless way they notice what really matters in life, even while she wishes for something different, something better for herself.

This story, "The Hundred Dollar Horse," written during this time period, offers a particular kind of appreciation for her children's innocent hopes, her husband's quiet assessment of country people, and perhaps her own begrudging tribute to what is truly important. Win's writing in this story is interesting on several levels. Like so many of her other stories, it is complete with detailed description, a twist of irony, and her farm neighbors' generosity of spirit, in this case when faced with her children's abject disappointment. Importantly, Win was not present at the events in this particular story. We can only surmise that she pieced it together from what she learned from Dave and the children upon their return home after the auction. Yet the vibrancy of the tale suggests she was there, that she saw it all. In the end, she marvels with her husband at the power of country kindness. Like hundreds of other stories Win wrote during the long years on the farm, this story has never been published. It does, however, offer a slightly more positive view of farm life than much of what Win was writing at the time and confirms that she knew farm life provided some important values for her family.

THE HUNDRED DOLLAR HORSE

Every child should have a pet. But on a farm where you can let your imagination wander, it is a problem to keep the pet population within reasonable bounds. At the moment, we have a turtle in a box under my bed, four tadpoles in the washbasin, and two caterpillars in a jar under the sink. Feeding these animals was a problem until I discovered the dime store variety of turtle food which we deal out indiscriminately, regardless of age, sex or breed. All the pets like the turtle food except the turtle, who will eat only freshly swatted house flies.

In the spring, we usually fall heir to four or five adolescent ducks and chickens. Our city friends are carried away with the cute pastel chickens that appear in the dime stores around Easter, but a month later when they have faded to a dirty pink and have reached unattractive adolescent proportions, it is difficult to explain to Junior that Pinky is going to have to have his head chopped off. The happy solution always seems to be to give them to the Horners who live on a farm. Since we are not emotionally involved in the situation, we provide food and shelter for the suburban outcasts and the rest is up to them. Their chances of survival, slim at best, rest on their ability to adapt. We had one duck who lived with us almost a year. He adapted successfully because he persuaded himself that he was a Beagle hound. He slept with the dogs every night, and during the day he flew and half hopped over the pasture hunting rabbits. We used to speculate on what might happen if he ever caught up with one.

Besides these transient pets, we have the pets who are more or less with us permanently. The children have two Beagle hounds, three cats, two goats, a cow and calf, 21 sheep, and, most recently, a horse. We used to have four cats, but one night Dave found a cat in the smokehouse eating one of our hams. After that there were three. When the children asked about the missing cat, Dave told them she died from eating too much ham.

We acquired the goat when Beth turned out to be allergic to cow's milk. After the birth of her last kid, the goat was stricken with acute gangrenous mastitis that left only one-half of her udder. A highly bred milk goat with half an udder has no justifiable economic reason for existence. So she was more or less put out to pasture, except when she jumps the yard fence to eat my evergreens or to lick the dew off the glass windows.

That's when Richard initiated the campaign for a horse one afternoon when he found a quart jar. Eager to help, Win labeled it a jar for a "HORSE," spelled "HOPSE." Win had a tendency to drop the tails on her R's, so the jar became their "hopse" jar.

"After all," I said to Dave, trying to help them out, "with all this free pasture, we might as well have a horse."

With that, Dave started the fund with a crisp new dollar bill. I added to it the next day when I cleaned out the junk drawer and found a quarter and two dimes. I also found my house slipper, a pamphlet of exercises for pregnant women, a 1955 calendar, and Richard's birth certificate. The next day, the mail brought a circular from *Reader's Digest* with two shiny new pennies in it, and that afternoon the vacuum bag and dirty clothes hamper yielded $.11. They all went into the "hopse" jar.

By this time everyone was getting enthusiastic. Win pledged a nickel out of her fifteen-cents-a-week allowance. Richard retired to his bank under his bed and emerged covered with dust and clutching two dimes and three pennies. Next, Beth came out of the bathroom with another quarter. I think she sneaked it from my purse, since I later found my lipstick in the toilet bowl. But in the burst of beneficence, no questions were asked.

During the next four or five months our fund grew. The children counted the money every three or four days. On counting days, we ate in the kitchen because the process took most of the daylight hours and the piles of nickels, dimes, quarters, car tokens, and play money covered the entire dining room table. Little David was allowed to watch but never to touch. But he was fascinated with the *Reader's Digest* pennies.

One day I was in the kitchen fixing sandwiches for lunch and the children were busy counting the horse money in the dining room. Suddenly, the peaceful morning was rent with bloodcurdling screams. Rushing into the other room, I saw David sitting tight lipped and puff cheeked in his high chair being attacked by his brother and sisters who were alternately beating him on the back and pounding him on the head. I fended off his attackers and eventually made out Win's indignant cry, "But mother, he ate the—" and she pointed an accusing finger at Dave. I knew what he had done. He had eaten the *Reader's Digest* pennies. With the skill that comes from long practice, I pried open the unrelenting jaws and extricated the loot from Davey's mouth. I was rewarded with a furious bite. The children moved his high chair back beyond reaching distance, and I returned to my sandwich making dripping blood and speculating moodily on the sweetness of little children.

After that, whenever the count came out short David was accused of having eaten the balance. Three months and four birthdays later, our fund approached the $100 mark and Dave began looking for a horse. When one of our neighbors was selling a riding horse at an auction sale, Dave went by to see it and decided it was just right, if it went for $100.

"Now Dave," I said, "if the horse goes for more than $100 don't bet on it. It's important that the children buy the horse with the money that they have. They might as well learn these things while they're young."

"Of course," said Dave, nodding his head in agreement. "The horse isn't worth more than $100."

The next morning, we recounted the money in the "hopse" jar, and Dave added $2.83 to make it an even $100. At noon, Dave and Win and Richard left for the sale, the children bright eyed and excited, with Richard clutching the "hopse" jar close to his bosom.

When they arrived at the sale, they headed for the horse lot where Win and her daddy looked over the finer points of the horse. Richard, in the meantime, was circulating among the crowd with the "hopse" jar.

"D' you know what?" he asked everyone he met. "Me and my sister are going to buy that horse. We got a whole hundred dollars in this jar and we're going to give it to that man and he's going to sell us that horse."

Dave heard him. "Richard, for heaven's sake." He drew him aside quietly. "Now listen, boy, we don't know that we're going to buy that horse. And for heaven's sake don't tell everyone how much money you have in that jar. Okay?"

"O.K.," said Richard. A man standing next to him asked, "What you got in that jar, Sonny?"

"A hundred dollars," said Richard, "and you know what we're going to do . . ."

Dave sighed.

By now, the auctioneer was painfully working his way over towards the horse lot, where Richard and Win were patting "their horse," then circulating through the crowd telling everyone that they were going to buy that hundred dollar horse. Dave spent the time picking up bargains. He bought a lampshade, an ax handle, and a French primer for $.10, all of which was really a bargain, except that we didn't need a lampshade, an ax handle, or a French primer.

Finally, the moment arrived. Dave lifted Win and Richard so that they can sit on the fence.

"Now, when I tell you, you can nod your head. But remember not a bit over $100. Okay?"

The auctioneer was in the lot now, rubbing the horse's ears. The owner mounted the horse and gave him a few turns around the yard. The crowds began closing in.

"All right, boys. What am I going to get for this pretty little mare? As pretty a one as I've ever seen."

There was a pause.

"Who'll give me $100?"

"We will," shouted Richard holding up the "hopse" jar, hanging onto the fence. Everyone smiled.

"Here's 50," Dave said, to start the bidding more appropriately.

"All right, boys. I have 50, who'll make it 60? Who will make it 60? Now I have 60. All right, kids."

The auctioneer turned back to Richard and Win. "How about 70?" "Sure," hollered Richard, shaking the jar like a castanet. The bidding went up to 80, then 90, and slowed down.

Only one man was bidding against the children, and Richard saw him standing at the back of the crowd. The children's bid of 90 held for a few minutes, and then the arm shot up in the back with the bid of 95.

Win and Richard held the jar and bid $100 together. They were jumping up-and-down with excitement. Dave was sweating.

"All right, boys. I have $100 over here. Do I have 110?"

There was a terrible silence.

"100 going once, going twice. There it is! Now I have $110 from the gentleman in the back. All right, kids. How about $115?"

That did it. Win's face crumpled and two big tears rolled down her cheeks, falling "plop, plop" in the dust at their feet. Richard looked at Win, and then he looked at the horse. The enormity of the situation overcame him. He closed his eyes, opened his mouth and roared. A stream of tears ran down his cheeks and sobs shook his body. Old ladies clucked sympathetically, and the men cleared their throats self-consciously. The auctioneer, completely unnerved, raised his voice above Richard's blasting cries and quickly closed the bidding.

When the two children came home, Richard was still holding the "hopse" jar, but now he held it lightly as though it were a thing of little value. Dave trailed behind them carrying the lampshade. At the supper table that night, Richard's tears made little pools in his mashed potatoes, and Dave blew his nose so many times that I thought he had a hay fever.

We were halfway through dessert when the telephone began ringing. Dave answered it.

"Well, yes, we are in the market for a horse, you might say." He paused. "Sounds pretty much like what we want. What are you asking for it?"

The children collected around the phone, silent and wide-eyed. "$100?" Dave winked at me.

"Well, how do we get to your place? We just might come down and take a look at her tomorrow."

Dave hung up the phone and had just sat down when it rang again. By the time we finally tucked the children into bed that night, we had had six phone calls.

"You know," said Dave as he laid aside his French primer on the stand and yawned. "I had no idea there were so many $100 horses around here."

And we both smiled.

End

Remarkably, Win never seemed to lose her sense of humor. The stories she wrote about family life on the farm, like this one about the horse, rarely indicate her growing depression or just how miserable she actually was during these years. Tucked in with all the carbon copies of the stories Win was writing, no doubt while standing at the kitchen counter with the children pulling on her skirt, were handwritten lists of the articles and stories she had already written. From these notes, it seems that Win was trying to construct a book that would include all of them. One such list is as follows: Introduction, Families, Huntsdale, Neighbors and People, Visitors, Life at the End of the Road, the House, Sick Animals, Sex, Pets, Cabin Fever, Finances, Schools, Sex, Money and Water, My Writing, Job at the Weather Bureau (Dave), Dave Goes Away (Washington seminar).

Although she includes sex twice as one of her categories, Win rarely mentions it at all. If she does, she will say, "Well, we won't go into *that*."

Most of the stories in Win's faded folders are delightful accounts of life with children, although many also deal with Win's frustrations, usually in a humorous way. One of the funniest is titled "The Afternoon I Took a Bath," in which Win tries unsuccessfully to take a leisurely bath, perhaps in anticipation of Dave's return from Washington. The day does not go well: the children steal her underwear and clothes, the phone rings, and someone comes to the door. Win is running around the house naked while Richard preaches a sermon on the steps and declares with a booming voice, "Mother, Mother, I declare. You have lost your underwear!" Beth leads the group in a hymn that sounds suspiciously like "Pepsi Cola Hits the Spot," but sung in measured, mournful tones. Richard falls down the stairs, and Win has to leap out of the tub to rescue him. Daughter Win answers the phone in very adultlike tones, telling the caller, "And, d'you know what? She doesn't have a stitch on—not a stitch!" Of course, at this point there is a knock at the door. Richard answers and conducts a lengthy conversation with a man whose voice Win cannot place as she struggles to find something to cover herself with. Crossing to the bathroom, she will be in plain sight of the door, so she stands to the side, completely nude. She calls daughter Win to the rescue: "Psst. Win, will you please get my bathrobe?"

"Of course, Mother," Win assures her, "just as soon as I get Suzie to bed." Win protests that she needs the robe *now*, but little Win disappears into the bedroom, "like the last lifeboat disappearing over the horizon." Knowing that baby doll Suzie would not go down for her nap easily or quickly, Win turns to toddler Beth to beg for a towel. Beth seems to understand and carefully brings Win her plastic potty, which must have been her interpretation of the request. That night, Dave asks about Win's day and she tries to tell him how difficult it was. But Dave is unsympathetic, apparently, remarking how strange it is that a woman could spend all afternoon taking a bath. Win, on the other hand, has murder in her heart as she slices the tomatoes for dinner.

Other stories are whimsical, like the time little Richard creeps down the stairs in the dark of night on Christmas Eve to cram the cookies left for Santa into his own pockets so that his sisters will believe Santa himself came to retrieve them. Both Win and Dave had fallen into an exhausted sleep and had forgotten the ritual of gathering Santa's cookies every year. The next morning, Dave whispers in wonder to Win, "And last night I was afraid he didn't understand." Another story, "Now I Lay Me Down to Sleep," tells of the children's nightly bedtime prayers, a tradition in their house even though the children most often seem to be saying, "Our father, Stuart and Evan, Halloween thy name ..."

Win's stories are not always humorous. One, titled "The Mistake," is about a time when Richard is given an overdose of morphine by accident when he goes to the hospital for minor surgery. The doctor tells Win that he has administered an antidote to the drug, but that Win must not under any circumstance allow the boy to fall asleep. Win is alone with the small child as his head drops lower and lower. She drags him down the long hallways, juggles him in her arms, sings to him, tells him scary stories, all to keep him awake. Richard, of course, has no idea what is going on and begs his mother to let him lie down. Win writes, "I went back to my son trying desperately, for his sake, to fight the panic that rose like nausea in my throat." She watches with horror as his body reacts to the various drugs the doctors have given him. "His eyes were wild and the pupils dilated," she writes, "as he moved in jerky, spasmodic movements." Two days later, her three-year-old boy is sleeping peacefully; four days later she takes a totally normal child home. Win writes of her reactions of anger and blame for the nurse who had given her son the incorrect dose of morphine, but she later realizes the problem is not the nurse, but that the small hospital has no resources, is understaffed, and is at the mercy of those, like herself, who do not vote on the bond issues because it is too difficult to go out in the cold with her children in her aging car. When the bond issue comes up again for a vote, Win calls everyone she knows and reminds them of Richard's close call, and this time, she writes at the conclusion of her story, "it passed."

Win and I spent some time chatting about all the stories she had written while living on the farm and raising her children. She was proud that some of them had gotten published, but ultimately she knew that if things stayed as they were, she would never be a writer or accomplish very much in her lifetime. She continued to talk about what her state of mind was as she contemplated her future.

It was about this time, I think, that I recall my father making a remark, one which I have never forgotten. Have I told you this? It really made an impression on me. He said, "You can pretty much tell what a man"—a man, of course—*"is going to do by the age of thirty-five." I was thinking about that a lot. By the age of thirty-five, I didn't feel I had accomplished very much. President of the PTA. Maid in a play. Member of a sewing club. Anyway, it didn't seem like very much. And I thought, this has got to change.*

Here's another little incident. We had an acquaintance from St. Louis, from my earlier days, who had married a sheep farmer from Australia. And they bought a large farm in our neighborhood. So, I visited their house and realized there was some difference in our circumstances. Their house was beautiful. And they had shades that had a city landscape on them. So she could pull down her shades and think she was in the city. And then, when she arrived at our house, she had on a fur boa. And our dog thought he'd treed a fox. He kept jumping and barking. It was hilarious.

Oh, and that brings up another time I've got to tell you about. This is a great story. When I was at Huntsdale, I went back to a reunion of my high school class. And they all had these little—I have a picture of this somewhere—they had these little fur capes. All of them! The typical "Win face" emerges here, indicating the humor she sees in this incident (and maybe a little envy she feels). *I didn't have a fur cape. I saw they were all buying sterling silver lamps, but not me. I'll never forget that reunion. They all had these little fur things on them! They all dressed alike. And you know what? They all had diaper service. I didn't have diaper service. They all had started out in little apartments, perfect little apartments. Then they started having children. Then they moved to houses. And I hated them. I wanted the diaper service. God, I was trying to, with not much water, trying to make do, clean diapers with cistern water. I was miserable. And somehow I figured we had missed out.*

It was very interesting, because here we were, trying ways to make money—eggs, tobacco, and lambs.

I was brought up with the idea that I was smart. And I was smart! Actually, I realized slowly, I was damned smart. I realized I'd been given a

*great education, and my part of the bargain was to go out and do something
special in the world to make things better for people. And finally I came to
the realization that canning beans and PTA meetings were not very special.
And I wasn't very good at being a farmer's wife. And finally and painfully,
I realized I was miserable. I wondered how Dave and I had wound up on
a dirt farm in central Missouri, this most unlikely of all places, given our
backgrounds as St. Louis city kids, and our early lives of children of com-
parative privilege in the midst of the Depression. And I was just miserable.*

*So then I thought, I've got to get myself out of this. So I started writing
out on the farm with four children. I started writing articles and sending
them off for publication. And I did pretty well, you know, I placed a lot of
little articles. In some small magazines, things like that. Mostly articles
about parenting. But you don't make money doing that. I'd sell an article
to a magazine, and they'd give me a hundred dollars. I wasn't going to get
rich this way. During that time, I was also listening carefully to what Dave
was saying about the difficulties of the farm. I would serve coffee to the
members of the local Farm Bureau. They would gather at our house and
talk long into the night. Pot after pot of coffee, I would hear them talk about
what was keeping them awake at night. I'm not sure when, but it occurred
to me that I could write about something besides raising children and sanding eggs.*

*So then, just out of frustration, mostly, I wrote this article that basically
posed the question, why is it that Dave and I, who are smart people—very
smart—why could we not make a living on a farm? And the Saturday Evening Post, which was the big magazine at the time, picked it up. It got so
much attention, I was shocked! Senator Stuart Symington read it into the
Congressional Record. And I became famous—ha!—in Columbia. But the
Post gave me eight hundred dollars for the article. When I told our banker
how much they paid for the article, he declared I should have held out for
more. But I was pretty pleased. I was pleased to have it accepted for publication, and I was very pleased with the money. I don't know which made me
more pleased.*

*You know, if I had looked around, and admitted it, I would not have been
happy with the life that most farmers lived then. Actually, that was not the*

life I wanted. We were not Gone with the Wind. *The track I had chosen was "whither thou goest, I will go," you know, "follow your husband." When I began to question that, I realized, with four little children on that farm, we didn't have any money. Some of my friends later on, if they weren't happy, they got an apartment and moved out. I couldn't get an apartment. We didn't have any money! I couldn't go back to my family with four kids. I knew that. Not to my mother. Not to Dave's family. I was stuck. I can remember throwing myself down on the bed in frustration. What am I going to do? I'll never forget that reunion. They all had those damn little fur things on! At the end of the day, at thirty-five, I was miserable. I thought about my father's remark, and I didn't think I had accomplished much.*

Win pauses a long time before continuing to speak.

I was just miserable. I had my four children. Dave had his farm. But I was miserable. Somehow, I was determined to try to do something different. But at that time, I really could not figure out what that might be. I continued to write—that was one thing I could do that I felt was worthwhile. Finally, in 1956, after the worst year we had ever had on the farm, I wrote that article for the Saturday Evening Post. Getting it published, and having it acknowledged as a well-written article, made all the difference to me. It set the stage for me to move in a new direction and, basically, change my life.

Win pulls out a large, bulky folder that contains copies of her article as well as many letters, even telegrams, from those who admired her work, including a letter from Senator Symington and one from the White House, signed by one of the president's advisors. The folder is also packed with faded, brittle articles clipped from the local newspapers about "Mrs. David Horner" who was published in the *Saturday Evening Post*. The *Columbia Tribune* headline reads, "House Care and the Care of Children Hasn't Prevented Mrs. Horner from Writing," and the accompanying posed photo shows Win and three children standing near her manual typewriter. In other photos, Win stands alongside the newspaper editor and several other male dignitaries. She stands tall and slender in a belted black-and-white dress, sleeveless with a high neckline, a headband in her hair, smiling as though her face hurts. She hands me the overstuffed folder and invites me to read her article, telling me to take it home with me and bring it back next time. I promise I will.

Win's article, published in the *Saturday Evening Post* in 1956, was titled "How Long Can We Stay on the Farm?" More than anything else, Win was proud of the byline, her first in what she considered a serious, major publication: "By Winifred Bryan Horner." I actually found several versions of her *Post* article in the yellowed folders from this period of her life. She labored over every word, scratching out one word and substituting another, replacing entire paragraphs with new ones in pencil. Her article is at times funny, at others sober, and is filled with both statistics and personal experiences. The irony is that Win wrote with compassion about the demise of the family farm and gained public attention and accolades for her plea for the economy to change enough to allow for sustainable small farms, when in truth she detested the farm and was miserable living there with Dave and her children. In fact, the article praising small farmers and chastising the government for not assisting them in their worthy efforts turned out to be Win's ticket off the farm.

To be fair, Win's article is a heartfelt tribute to her husband and his love of the land, and to all the farmers she knew who couldn't survive on their family farms. She notes how well educated she and Dave are, and that they come from generations of lawyers, engineers, and teachers in St. Louis. Win writes that their move to the farm was never about making money, but about raising their children in the open air and being "their own bosses." They had expected to make "a decent living" and to have "a good life," and they had acquired many blisters and calluses, as well as some know-how, but they had certainly not gotten rich. These are honest sentences. In true Win form, she is able to find humor in her situation: "We needed a permanent home for our growing family. I had been making loud, clucking noises like a broody hen that wants a nest for her chicks—a four-year-old, a two-year-old and one on the way."

The readers of the *Saturday Evening Post* loved Win's article. They thought she was funny but that her message was serious and timely. Perhaps they felt they were hearing the farmer's wife's story for the first time. Although in the article Win claims that the shine of the city had worn off them both, she often told me how she loved the city noises, the shops, the sounds and smells of restaurants. Perhaps at this point Win was trying to convince herself that she loved the farm. Certainly, she could see no life for herself beyond that of a farmer's wife, because she still did, very much, want to be Dave Horner's wife. Win might have preferred a cracked windowpane in the city to the house with no bathroom or running water, an overheated flat to the potbellied stove that devoured large logs of wood but still did not heat the house. None of Win's pain and depression are in evidence in this well-received article published in a national magazine. In fact her readers would have been quite confused if they had known what was actually happening to Win Horner out there on the farm, delivering babies, sleeping with newborn lambs to keep them alive, and washing diapers in cistern water shared with a family of frogs.

When I returned to continue our conversations, I told Win I had read her *Post* article and thanked her for sharing it with me. I wondered if we would discuss the article and my response to what I felt was the subtext of her writing, but she appeared not to want to discuss the article in depth. Instead she was prepared to talk more about what life on the farm during this time was like for her and Dave. She closed the folder and was ready to move on.

So that's that.

By this time, I had recognized that not only was I depressed on the farm, but Dave was depressed about farming as well—for different reasons. I was depressed because I could not believe how I was spending my days working, sanding eggs, cleaning out the cistern, washing diapers in the kitchen sink, and bundling the tobacco. Dave was depressed because we simply could not make a go of it on the farm. Farming was not going to pay the bills and provide enough money for our now rather large family to live. Both of us were depressed about the lack of money.

I had no hopes, really, when I sent my article on the family farm to the Saturday Evening Post. After all, it was one of the premier magazines at the time. But I typed it up and sent it off. The first I knew the Post wanted to publish my article was when a photographer showed up at the farm to photograph me, Dave, and the children on the farm. He actually spent four days with us following us around and taking pictures to accompany the article. I thought I was the cat's meow. That was so great. I loved it all.

For a brief period of time, Win became something of a local celebrity. To have an article published in the *Saturday Evening Post* was a notable

accomplishment, one that Win must have felt her father would have recognized as such. But at this point Win had no idea what might lie ahead
for her. She felt something had to change; she had to find a different path
than that of the farm wife who only wrote between sanding eggs and harvesting the tobacco crop. As she pondered her predicament and counted
down the days until she would turn forty, Win could not have guessed
how her momentary fame might open a door to a new world, or that her
career might now actually begin.

Winifred, age three, St. Louis, 1925. *Courtesy of the Win Horner family.*

Winifred (*in center*), age five, Water Oaks summer compound on the Meramec River, with future husband David Horner (*on Win's left*), her brothers, and his. *Left to right*: John Bryan, William Bryan, Robert Bryan, Winifred Bryan, David Horner, Richard Horner, and Linscott Hall (friend), 1927. *Courtesy of the Win Horner family.*

Winifred, age seven, at Water Oaks, riding behind her friend, Marcia Toensfeldt, on Marcia's horse, Roux, 1929. *Courtesy of the Win Horner family.*

Winifred's high school graduation photo, Mary Institute, St. Louis, 1939.
Courtesy of the Win Horner family.

Winifred Bryan and Marcia Toensfeldt settling the problems of the world .... a continuing project.

Winifred with her childhood friend Marcia Toensfeldt at Water Oaks, 1940. Handwritten note on photo reads, "Winifred Bryan and Marcia Toensfeldt settling the problems of the world . . . . a continuing project." *Courtesy of the Win Horner family.*

Winifred's family at Water Oaks, 1942. *Left to right:* John (Win's brother); Winifred (Kinealy) Bryan (Win's mother); Walter Bryan (Win's father); Winifred; Bill (Win's brother). Missing from the photo is Win's third brother, Bob. *Courtesy of the Win Horner family.*

Winifred with Dave Horner, engagement photo, St. Louis, February 1943.
Courtesy of the Win Horner family.

Winifred's wedding photo. She was married to Dave Horner at Grace Episcopal Church, Kirkwood, Missouri, on June 15, 1943. *Courtesy of the Win Horner family.*

Winifred in her "going away" outfit at her wedding reception at the home of Bill and Ginny Bryan (Winifred's brother and sister-in-law), Glendale, Missouri, June 1943. *Courtesy of the Win Horner family.*

Winifred with Dave and his friend John Hornseth, visiting from the military base in Salina, Kansas, 1944. *Courtesy of the Win Horner family.*

Horner house on Huntsdale Farm, near Columbia, Missouri, 1946.
Courtesy of the Win Horner family.

Winifred and Dave on their porch, 1946. *Courtesy of the Win Horner family.*

Win with Dave and their newborn daughter, Winifred, 1949.
Courtesy of the Win Horner family.

Win with daughter Winifred and newborn Richard, 1951.
Courtesy of the Win Horner family.

Win with Winifred, Richard, Dave, and newborn Beth, 1953.
Courtesy of the Win Horner Family.

Win with Beth (on her lap), Winifred, Richard, Dave, and David (on his lap),
at the Horner home on Glenwood Avenue, Columbia, Missouri, 1963.
Courtesy of the Win Horner family.

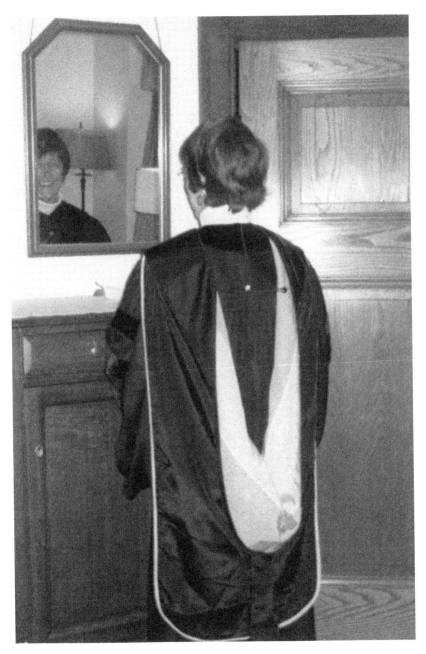

Win donning her robes for her doctorate graduation, Ann Arbor, Michigan, 1976.
Courtesy of the Win Horner family.

Win, age fifty-two, walking in her PhD graduation ceremony at the University of Michigan, 1976. *Courtesy of the Win Horner family.*

Win and Dave, Fort Worth, Texas, taken while Win was on the faculty at
Texas Christian University, 1987. *Courtesy of the Win Horner family.*

Win receiving the Distinguished Alumni Award from the University of Missouri Alumni Foundation, from Bob Dixson, foundation president, 1990. *Courtesy of the University of Missouri Alumni Foundation.*

Win with Dave and one of his beagles at their home on Tremont Circle, Columbia, Missouri, 1992. *Courtesy of the Win Horner family.*

Win on her seventy-third birthday, with two of her grandchildren,
John and Alexandria Horner, August 1995. *Courtesy of the Win Horner family.*

Win with Mary Lago, her friend and colleague in the University of Missouri
English Department, in Win's home on Tremont Circle, 2000.
Courtesy of the Win Horner family.

Win, featured in the *Columbia Daily Tribune*, Columbia, Missouri, 2003.
Photograph by Michael McNamara. Courtesy of the Columbia Daily Tribune.

Win teaching memoir writing on the University of Missouri campus, 2009.
Photograph by Elaine J. Lawless.

Win, second row from the front, third from left, holding up fingers in "victory" signs, with Dave to her right, at Bryan family reunion, Potosi, Missouri, 2011. *Courtesy of the Win Horner family.*

Win on her ninetieth birthday, with Dave, surrounded by their four adult children, Beth Horner, Richard Horner, Win Grace, and David Horner, August 2012. *Courtesy of the Win Horner family.*

Win on the porch of her and Dave's apartment at TigerPlace, Columbia, Missouri, fall 2013. *Courtesy of the Win Horner family.*

5

—— ∂ ——

Win's Ticket off the Farm

Once I got the children out of the house, in school, that's when I started my career at the university. And I loved it! At least, I loved it for a while, until I realized just how much they were using me.

—Win Horner, on working at MU

IF YOU WERE TO ASK Win Horner how she managed to get off the farm, she would, without a doubt, begin by telling you her "how I came to teach at the university" story, a narrative that lays the foundation for her life as a writer and an academic. This story was one of her favorites. In typical Win fashion she always turned it on its head and made it funny. No matter how many times I heard it, I still enjoyed it, in part because the people Win was talking about were also my colleagues in the English Department. Early on we agreed that in her account of university life, all names of individuals, except for family and friends, would be "changed to protect the guilty." That was the way Win put it, and that's what we did. She and I worked out appropriate pseudonyms together. Typically, when Win began telling this story, she would ask, "Have I told you this story about how I got a job at the university?" No matter the answer, she would quickly add, "Well, it's a good one." True to form, Win begins the story this way for me as she launches into her favorite on cue.

Have I told you this story? I probably have, maybe several times! But it's a good one. It started by meeting this one professor from MU at a party. I had just published an article in the Saturday Evening Post, which was a pretty big deal—kind of the height of my writing career, at that time, the one I was trying to combine with the children on the farm. And he, that is, this professor, said to me, "Do you like students?" And I said—well, you know, what do you say to such a question, "Do you like students?" Well, of course you like students. So I said, "Oh, yeah. I just looove students." And, I'll have to add, we were both a bit "in our cups," as we used to say. He was having a great time, and, well, so was I! So then he leaned over out of his chair toward me, and he said, "Well, why don't you come over to the university, and you can teach a composition course."

And I thought about that for about a year. And then I went a year later to his office, and I said, "Well, here I am." And he didn't seem to remember who I was. He looked at me like, "Well, hello." He was probably, you know, being polite. Really, he had no idea who I was.

And I said, "Well, I came to teach."

Confused, he said, "Well, we don't have anybody teaching that doesn't have a master's degree."

So I said, "Well, I'll just go next door and get one of those!"

I can't help myself, I am laughing so hard, repeating what she has just said. "'So, I'll just go next door and get one of those?' That's what you said?"

Win laughs with me. *Well, I did.*

"What was next door?" I ask her.

The graduate director's office! I think it was Hudson Ames who was the graduate director for the English Department. I think it was, but I'm not sure. And Bradford, who I had met at the party, was the composition director. There were people like that all around the country, these gruff old men who handled the graduate students, you know, all the grad students who teach the composition courses. Not usually much of a scholar, but they could handle—well, they thought they could handle—the graduate students. Which, of course, when I became composition director, they didn't think I could handle them—that is, the graduate students—but that's another story! In fact, one of my colleagues—you remember James Cord? He said, "She can't tell them they can't sleep with their students." And I thought, hell, I can tell them that as well as you can. But that was later on.

But first I had to get the master's degree. I actually didn't write an MA thesis. At that time, we had an exam. And because of my interests, which were language and linguistics, even then, nobody really took me seriously. You know, they thought I was just a dilettante. And I know I got a B on the exam because I don't think the grader ever read it. I know that because it was not a B exam. It was a hell of a good exam. And I loved writing it. I knew I was in just the right place as I worked through the texts and wrote my answers. They didn't care, but I did.

During that time my husband, Dave, who was always a tremendous supporter, hired a young woman from Germany who lived with us to help. I would leave at eight in the morning, and I would go to my classes. And I would spend spare time in the library. Then I went home at four thirty. This girl was taking care of the children, who were now mostly in school, but she would be there went they got home. She would be there, and she would have dinner ready. In that way, I got through with my MA in one year. Because I had help at home, I learned to stay over at school to get my work done, and then when I went home, I was the "mother superior." I didn't do anything after supper, because I did it all during the day. So, as he'd promised, Dave provided the help I needed to get all my work done.

Win doesn't tell me much about the challenges she faced as she worked to get her MA, but we can get a hint of it through a story told by her daughter Beth. A professional storyteller, Beth depicts this period of Win's life as frenzied as she juggled managing the farm, raising small children, studying for her MA, and starting to teach at the university. I recorded Beth's version of her mother's story at the University Playhouse on the University of Missouri campus, on June 14, 2014, an evening held in tribute to Win following her death in February of that year. In this telling of her mother's story, we can hear Win's humor and turns of phrase, even while we also hear the ways in which Beth changes the story to fit her venue and storytelling style.

My Mother, the Writer

With the devastating drought of 1954 and other difficulties, Mom and Dad were not making it on the farm. Dad got a job in town to supplement their income, but that wasn't enough to pay off the debt caused by the drought. So my mom said, "I've got to do something too." She started doing what she wanted to do. She started writing. And actually, she was a good writer. In 1956, sad, depressed, tough times on the farm, she wrote an article that was published by the *Saturday Evening Post*, titled "How Long Can We Stay on the Farm?" I am sure that Mom's answer to that question at the time was, "Not long!"

This article garnered quite a bit of attention, including a letter from the White House and an invitation to Mom from the Canadian Parliament to speak to them about family farming and agriculture. And dozens and dozens and dozens of telegrams from farmers around the country. But Mom knew that if she was going to really make her living as a writer, she'd have to get an agent. She'd have to start traveling and she couldn't do that. She had four little children.

Then she met a guy at a party. This guy said, "So, you're a writer?" By now, in addition to her big splash with the *Saturday Evening Post* article, Mom had also won an award from the University of Missouri Journalism School for another article, titled "I Am Fed Up with Family Togetherness." It had to do with the frustrations of parenting. This gentleman said, "You seem to be a writer. I run the freshman English composition program at the university and we need people to teach in the program." Mom quickly asked, "How do I get that job?" He replied, "You have to be a graduate student in the English Department, working on your master's degree. You have to enter the master's program. And then you can teach." Mom's thought was, "And I can make some money!"

So Mom decided to go back to school. Whenever anyone mentioned this time in my mother's life, she would get a kind of crazed, faraway look in her eye: "How did I possibly think I could do that?" Just getting to the campus was difficult enough—from a rural farm. It was a tough, long drive on little dirt roads—with mud in the springtime and ice in the winter. In the wintertime, she'd have to put chains on the tires, drive (or slide!) down a steep, long hill which led to a tiny, narrow bridge over a creek, and then rev the engine and attempt to make it up another steep, long hill without sliding back down toward that narrow bridge. Sometimes she couldn't make it up the hill and would have to carefully back down and make a run at the icy hill again. I can just hear my mother saying "Just do it" as she charged back up the hill. Of course, when she arrived on campus, she had to change out of her jeans and boots and into stockings, heels, and a dress. For there was a dress code for women attending the university.

She told us, "Just getting there was hard enough, but how I thought I could possibly study while raising four little babies in an isolated rural home—not to mention while running a farm. I don't know how I did it." I remember that she kept her typewriter and all of her books and papers either on the kitchen counter or on a high buffet in the dining room—out of reach for little children. "I could *not* sit down," she later told us. "If I ever tried to sit down, inevitably one of you kids would come over, dragging a book and wanting to be read to."

It wasn't that Mom didn't like to read to us. She had grown up in a family that read the dictionary aloud to each other. It's just that our taste in reading did not jibe with what she was trying to study. We liked, "I do not like them, Sam-I-am. I do not like green eggs and ham." "Hundreds of cats, thousands of cats, millions and billions and trillions of cats." "King John was not a good man, he had his little ways, and sometimes no one spoke to him for days and days and days."

It all came to a head one night when she was desperately trying to study for an exam on Milton. She had to do well on the exam because she had to stay in the master's program so that she could keep teaching so that she could make money. She made the long, treacherous drive from the campus back to the farm. By the way, Dad was now working at the US Weather Service in addition to farming. He had long and unpredictable shifts at the Weather Bureau that went late into the night. So Mom slipped and slid home, relieved the babysitter, made dinner for four children, and then bathed four children. Bathing four children in the makeshift farmhouse bathroom was not an easy task. Our hot water was pumped up the hill from out of the pond. The pond had a bit of an algae problem, so the hot water was rather green. The cold water, also our drinking water, was pumped from the cistern, a hole in the ground that stored water that drained from the house gutters. The cistern water was rather brown due to it being stored in a hole in the ground. (When we moved into town, us kids were always very suspicious of the clear water. I digress.) Anyway, she bathed four kids, read to each of us four kids, led and carried us up the steep, steep stairs to the long attic room, put us into the metal cots left over from a railway strike, and got us to sleep.

Back downstairs . . . did the dishes . . . made everybody's lunch for the next day . . . prepared everyone's clothes for the next day . . . graded two sets of freshman English composition papers that she was to return to her two composition classes the next day . . . prepared what she was to teach to those two classes the next day . . . and finally, she sat down to study Milton.

No sooner had she sat down than she heard feet on the floor of the attic above and small footsteps coming down the stairs. "Mom! Richard is terrorizing David again!" More feet on the floor. More footsteps coming down the steep stairs. "Mom, Beth peed in the bed again!" More feet on the floor . . . more footsteps. "Mom, Win is snoring so loud I can't sleep!" And a fourth pair of feet. "Mom, would you read to me?"

It wasn't that my mother didn't love her children. However, as she looked at us looming toward her, she began to have very, very dark thoughts. But in a sudden moment of inspiration, she reached out, scooped up all four kids, threw us into the playpen, climbed into the playpen herself with a book, and proclaimed, "All right, all right! I'm going to read to you. And we're going to read . . . Milton!"

"Infinite wrath and infinite despair, which way I fly is hell? Myself am hell. And in the lowest deep, oh, lower deep, threatening to devour me in misery. Oh, is there naught for me but Hell . . . Hell . . . Hell?"

She said we rather liked Milton. Very dramatic.

Certainly, Beth and her mother tell these stories differently, but it is easy to see how the stories became family favorites. While Beth emphasizes how difficult times on the farm were for her parents, Win was more likely to talk about how fabulous it was for her to escape the farm, bad roads and all, in order to find a new life at the university. There, once she had earned her master's degree, she both enjoyed success and endured frustration for more than a decade.

Once I got the children out of the house, in school, that's when I started my career at the university. And I loved it! At least, I loved it for a while, until I realized just how much they were using me.

But I kept at it. I wrote a grant and got it. It was to visit other universities and document the way they were teaching writing. I had the rare opportunity to visit those other campuses. It was such an eye-opener. When I returned, I turned in an excellent report. It blew everybody's mind—even my boss, who didn't even really want me to go because I was doing all his work for him. He said, "They don't see a report like this very often." I turned in my report to the full administration, all the way up to the provost. After that, the provost wanted me to work in his office for the summer. He had seen this report and wanted me to work with him. My boss in the English Department objected, saying, "Well, they can't just send you over there. They can't do that!"

But I did go over there. I worked all summer, every summer, with no salary just so I could work with the provost. Those summers, we kind of bonded. We worked well together, and that eventually paid off for me. However, in my own department, although they liked the fact that I was getting grants, there was also this kind of pressure because there was a general feeling that I was really getting out of my place. You know, everybody loved me when I kept my place. When I tried to play with the big boys, whoa, no one was quite comfortable with that. I really devoted my life to that at the University of Missouri, that is, to teaching composition and visiting classes to evaluate the teachers. It was supposedly snooping on—rather, "evaluating"—the graduate teachers and reporting to Bradford if there were any problems. But I soon found out, and I wrote an article about this, I learned that they really were trying, the graduate students were. They all wanted to teach well. And I decided I was going to help them do that. So I decided, the best thing for me to do was to help them rather than report on them. So, anyway, I did that, and I loved it—for a while. I was teaching as well as supervising the other graduate students, quite a trick. And then I really began doing more and more of Bradford's work. Now, here's another little "lie" that I usually don't tell. She leans toward me to emphasize what she is about to say. *It was through a fluke that I got tenure.* Her voice has gone conspiratorial again.

"Oh. I don't believe that," I say.

Well it was! I was doing a lot of his work, a lot of the work connected with composition. And I was eager to do well and to help the composition program. So I wrote and I got a couple of small grants, and also every year Bradford would give me a little better salary by maybe two hundred dollars. And he would also give me a little better title. And then sometimes I just "assumed" a better title for myself, based on what I was doing, you know. I think by then I had the rank of assistant professor, although no one with an MA could really be an assistant professor—but I was.

Win is really laughing, remembering how she had pulled herself through the ranks.

So I was playing dumb a little bit, and one day I went into Bradford's office, and I said, "Well, what about this thing called tenure?" He responded with, "Oh, okay. You want tenure?" He says to me—you won't believe this, but he said, "Okay, I'll talk to the dean." So he talked to the dean. And he came back later—I really kind of forgot about it, but after a while he came back—and he said, "You have to work full-time for three years to get tenure."

Well, believe me, my contract read half-time or three-quarters time, but I was working full-time and then some. But I said, "Okay, so put me on full-time." And he said, "Okay." And three years later, I got tenure.

Having gone through the tenure process in this same department, it is hard for me to believe this story. "But surely they had to vote on you? Did the department have to vote?"

Yeah, I guess so. Win shrugs and grins like a Cheshire cat.

I'm still a little skeptical. "So all this is before you went to Michigan for your PhD, right?"

Win is nodding her head. *Oh, yes. Yes, all of this was years before Michigan.*

My responses now seem a little wacky. "Oh, okay. I didn't know that. That's not a fluke! Why do you call that a fluke? They had to vote on you."

Well, Mike Sanders, you know him, said to me one time, "Well, Win, you know you got tenure as a fluke." And I said, "Then so did you at that time." You know, they tenured anybody who breathed then, you know, anyone who could walk and chew gum, so to speak! Win and I have a great laugh over this. *And anyone who could stand in front of a class got tenure. Anyone, that is, that they liked. My tenure went through the college just fine. I re-*

member a good friend of mine had to vote, maybe at the college level. And he said, "I was opposed to it." But they were just beginning voting on tenure at that time. I had no scholarship. None. And they were just beginning to get into that bit about counting published articles in professional journals, and books. This was way before that. He said, "I voted for you anyway." I never knew why he voted for me.

"What year was that?" I ask her.

Win shrugs her shoulders. *I don't know, maybe '65? I'll have to look it up.*

"Well," I venture, "when did you go to Michigan? That will tell me the date."

Oh, no, no. It won't! That was '73, but that won't help.

"Really? Why not?"

Turns out, she was right.

Because, let's see, let's go back. Bradford retired. And Mike Sanders was chair of the department at this point. And then he asked me to be director of composition. So, with tenure, I actually became a member of the English Department. I think that was in 1964, maybe a bit later.

I didn't have my PhD, but I had tenure. But nobody knew, really, or cared, that I had gotten tenure. I was never asked to go to a meeting; I never went to a department meeting, even though I had tenure. I wasn't asked. And I just didn't know if it was appropriate. Well, that's not exactly the truth. The truth is that James Cord said to me, "There will be trouble if you come to departmental meetings."

I am appalled. "You have got to be kidding me!"

That's right. There was only one other woman in the department at that time, and that was Mary Lago. And I can tell you how she got up through the ranks. She was legitimate. You know, she had published on the Indian poet Tagore, and Harvard had published her book. She was the real deal. She was legitimate. I mean, they really wanted her in the department. She was good. On the other hand, I was just useful. Ha! So I devoted my time to the composition program for years, by getting some grants and everything. At one point, I was told by a member of the department that I was a disgrace to the department, because I only had an MA.

At that time, Mary and I were not close friends, but at some point she came back from England doing her research and I think I told her I had been told not to attend faculty meetings or "there would be trouble." Mary said that was nonsense, so I think we both began to attend the faculty meetings together. Mary and I, we tried to make all the trouble we could. That was great. Mary would sit in the back during faculty meetings, mumbling the whole time, knitting. She would say, "Well, I want to get something useful done with my time," or some other disparaging remark to let the men know what she thought of them. She laughs with pleasure at the idea of making trouble in the department.

I remember I grew up in an academic family, well, they just loved academics. Oh, they just thought professors were the best—the leaders of the world. And there was Mary and me, sitting there in those meetings, listening, and we began to figure out that, actually, we were smarter than these jerks. It comes to you gradually. First you say, I'm as smart as they are. And that will take you about two weeks before you figure, no, we're smarter than they are! Anyway, so now I have to go back and digress. But those years back there, that part was fun, with Mary. But it was also hard, sometimes very hard, because I did not have the PhD and, in many ways, they, the other department members, did not respect me or anything I did.

Now, the way they ran the composition program in those days, there were two semesters of required composition—freshman and sophomore. Every new student who came in had to take those two courses. So it was a huge program. If we need to guess these figures, I think we had about one hundred and twelve classes each semester. Now they just have one semester. We had two semesters, and there were no computers.

And we did all the scheduling by hand. And that was a job! It was mostly staffed by graduate students. And every year they would have a few composition courses, maybe ten or twelve, and not enough graduate students, so they would hire a few outsiders. So I became one of those outsiders, you know, an adjunct. And then they decided I was okay. Here Win reflects again on her earlier time in the department. *After one semester, I was hired to go and visit the other classes and write reports to give them to my boss. And I would be walking down the hall and a graduate student would come up and make a comment about, "with all of your experience," assuming I'd been around for a long time, but I'd only been there one semester. Ha! That was great. I loved that! Anyway, with "all my experience," I began visiting classes. And I really learned a lot, mostly from the graduate stu-*

dents. So I taught from about 1961 on. I got my master's degree in 1961 and that's when I joined the English Department. That's when I became "legit," well, almost legit.

It was interesting because the University of Iowa, the University of Illinois, all of those universities had the same kind of setup. They all had a kind of a curmudgeonly director who kept all of these graduate students in line. A very powerful job. And at some point, I started doing that. I had studied other composition programs through a grant I got. I learned how to apply for grants by working on them with a friend, a good friend who was chair of the German Department, which was right downstairs from the English Department. Together we had a little lunch group. We would go out for lunch every day. She was one of the people in the humanities who I knew got grants. At first, I helped her get grants, you know? Later, she would come over after school, and we would write up her grants. We were good at it, and, of course, we also had a couple of martinis as we wrote. That helped a lot. For these grants, our great line was, "For the language teacher, her laboratory is the country of the language." Because then, as now, all the grants were going to the sciences. So we had to work that in somehow. We were brilliant. Truly brilliant, Laverne and me. She helped me get some grants to study other composition programs.

Now, I'll tell you what happened. Whenever any other professor got a grant, the secretary, our secretary, took care of the finances. You know, the male professors did not bother with that. But when I went to the secretary for assistance with my grant funding, she said, "I don't do that."

I said, "You don't? I thought you did."

"No," she quipped, "you have to do that."

"Oh, okay," I meekly responded and slunk away.

But I started figuring this out. It's very complicated—well, really, it's not so complicated at all. It was because I was a woman! Eventually I found a sympathetic secretary, a finance person, in the dean's office, who helped me. She realized what was going on. She knew I should have been helped in the department, but the secretary did not want to help me, a woman professor and someone with only an MA. There were always little things like that going on.

But I determined to be the best evaluator I could be, and it soon became really apparent to me that these graduate students really, really wanted to *do a good job of teaching. So I decided I was going to help them and not turn in negative reports. The first thing I learned was to walk in with the instructor so they'd assume I was on his side or her side—mostly "his," by the way. The other supervisors would go ahead of the instructor and sit in the back of the class. The instructor would come in and here was the "judge," sitting in the back. So I learned to wait for them and walk in with the instructor to avoid that situation.*

But before I learned that, I would go and sit there. And because it was awkward, I would be introduced as the instructor's mother, his grand-mother, you know, whatever. And the students, realizing exactly what was happening, would really misbehave. Win nearly chokes laughing at this. *I remember, there was one class, and all the students decided to fart together. And it was just "boom, boom, boom."* Now Win and I are both laughing at her story. *That poor instructor, it was like high school or junior high! Anyway, it was very interesting. In the meantime, I was also teaching. From my ignorance, I taught strictly from the textbook. I would try to read it ahead of the students, and the classes were all over the campus and sometimes I couldn't find the classroom. Sometimes you get stuck in a lab or something. Some of them are pretty bad. One semester, they had little cages outside in the hallway across from the classroom. I never did figure out what those little cages were for. Not only was the room terrible, but the students in this class wouldn't talk. One day this student who had never opened her mouth raised her hand. I thought, oh, this is a breakthrough! Yes! And she said, "Mrs. Horner. There's a snake on the pipe right behind you." So I turned and, sure enough, there was this snake.*

So, very calmly, I went to the door, and I yelled as loudly as I could, "HELP!" And somebody appeared, just like that. He came in and he kicked the pipe, and the snake went back into the wall. Three students dropped the course that day.

Win pauses to laugh at her own misadventures.

Another time I taught in kind of a chemistry lab, which had really steep steps up the enclosed stairwell. So all the students up there came to class and promptly went sound asleep, because that's where all the heat was. And there I was lecturing away to no one. One day they were supposed to read some essays and they hadn't read them. So I slammed my book. I walked off this platform and I stepped straight into the wastebasket. There I was, stuck, my shoe was caught in the wastebasket. I even had to sit down and take off my shoe—it was very embarrassing. But the students loved it.

But that seemed to ease the tension a bit in that class. Another time in that same class, I went in and I had not read the assignment, this time I hadn't done the reading. You know, I was teaching three classes of composition and grading all those papers. I'd have about twenty-five to thirty in each class, so I had about seventy-five to a hundred students total. So I said, "You know what, class, I haven't read the assignment. So tell me what it's all about, will you?" It was the best class I ever taught, because I didn't teach it! They took it over. They discussed—that is, the ones who'd read it, discussed it. It was great. I was teaching sometimes three composition classes in the same semester. And it was very confusing. You know, I'd get to the third class of the day and I'd think, you know, did I say this before? So I learned to say, "I may have said this before, but it does bear repeating." So I got by with a lot of that!

Those are a few of my most interesting teaching experiences. I learned a lot during that time, because I was visiting the graduate student instructors' classes. I was supposed to tell these other people how to teach. I kept turning in reports, but if I had negative things to say, I didn't put it in the report. I would talk to the instructor afterwards, and we would work out something, because they really, really did want to do well. And I recognized that. I was not about to report anything negative—anyway, they were happy. And my boss was happy because he thought he had these brilliant instructors who had no problems at all. Ha!

I found out something during that time about English departments, too. Those of us teaching composition quickly learned that teaching composition was not the big thing. The big thing was literature. But I was really interested in composition and what writing does to our minds, and how we use language and are used by language. That was really what I was interested in. I thought the literature was lovely, but you know, we were up in the ether with that, out of touch with the real world. I was much more interested in linguistics and language, how we use it and what that does to our brains. This truth about what I wanted to learn and teach helped me dream about getting my PhD someday.

In all, Win spent more than ten years at the University of Missouri before she left to get her PhD. From her start as a master's student and a graduate teacher, she had taken on more and more responsibility, gotten tenure, was a teaching supervisor, and eventually served as director of composition studies. Through all this time, the fact that she would never be truly respected in her department and be "legitimate" without a doctorate wore on her mind. Yet she knew she could never get another degree at Missouri, especially in the areas of study she loved and longed to pursue: language and linguistics. By this point three of her children had gone off to college, but young David was still at home. She pondered the possibilities, even as she turned fifty. Then one day, unexpectedly, a new door opened. Win was both excited and terrified when the provost called her into his office to talk with her about a plan he had to improve the writing programs on campus and help Win get a PhD at the same time. Her determination, her hard work, and her grant-writing skills would all result in an offer she could not refuse.

A Room of Her Own in Michigan

The brain doesn't get older, it just gets better.

—Win Horner, reflecting on graduate school at age fifty

WHILE WIN WAS HAPPY TO tell me about the party encounter that got her off the farm and into the English Department at MU, she was even more excited to share with me the next segment of her life story. It may have been a leap for Win to leave her children in the care of a nanny, drive into town to teach at the university, and complete her master's degree in one year, but what Win did next was truly risky and unexpected, and she knew it. She might have started her married life thinking she would be a traditional wife and mother, but by 1973 she was ready to not only leave the farm, but to leave the state as well. Much like Win's story about how she got to the university campus, her story about how she left Columbia for the University of Michigan to get her PhD is carefully constructed to suggest that her move to seek her doctorate was not (entirely) of her own making. In truth, even while visiting other big state universities she had kept an eye out for programs that might offer a PhD in the areas she loved—language and linguistics. Although Win did not initiate the next step in her education and liberation, she had been contemplating it for a long time and had been careful to make a positive impression on high-ranking university administrators. In her story about this phase of her life, Win is also careful to note the many difficulties she had to overcome to actually leave Missouri and head for Michigan.

Now my story takes a turn. In 1972, I think it was, the provost offered me a full year's salary to go to Michigan and get a PhD. Can you believe that? I couldn't! He was the one I had worked for during the summers. He had a real interest in the composition program and he had some ideas about how to make it more substantial, how to bring it up, so to speak. One of the ways he thought he could do that was to help me get my PhD. That's right, but nobody in the department believed it. I was over fifty years old! The department couldn't believe the provost was so supportive. Actually, the department didn't want me to go that year. They wanted me to stay and direct the program. I was doing such a good job! Ha!

At first I was having second thoughts about going myself. David, my youngest, was still in high school, so I thought maybe I should put it off a year. But then it just seemed a little tricky, so I thought maybe I should go while the offer was there. Provosts don't often last very long.

It turned out not to be so easy just to go, anyway. I had just gone to the doctor for a checkup and learned that I had something, maybe cancer, in my throat. The doctor told me he thought I should have surgery right away. I told him I was going to go off to get my doctorate, and I could come back at Christmas break and have it done then. But he looked very grim and said he thought I should do it now. So I did. I had the surgery, and they did a very thorough job taking everything out they could. I couldn't talk for a while, and it was biopsied and it was malignant, so for a bit I was sitting around feeling sorry for myself. We had moved into town on Glenwood by then, sometime around the time I started working at the university. I had found this house, and I'd finally convinced Dave to move off the farm, although he kept it and continued to go out there every day to work.

I was having second thoughts about Michigan, big time, but Dave said, "I think you should go ahead and go. They are never going to take you seriously if you don't go get the PhD." In fact, this is a great story. We all love to tell this story. I was not moving, so one morning Dave pulled his truck around to the front of the house and he said to me, "I'm going to go up to Michigan and look around. Do you want to come with me?" Well, I wasn't so sure about that, but I could see he had put a mattress in the back of the truck under the overhead cab, so I crawled in there and told him to go ahead and drive. After a while, I got tired of being in the back so I banged on the window and told him I was ready to come up front and ride with him. But you see, that was the way Dave was. He knew I was unhappy and he also knew I wanted to go to Michigan and get my PhD. So Dave said, "Go." And I went. Win stops talking and looks out the window with her hands in her lap, smiling widely. *And I loved it. I just loved it. You know, I was older than everybody there. They all took care of me, and I took care of them. And I mothered them, and they mothered me. It was just wonderful. And so that is another part of my life. That's another story!*

We pause a moment and drink our water. I ask Win if she needs to take a rest. No, she tells me, she is okay to continue.

"So how long were you at Michigan?" I ask.

That first time, a year. And then I came back because I had to run the damn composition program. Mike, the chair, was very worried, you see, because Bradford had half a semester left before his retirement, and I thought he could handle it, but Mike was very uneasy about that. Rightfully so. I mean, in addition to the way he ran it before, he just didn't care anymore. So I was away for a year, and I got all of my coursework finished. Yes, I did! I wasn't teaching, you see. I remember one of my fellow graduate students was so surprised that I took the comps at the end of my first year. "How did you do that?" he said. And I said, "Look. I decided who I was going to sleep with years ago. And you have to decide every night, and that's a strain." And that's the truth!

It's the truth! I love to tell that story.

So anyway, I came back for half a year, for a semester, and ran the program. But I learned. It just took me quite a long time to put myself first.

In addition to the pressure she felt from the provost's offer, Win fretted over what young David might do or think if she left Columbia. But, laughing, she tells me that Dave and David went to the local Bullpen Restaurant every night for dinner when she was gone. There, Dave met all his farmer friends, and David learned a great deal just by sitting still and listening. Both she and Dave are quick to say that this experience did not hurt young David one bit. He never got in trouble during his senior year, and although they both missed Win, they did just fine taking care of each other.

Although it was Dave who took Win to Ann Arbor to visit the town and the university and to secure a small apartment for her, it was actually Beth who took her mother to Michigan to settle in before classes began. After a day or two, Beth had to go back to her own school, and Win drove her to the airport. Win wrote in her first letter home that having Beth leave her there was a bit overwhelming. When her daughter left her in Michigan, Win realized she was on her own, perhaps for the first time ever. She also realized she was going to be just fine.

As you may have expected, I dearly loved graduate school. It was just wonderful. Going to graduate school began another important part of my life. I had no responsibilities outside of my coursework. It was pure heaven. I spent eighteen hours a day working, and loving every minute of it. I was really engrossed in the courses and the languages.

The University of Michigan was wonderful. It was a wonderful experience. To be honest, when I got there I was scared to death. I'll give you a little bit of information about why I was so terrified and how difficult it was when I first began the classes for my doctorate. My first class was in Old English, and here were all these kids from Stanford, from Harvard, from Yale—all young kids, well-educated, and smart. The professor gave out copies of the Lord's Prayer in Old English, asking, "Can anyone read that?" And all these hands flew up in the air. Not mine. I sat there and thought, oh my god, what am I doing here?

As the students translated the passage for him, he chided them, saying, "Well, that's good, but I think you're reading the German in the footnote," which was another thing I couldn't do! I can laugh now, but I was definitely out of my element. I was thinking, what am I doing here? How did I get here? The good news that I can tell you now is that I survived, and I loved it!

But, again, I had to fight for what I wanted to study. Some of the professors and administrators kept trying to move me into this one-year program that was not the same as the actual PhD program. You could do your coursework and write a thesis all in one year, a kind of "less than" degree. But my mentor and friend, Laverne, my martini-and-grant friend in Columbia, cautioned me against that path. She told me, "Don't do that! Get the best there is! Don't you ever settle for a less-than degree." She was so right. And that's what I did.

Now I can realize what I didn't see then, and that is that the department at Michigan may have been initially upset at having a graduate student who was an experienced teacher and a tenured member of a university English Department. I was the most unusual student. They probably were uncomfortable, thinking I wasn't up to par, but also wondering how I would fit in, and if I didn't how could they fail me? Oh, man! That must have been difficult for all of them, as difficult as the whole situation was for me—but for different reasons! It took them at least six months to get used to me. There was a point, however, when the head of the English language program said I was the best thing that had ever happened to their program. He said that because I was a good student, and I worked hard. I think I surprised them. I was not teaching, and I had no family to care for during that time, so I had time to devote to my studies. I'll have to say, too, that I learned as much from my fellow graduate students as I did from the professors. It was a wonderful program in so many ways. That's where I got to know your friend's daughter, Kathy Loring, when I was at Michigan. We solved many of the world's problems over more martinis. We became great friends.

In some ways I designed my own PhD at Michigan. I was in both English language and linguistics, which was an interdepartmental degree there. But my main interest was rhetoric. This is why it's really important to me to know what my audience is when I write—what my purpose is and for whom I am writing. Rhetoric and language were the basis for my love of writing and why I felt it was so important at the university level. To me this is where and how rhetoric and composition complemented each other so well.

I have a full folder here of the letters I wrote home to the whole family, which included Dave and the four children—now scattered—my brothers and their families, and my mother. I think these letters were quite marvelous. I wanted them to know everything I was learning. Probably bored them to death. I don't think I ever asked the family if they enjoyed reading them, but I certainly enjoyed writing them! This was my way of documenting my life in graduate school away from Columbia, the family, and the university.

Are you ready? I am now going to read to you, for the record, the first letter I sent home. I don't think you need to change any of the names in here. Everything I say is very laudatory!

September 9, 1973

Ann Arbor, Michigan

Dear Family,

It's been a long and eventful week since last Saturday morning when Beth and I pulled out of Columbia, Mo. onto I-70 headed east and north. We arrived in Ann Arbor Sunday about noon and were lucky to find a parking place in front of the Maynard House to unload our stuff.

It was wonderful to have Beth's help. She had decided to drive up with me on the theory that I had taken Win to college her first year, Win had taken her, and now it was her turn to take me. She knew all the getting-settled-at-college ropes and helped me plow through the K-Mart stores to find the little necessaries for even this kind of simplified apartment living—measuring spoons, scouring pads, laundry soap, dishcloths, toilet paper, bookshelves and extension cords. In our shopping trips we saw lots of other mother-daughter pairs selecting the same kind of college light housekeeping items and wondered if there were any other daughters taking mothers to college. Beth said she kept wanting to announce something like: "Would you believe . . . ? I'm taking her to college!"

I dreaded telling Beth goodbye at the airport. It was the last goodbye of so many. Saying Goodbye was really a gradual process. I did it in such bits and pieces. Goodbye to friends at lunches and dinners—to Win at my birthday party, a sleep-smelling kiss from David Saturday morning, waving a last Goodbye to Dave as I drove down Glenwood and now Beth. I crumbed up the poignant moment though by neatly tearing off my big toenail on a doorstop at the airport. Beth came up with some Band-Aids and I told her Goodbye at the gate and limped and bled my way back to the car cursing myself for an utter fool, wondering how in the world I would ever get through registration. I decided to go to the emergency room at the hospital, where a kindly surgeon shook his head over my foot, bandaged it, gave me two codeine and told me that it would probably hurt a lot. I had no difficulty walking across campus that night to the meeting for graduate students; I figured my foot must still be in shock. But I went to bed and slept soundly that night. I never needed the codeine and I can walk very comfortably in my sandals although the pressure from regular shoes does make it hurt a little. At any rate, my toe trauma got me through that last goodbye. The homesick times, I find, creep up at unexpected moments over unexpected things—like eating the last tomato from home, and seeing the pictures in Win's album of David with his paper bags or Dave picking yellow daisies on the farm.

But mostly I have been so busy that there hasn't been much time to be lonesome. I have been doing the whole bit and attending all the meetings—for new graduate students, for women graduate students, for English graduate students, for Doctor of Arts students and for new T.A.s. In finding the meeting rooms I'm finding my way around the campus although I still never venture out of the apartment without my campus map. Also I'm picking up all sorts of information—things like there is a map library with 130,000 maps and there's the book checklist in the Graduate Library which lists all the books that are out on loan or in storage which saves you a fruitless search in the stacks. I come away from all these meetings with stacks of literature. From the graduate students' meeting the other night I came home with pamphlets on Ann Arbor events, the Campus Film Series, parking facilities, city bus lines, student services, family housing (new liberated term for married student housing), and contraception. There is every kind of interest group you can imagine—ecology, weaving, macramé, yoga, dog training, jogging, and needlepoint. There's an ombudsperson for students and everyone has an advocate. There is a Black Students' Advocate, a Chicano Advocate, a Disabled Students' Advocate, a Gay Advocate, a Women's Advocate, and even a Native Americans' Advocate. It's a crazy and exciting place. You can almost smell the brain cells around you.

I worked Tuesday, Wednesday, and Thursday on getting my courses planned and seeing various professors to get their advice, okays, and signatures. Since all of my courses are graduate level I have to get the permission of each professor and sometimes talk my way into a section that is already filled. Also I needed to decide which program, the D.A., the PhD in Language and Literature or the Individual PhD program, I can and will go into before I could even begin to select courses. It looks now as though I may be able to do the Individual PhD which means I can plan my own program as an interdisciplinary degree between Rhetoric and Linguistics. This is still very much in the "maybes," but it has the informal okay of the Grad. Associate Dean in charge of the special programs. Dr. Downer in English and Dr. Becker in Linguistics have agreed to act as advisors. My next step is to write a petition and arrange a meeting with these three men and my mentor, Dick Young, who is chairman of Humanities in the Engineering College to work out a program. This possibility is really exciting but will take some work.

In tracking all these people down I have hiked miles every day. I have learned to use my legs and I feel like a new person. I can't help laughing about my original worries about getting enough exercise. The first thing I learned was to shed some of the accoutrements I have been carrying around—like a comb, two lipsticks, a nail file, two checkbooks, at least a quarter pound of credit cards, a half pound of loose change, and my big leather purse. Now all I carry is a Kleenex, 3 dollar bills and a dime, a pen, and a pad of paper with my map and ID card stuck in the back. My apartment key, mailbox key and carrel key I wear on a chain around my neck that Beth gave me as a going away present. I've learned to travel light, walk free and I have developed a new respect for pockets. I live in my Dr. Scholl's sandals and fear my feet have become so liberated that they will never again be squeezed into high heels without some violent protesting.

This week has been so full of new experiences that it fairly boggles the mind. One morning I went in to see Dr. Becker, who is to be one of my advisors. One of his offices is in the building for Southeast Asian Studies which is very big here. His office is very American conventional—dark brown leather-covered chairs—but the secretary, a solid-looking PTA type, asked me to wait in the hall. The hall had two large square areas surrounded by translucent curtains. Inside the curtained area there was a platform raised about one foot off the floor covered with carpet and ten or twelve flat square pillows. There were no chairs. I sat down on a pillow next to a student with a really wonderful natural hair style, naked from the waist up, with a huge glass cross which, because of his position, hung over one hairy armpit. I smiled pleasantly at him. "You've come a long way from Missouri," I thought to myself. I made a mental note that this would be a good rest stop in some future time of need.

I am developing a new sympathy for students. For one thing it takes so long to get anything done. The student is presumed to have infinite blocks of time. He must stand in endless lines, appointments are not kept, or professors won't make appointments so one waits. Secretaries are often snippy. All this I have noticed in spite of the fact that my advanced age, dignified demeanor and sore toe often get me special consideration. Every once in a while in the midst of the crowd you come across a kind and gentle person who smiles with his eyes as well as his mouth, someone who says, "May I help you?" and really means it. Those rare characters are unforgettable.

On Thursday I registered and "went through the gym," a phrase that everyone here uses that makes registration sound like giving birth. Actually I didn't find it difficult, probably having been on the other side of it for so long. I just stood in lines which weren't really so long, held all my cards and forms "at the ready," and let them move me along from line to line to line. The only bad moments I had were when I had my fee card stamped with the out-of-state tuition figure and, for some reason, was directed to the "lost card line." You get very friendly with the people around you, since you move along in clumps. I was with two graduate students, one from Germany, the other from Ireland, both utterly confused and a little terrified. Almost everyone preregisters here so most of the people going through regular registration are either new graduate students or freshmen—both equally unable or unwilling to cope with lines and machines and forms.

Friday was the first day of class. That morning I put away my University of Missouri faculty card and got out my University of Michigan student ID. I took my notebook, pencils, my dime and Kleenex, put my key chain around my neck and hiked off to class in my Dr. Scholl's sandals. My schedule couldn't be better and my classes really sound interesting. My professors sound like the Who's Who in linguistic scholarship. Dr. Markwardt is the "grand old man"' in the history of the English Language and Dr. Burling is the leading authority along with William Labov and Raven McDavid on forms of Non Standard English. His particular specialty is Black English. All of my classes are on Monday, Wednesday, Friday.

9-Dr. Burling: Non Standard English

10-Dr. Fodale: Generative Grammar

11-Dr. Robinson: Old English

1-Dr. Markwardt: Development of the English Language (Audit)

2-Dr. Becker: Language and Culture

Old English will probably be my hardest course. There are three sections with about 30 students in each—mostly bright new students in the English M.A. program. Before the professor came, I listened to them exchange information about themselves. They came from places like Yale, Berkeley and Stanford and they're all bucking to get into Michigan's PhD program. They all seemed very confident and very bright and I sat there feeling very unbright and very scared. However, being older and wiser in the ways of the world, I quickly came to the conclusion that with ninety students showing up in a class with an anticipated enrollment of only thirty, there was going to be one hell of a text book shortage. So as soon as class was over I walked fast to the three book stores. I was right. They were all sold out of the text. I know Old English will be hard enough for me—learning ten declensions and eight personal pronoun paradigms, but starting with no text seemed like too much. Then I thought of the University of Michigan library. I almost ran and sure enough—nestled there gathering dust in the stacks was a copy of the text. That is a relief. If the professor calls in the text to put on reserve for the class (and being old and wise he probably will) I will just have the first lessons Xeroxed. At two pages for 5 cents—the going rate up here—that will be no problem.

In these days that have been so full of frustrations and satisfactions and new experiences my apartment has been a source of joy and pleasure and a place of retreat to grab a sandwich, or soak my feet, or just generally to reshuffle my papers and regroup my forces. In an eighteen by fifteen foot space I do my sleeping, studying, cooking, living, and eating. The bathroom has a small dressing room area. The kitchen which takes up the north wall has all the necessaries except counter space. If you mix a salad you use either the sink or the stove and if you're using the stove you can't drain the dishes and if you take something off the stove you have to put it in the sink, hold it in your hand, or eat it. But everything you need is there and if you're eating at the breakfast table you can serve yourself from the stove with one hand and put the dirty dishes in the sink with the other. My bed-couch is along the east wall; two easy chairs and a table on the south wall and the entire west wall is my study. Going from left to right, there are two bookcases, my desk, a typewriter table, and another bookcase.

But the real bonus is my view. I'm seven floors up and from chair back height up, the whole south and east walls are glass. All the clouds go right by my window and in the early morning the sun comes up through gray and pink veils and shines through the Celtic cross on the top of the church steeple across the street and comes streaming in my window. In the afternoon the south sun bathes everything in the room and at night the moon hangs right outside the window.

On the south I look up Maynard Street toward the back of the Student Union and a constant stream of students. In the Union courtyard is a contemporary sculpture which is a huge black cube about 14 feet high which pivots on one corner. The students keep it turning all day and most of the night. Everyone who passes by gives it a whirl. The other day I saw a bicyclist circling it. He really had it turning and this morning a little boy was perched on top while his friends were pushing it around. The only time it rests is early in the morning. It has become a familiar part of my view. I've seen it turning in the moonlight and wet and shining in the rain.

To the east I can see over the slate and red tile roofs of two small residence halls to the trees on the central campus and Angell Hall where most of my classes are. Along the top of Angell Hall are the words: "Religion, morality, and knowledge are necessary to good government and—" I can't read the rest until the leaves go off the trees. Then I'll let you know what else religion, morality, and knowledge are necessary to.

Yesterday I bought a begonia and a bunch of brightly colored dwarf zinnias for the apartment. With my music box and my pictures of the family, it feels a little bit like home. But I really don't feel so far away, because I still feel supported and cherished by your love as you all are by mine.

God bless and keep you all . . .

Mom/Wini

Years later, in her book *Life Writing*, Win wrote, "Letters are a testimony to the enduring attempts of human beings to bridge the communication gap between themselves and others across time and space." It seems in her letters home to her family she was modeling what she later developed as a theory about the importance of letter writing.

That is just one example of my letters home. Isn't that great? Every Sunday night I would sit at the table in my little apartment and type a letter to my family. I think most of them were pretty much like this one. I wanted them to know how happy I was, and I wanted them to know what I was doing in Michigan, the courses I was taking, what I was learning. When I was in graduate school, I sent my letters home to a bunch of people, not just Dave and the children, but also my brothers and my mother. I will tell you how my letters relate to my mother's death. I told you how I learned about my mother's death, right? I had my PhD committee to my tiny apartment for lunch. That was the only way I could get them all together. So I made this really nice little lunch for them, and there we were at my small table discussing my dissertation, when the phone rang. I think it was Dave. My mother had died. I thanked whoever had called, but I did not do anything at the time. I went back and we finished our lunch and the meeting. I didn't even tell them right away. Did I tell you this?

As they left, I remember we were standing in the hallway as they were leaving, I distinctly remember that, after lunch. You have those—you have these little visions, past memories, that stay with you. I remember in the hallway telling them what the phone call was about, that my mother had died. There's a letter that predates her death, a letter that I had not sent out yet that was intended for Mom too. I had written it for everyone, but it would have arrived after she died. But everybody told me to send it out. So I did, but I amended it. I added something—I wrote and said something about how this letter is a bit outdated now, because it was written for Mom too. I wanted them to know that it was intended for Mom as well.

And I'll get back to that letter and my mother's death in a bit. But after that, let's see, it's hard to put the week she died into the context of our everyday lives. It was hard then, for me. I had to leave Michigan and go to St. Louis. I flew home for the funeral, and when I flew back to Michigan, I found flowers from my advisors and a box of candy from a classmate, Kathy Loring. They were so good to me. Kathy and her husband came by Saturday night when I got home just to see how I was doing. Somehow I didn't, or couldn't, allow myself to think too much about her at that time. There was so much to do. But I do remember thinking about my mother. I knew I really should think about her and her suicide. I needed to think about that but it was difficult. I do remember doing a lot of walking and thinking about my mother. She was really wonderful.

The next week, Dave came up to visit me; that was in October. I think my mother died on September 16. So the past month, just prior to this, had been a full one, with lots of exciting things and new things, and scary things, being so old in the classes, which I'll get to. But I remember Dave came up to visit, and mostly I spent the week planning for Dave's visit. I was very excited. I did my laundry—which consisted of one dish towel, one bath towel, two washcloths. That's all I had to wash up there! Can you believe that? One pair of slacks, and fourteen underpants. That's what I took with me. Not much to wash. On Thursday, I cleaned the apartment like it had never been cleaned before. I scrubbed the floors and washed the kitchen walls. I did! And all of that took me forty-five minutes! So I planned to get everything done ahead of time and save Friday evening to take a leisurely bath before meeting the plane at eight thirty to pick up Dave. And would you believe it? I was ten minutes late. Isn't that hysterical?

I was ten minutes late. How embarrassing. On Saturday we walked all over my world. We tramped through the rain to see White's Market, where I got my groceries. We went to the bookstore, up in the library to see the view from my carrel, the microfiche machines, and the law library, and I took him to see all the campus spots.

On Saturday night, I put on a dress, a real dress, and we went out for dinner. Dave arrived not with a suitcase, but with his clothes in a grocery bag. True story. Typical of Dave. And I only had one pillow and a single blanket. So I stuffed my extra pillowcase with coats. Dave woke up the next morning with button marks on his face!

So that week I didn't have to worry about writing my letter because I had Dave to talk to. It was always nice when Dave came to visit, to have somebody buy my groceries and take me out to dinner.

After Dave left, I had a good dinner with some of my fellow students. One was Gail Fu, who I kept up with for years. She's from China, and she went back there, eventually. Both she and her husband served as presidents of the University of Hong Kong, or one of the large Chinese universities. I can't remember which one, but they each had a three-year term. And then there was Marjorie, who lived two doors down in my apartment. She was enrolled in the English as a Foreign Language program. She was very inter-esting. She had just discovered sex. She told me all about it.

Anyway, it was fun. They were all wonderful. It was interesting to talk about our work and the new and different lifestyles that our work involved. And no one really talked against the graduate program and the professors. I heard a lot of that at Missouri, but these people never did that. They re-garded the professors as kind of interesting, but very human and very im-mature. They really did. We had a transfer student from Germany who was very attractive. And oh my god, they all did acrobats around her. Everyone just regarded this as kind of cute. I guess this was way before sexual ha-rassment or rules about that sort of thing had become standard. And you know, these were all outstanding scholars, but they were also flawed human beings.

One evening, I went to my friend Kathy's house to celebrate the fact that the zoology comprehensive exam was over and her husband had passed it. Now there's a good reason for a party. I was really pleased to be includ-ed, because they were all much younger than I was. But the only one who seemed aware of my age was me, I realized.

Here's another thing: I was still looking for the marijuana that everybody talked about, expecting to see it everywhere. But I hadn't seen much of that yet, except out on the main quadrangle of the campus, where a few scruffy-looking characters hung together, rolling cigarettes in little clouds of sweet-smelling smoke. Everyone seemed to tolerate the drug groups. They were sort of the campus clowns. But they didn't seem to figure in the mainstream of things around where I was. That seemed surprising to me, because that really is the height of the drug time, in the early seventies, and surely it was on the Michigan campus.

And for all of us over thirty, I really didn't see that much alcohol, either. A little wine, and occasionally a little beer. That night, Kathy had two six-packs of beer and two jugs of cider for twelve people. The most alcoholic thing she had was a six-layer rum-and-almond torte she had made that morning. Drinking was not a priority, really. I was really impressed with the young people I met. They were interesting and hardworking and very gentle-hearted. They were really a wonderful group.

Now, this is important, and kind of funny. During this time, I also had to learn some new ways of thinking and talking about various couples. There's always a question about what you call the person who is living with another person but they're not married. Now this was a new problem at that time. But it became important to know how to refer to these various people. I noticed it first when I went to this one professor's party. He was hosting the party for the people who were going to be in the one-year PhD program, which I decided, in the end, not to do. At any rate, he was hosting the party for those who were going to be new in this program. I'm not sure why I went; maybe I was still just checking things out.

At any rate, when I arrived, this lovely young woman came to the door and I said, "Oh, are you Professor So-and-So's wife?"

"Well, no," she said, "I'm not, but we've lived together for two years." And then, as though in explanation, she said, "It has worked out very well." Which was a little more information than I wanted, but clearly I needed some new words for these situations. With Beth, you know, I like to use "partner" for her significant other. I like that, because that makes them— people, I think. That's right. But up there, at that time, I was learning very fast that when a couple is introduced with different last names, it could mean anything. And that was perfectly fine with me. I had never wanted to judge anyone or call attention to different ways of doing things.

This made me think about the way Dave and I had raised our own children. One of the wonderful things about being older is that I really don't feel like I have to stand in judgment of anybody. I think as parents when our kids were small, we did stand in judgment sometimes because we were trying to teach them certain values. Although, in a way, Dave and I didn't do that a lot. I think the fact that we didn't do more of that was somehow confusing to our kids. I've always thought conservative parents really did it right. Their kids were better adjusted. It was clearer, I think, because there was right and there was wrong. For Dave and me, it was more difficult. I remember Richard came home and somebody in his class, when he was about ten years old, had stolen some money. So I went into this long spiel about maybe he needed it for his lunch and blah, blah, blah, blah.

Richard listened to all that, and then he said, "But was that right or wrong?"

It's really interesting, all these things you think back on. For some things, you can say it's right or it's wrong. I think that's a very safe thing for a child to hear.

Anyway, at Michigan, I had a great deal to learn and I was very, very unsure of myself for a long time. I was around all these young, smart people. But you know what, I soon found out I was as smart as they were. And smarter in a lot of ways. In fact, I was smarter than some of those professors. But it took me a long time to realize that!

I learned a lot, and I did really well. I also had a lot of support from the other graduate students and from the professors. My Old English professor was such a great guy. We had a quiz once, and when the professor gave my paper back, it was marked "Excellent." And he said, "It always makes me feel good when you do well." Can you imagine? The only way I can explain it is that many people identified with what I was doing. Maybe I was struggling, but I was living proof that you can learn Old English at fifty. The brain doesn't get older, it just gets better.

While we were taking the Old English exam, there was a protest movement right outside the classroom in front of the library. The loudspeakers were blaring and the crowds were big. There had been protest rallies regularly every week up there, but the recent ones had an air of urgency. I think it was when Nixon was being urged to resign. But I was not involved at that time in politics. I was busy being a graduate student and that was about all I could handle. I never thought I would take kindly to being a recluse, but I found I kind of enjoyed it. Old English verbs and sentence trees are very reassuring. They have an air of permanence in a changing world, and they never talk back.

One day I came home for lunch, as I usually do, but the carpet cleaners were in my building. So I went to a restaurant, got lunch, and went back to the library that afternoon. That night, when I went to bed, I realized the only words I had uttered all day were, "I'll have the cottage cheese plate, please." All day! Isn't that amazing? At the time, it was enough for me, and I was very, very happy and content.

At the end of that semester, they decided I should take my written exam. That was okay with me. I decided to go ahead and take it. I could have put it off to the end of the year, but they decided it would be better to take it at the end of the first semester. So I took a week off for Christmas at home where I didn't study or do anything. And then I came back a week early to study. So, for three weeks, it was pretty constant studying. Work, reading, hunting

down books in the library, translating in Old English, writing and rewrit-
ing various answers, sharpening my pencils. And it was really interesting.
It was the first time in my life that I really enjoyed studying. You know, I
could put all these things together that I had never been able to do. I really
enjoyed it. I knew I had the material in my head. And I knew I could write. I
had studied all the things I was supposed to study, important dates stacked
up on a few notecards, appropriate quotations to put in here and there. And
wow, this is a little bit odd—I was hoping "the guy upstairs" wanted me to
pass. That's not like me, usually. I must have been a little more desperate to
do well. I wouldn't do that now, relying on "him." Now it would be more like,
if the guy upstairs thinks I'll pass, I'll pass. A little different.

At this, Win makes a raspberry sound with her lips, dismissing this notion as pure rubbish.

Actually, I was so cool I began to worry. I knew I worked best under pres-
sure. So I thought maybe I should try to work up a little more pressure. I
remembered the horror stories of other graduate students. So I was trying
to work up some desperation. I would get up and either eat or start cleaning
the apartment. So far that week I had wiped down the kitchen walls twice,
I was so bored. And I polished my brown shoes several times. I also took long
walks in the snow. Then I would get in bed and start reading, and I would be
asleep within five minutes. That wasn't so good, I thought.

Anyway, the best advice my advisor gave me about exams, he said, "We
are not testing to find out what you don't know; we are testing to find out
what you do know." That was really good advice, particularly when you hear
what happened with my exams.

So, this is February 3, 1974. Now, we're going to get into this exam. The
exam was scheduled for six PM, Friday. I trudged over to Mason Hall in the
snow. The first thing you have to do is to get there, albeit your body is quiv-
ering and shaking. Now, in any civilized society, everyone knows six PM on
Friday afternoon has been reserved for "the cocktail hour." But, hey, there it
was! Anyway, I got to Mason Hall—in the snow—feeling pretty good. I re-
member this as clearly as if I were there now. There were about twenty-two
students in the room taking various language and literature tests—and in
all the various stages of panic and disarray. The guy sitting next to me had
on a flowered shirt that was in shreds. He told me that he had worn it to

every exam he had taken since high school. The man on the other side of me was carefully lining up four bottles of orange soda in front of him. I couldn't help smiling as I took out my can of nuts, my banana, my three pencils— one saved from the French exam, which I had passed—and my good-luck horse chestnut. I still remember my number was thirty-one.

And then the roof caved in. I was asked to answer three out of five questions. Two of them I could handle, but the other was on phonology, which was not even in my PhD program. This other question was on sixteenth-century London dialect, and my program of study specifically stated "American dialects." I couldn't believe it!

First I thought of walking out. Then I thought of murder. Then suicide. And then I read the exam again and decided I would take it. I took a mouthful of nuts and plunged in. I felt confident I was at least doing the best I might. The first question was right up my alley, and I could have written four hours on that one. The last question was, "John promised his mother to go, and John persuaded his mother to go." Well, I could write on that too, in terms of the five grammar systems. That was easy. Traditional, Jefferson grammar, early transcendental, you know, all that. So I finished those, which left me only sixteenth-century London dialects, about which I knew nothing. My first sentence was, "The sixteenth century was a time of great social unrest in London." I figured no one could argue with that. Then I took off on a discussion about dialectology by William Labov. After that, I said that sixteenth-century English was a language brought to this country, and that many Elizabethan forms have dropped out of British English but are preserved as relic forms in American English. And from there, I went into American dialects. I brought it right back to what I did know. It was brilliant. Remember, he said they wanted to know what we knew, not what we didn't know. So I gave them that! I told them what I knew.

But then reality hit! I went home like a deflated balloon. Dave called and I told him that I hadn't passed the exam. Then some students from the exam came by and they were all bemoaning the fact that they, too, had flunked. I knew they were kidding. I kept telling them that I had really flunked, but no one would pay any attention.

Somehow I had to get through the month of January. For the next few days I must have written that answer to the question on sixteenth-century

London dialects in my mind one hundred times, including all the brilliant and insightful things I might have said. It didn't help my morale any when I realized that one of the women I'd taken the exam with was an honor student from Wellesley and had been in the language program at Michigan for a year and a half. We drank coffee every day together, and she was sure she had flunked as well. After four days, I went in to see the chairman of the English language department and told him how badly I felt about the exam and that I was disappointed in the exam itself. I felt it failed to test my areas of competency. He looked sad and agreed. Then he told me to keep the faith. Lot of good that did!

I tried to get back to my work and put the exam out of my mind. And a miracle happened. From all over that great, big, mammoth university in the big, ugly world appeared friends, people I had met in classes, people there in the apartment building, people I took the exam with. And, above all, my wonderful, loving family. There was Danielo, a linguistics student from Indonesia who kept telling me he was praying for me. I never found out which language that was in or which church or to which god he was praying, but somehow that didn't seem to matter. There was Margie, my apartment friend, who brought me late-night snacks when I was studying. There was Kathy, who took me out for dinner Saturday night after the exam. There was Gail, my friend from Hong Kong, who sat with cigarette butts in the hall that night waiting to walk home with me after the exam. Then there were the people who told me they had flunked their exams and had survived.

Best of all, Dave came up to visit. This time he brought a suitcase, because I had objected to his paper bag full of clothes. He opened up his suitcase and all it had in it was a pillow, because I only had one. Finally, that Wednesday night, the head of the program called to tell me I had passed the exam. I still can't believe it, to this day. I passed that exam. It was great! It was just great! It was a good semester. I passed my French exam, my English exam, and my grades were three As and a B-plus in Old English. I could not translate the damn section they gave us. They gave us a section to translate, I got it all wrong. As it was, I think everyone involved was very glad I had done well. I think they were worried about my success. They did not want me to be an embarrassment. Some of them had tried to get me into this other one-

year program, but then I think they found out I was a really good student and they changed their minds. Then they were very supportive. And I will tell you that they liked me, and I liked them. I don't know why, but people usually like me. But the people here, at Missouri, they didn't like me. I could never figure that out. People usually like me.

Win stares at me over the top of her glasses as if to ask why people like her—as though she does not understand. I laugh at her. In truth, Win knows that she's extremely likeable. And both of us have a pretty good idea of why the men in the English Department at Missouri did not like Win—probably because she was smart, witty, and headstrong. Thirty years later, the very same men also did not like me. Some things do not change quickly.

Win was very proud of her new friends at Michigan. She and several other female students began to meet on a regular basis, often late in the evenings after they had all worked hard in the library on their various papers and assignments. One friend was going through a divorce; another was pretty certain her fiancé had a new girlfriend. Of course, Win became their confidant. One story she loved to tell is that once when Dave visited, Win took him to her favorite restaurant where she and her friends often gathered. When she and Dave arrived at the door, the waiter welcomed Win by name and asked if she and her date would like to sample some of her favorite martinis. Dave was surprised by this encounter, saying he was led to believe that Win studied morning, noon, and night. How, then, did she have time for martinis? And moreover, how was it the waiter knew her name and what her favorite drinks were? I have heard Win, Dave, and Beth all tell this story with much appreciation for Win's ability to study hard but to also find time to drink with her friends. They all tell this story with a laugh, as though Win had been partying on the side and Dave had "found her out," but in truth they all knew Dave was happy if Win was happy.

From all accounts, it is evident that Win was exuberantly happy while at Michigan attending seminars to get her PhD. Although she was terrified that the other, younger graduate students knew far more than she did, still she persevered, studied hard, and loved every moment. It's possible that she had not felt this happy since her summers at Water Oaks.

And she was pleased that she was able to maintain her relationships with Dave and her children, now mostly grown and, as she would put it, "out of the house." She even stopped worrying about young David, trusting that Dave and David would manage without her.

In her letters Win told her family that she missed them, yet she also declared that she was never lonely a single minute. For the first time per-haps since college, Win was enjoying making new adult friends, other graduate students who helped her when she was feeling insecure. She was sought out for her ability to give mature advice to the younger women who came to her with husband or boyfriend problems, and she enjoyed talking with these same women about graduate school, professors, and the library for hours into the night over tasty martinis. She was in her ele-ment. She told me over and over how much she loved it. Her broad smile, her sparkling eyes, and the lilt in her voice were testaments to the joy she found during this year and a half away from Missouri pursuing her own passions. Perhaps she felt her father could finally say she was doing some-thing with her life.

In the fall of 1974, Win returned to Michigan to write her dissertation. She spent most of her time in her library carrel or typing at the kitchen table in her small apartment. When she returned to Ann Arbor the sec-ond time, she felt less insecure. She had, after all, passed all her courses and exams. She had graduate student friends who treated her as a peer; they encouraged her and she encouraged them. If Win had enjoyed her first year at Michigan, she found even more pleasure when she returned with complete free time to write her dissertation. She had learned the ropes. She knew what she had to do.

At any rate, after I had passed all my courses and my exams, I was "en-tered into candidacy," that is, for the PhD, and I was ready for the disserta-tion. After returning to Missouri for a summer and a semester, I wanted to go back to Michigan to write the dissertation. That is quite a story! I never really had my dissertation proposal approved. Never did. They didn't like my first idea and probably for good reason. Someone had suggested it and I thought, well, no one has written a thorough study on that particular scholar, so I'll do that. But luckily one of my advisors said, "That idea is so dull!" Well, I also had thought it was pretty dull, but it was also pretty easy and I knew I could do it fairly quickly, because I had to go back to Missouri. I didn't have a lot of time like some of the other graduate students. But he made me think about it, and eventually I came up with a better idea.

I do remember the day he told me my dissertation idea wasn't a good one. It was a very discouraging day, cold and clear. First there was a big mix-up at the library. I got there early, around eight thirty, and around ten o'clock this man comes in, an instructor or something, saying I was in his carrel. Now, I'd been in this carrel all year. I couldn't believe it! I was furious. But Carol, the librarian who liked me, worked it out and I got a good carrel on the next floor, right next to the copy machines, which is good. But all the discussing, calling, moving, et cetera, took all of my time until three o'clock. What a waste of my work time. Then I had this appointment with my advisor about my dissertation topic. I waited until four thirty to see him for ten whole minutes. He came in, he very firmly did not like my dissertation idea, and then he left. I went to his five o'clock class, which was very good, although I was still angry and frustrated. Then I think I went home to my apartment, had two martinis, and smoked a pack of cigarettes. Very childish reaction, but it was a big deal. Soon I had it figured out.

Win was not at all daunted by the idea of writing a book-length study on her own. After all, she had been writing, or longing to write, her entire life. Luckily one of her advisors told her, "Write something you want to write. Write about writing. Write about rhetoric. You have put together an interdisciplinary degree here at Michigan—put your areas of study together and write your dissertation about that." This must have been a magical thing for Win to hear. She was being told to write about writing. Could there be a topic dearer to her heart? She could write about the power of words, the beauty of language. She had once written on a notepad, "3/24/74—Philosophy, linguistics, and rhetoric are closely connected because language has to do with the nature of man." Several pages later she had written, "4/4/74—Philosophy, rhetoric, literature, psychology, and anthropology—all connected with language because language has to do with the nature of men." Win was making sweeping connections in her mind about the nature of man and the nature of language. On the next page she added, "So many new ideas all at once."

Okay. I ended up writing about text act theory. Are you familiar at all with that? It had always been applied to speaking. Win pauses and then continues with an unabashed smile. *My dissertation was really good. It was! The thing was, my dissertation started at that point where linguistics was always concerned with spoken language. There were a number of scholars who indicated that written language was just a bunch of symbols, but I wanted to prove that it was much more than that. I wanted to show that you could do things with written language that you couldn't do with spoken language. And how differently we read the written language, such as a poem we read at the age, say, when we're fifteen, and when we're thirty, or when we're sixty. Anyway. So that was my dissertation. It was brilliant. At least, I thought it was.*

When Win returned to Michigan she hunkered down to write the dissertation. Her letters home were clear—she was having the time of her life. She now had, as she put it, *permission* to do nothing but write while sitting in a tiny studio apartment in Michigan, hundreds of miles from home. How long had Win waited for this moment, to be able to write uninterrupted in a quiet place? She had a topic; she was on a roll; she was happy. This undated letter that Win wrote to her family several months into her dissertation illustrates how she was feeling:

As I was walking across the campus the other morning, I realized in a burst of joy—that I was going to make it, and the year is going to be a good one. I realize that I have several things going in my favor to offset the fact that I'm a little more agey than the general run of student. First, I can think faster than most—not all—of the people around me. Second, I have more money than most of the students and that's a real advantage. Third, I don't mind working. I even like it. Fourth, I know that even though I have less life time left, I know, probably better than most students do, that there is no instant anything—it's the long pull that counts. I know that and it's okay. But most important of all I have a certain philosophic perspective that comes, I suppose, with age. I've done enough dumb things in my life to know that one or two more dumb things won't kill me and I've failed enough times at enough things to know that individual failures make very little difference in the long run. What really matters is if I can pick myself up and brush off the dust and go on. As I was walking along, I realized that I wasn't really afraid anymore of looking stupid or failing, and that probably I will do both many times before this year is over. But at that moment I was sure, for the first time, that I was going to make it. And I felt good all over.

Friday I bought a poster that has a picture of a small, scraggly, frightened-looking kitten hanging for dear life onto a pole. The words are: "Hang in there, baby!"

So, to all of you—Win and Herm with your jobs, Richard with your Spanish American studies spread all over the east coast, Beth with your studies and your apartment, David with being on your own in this last year at Hickman, and Dave with the weather and the farm and the family,

Let's all hang in there together.

God bless you and keep you all,

Mom, Wini

Win titled her dissertation "Text Act Theory: A Study of Nonfiction Texts." Although it is rather technical, her introduction is fairly straightforward and insightful. In it, we are reminded of Win's interest in words and language, the joy of putting pen to paper that was evidenced in her first childhood journals. She writes,

This study arises out of two original concerns—an interest in persuasive discourse, and an interest in the linguistic analysis of written language. It is significant that editors and literary critics generally agree that certain essays are "persuasive," in spite of the fact that they often do not actually persuade certain readers to either a point of view or a course of action. Speech act theory has demonstrated that the speaker's intentions, feelings, and beliefs within the illocutionary force are reflected in the syntax of such utterances as requests. It also appears that in political speeches and advertising, where the intention is to persuade someone to vote for a candidate or to buy a product, persuasion can best be effected if the intent appears not to be persuasion. Thus, a speaker often may achieve the effect of persuasion best if his hearer does not recognize that intention.

Text act theory extends the concepts of speech act theory to provide a network of participants and a framework of relations within which both the intent and effect of an utterance can be considered.

Quite a mouthful. More simply put, Win wanted to link the concerns of scholars who studied persuasive speech texts and those who studied written texts. She claimed that certain procedures must be accepted by both the speaker and the hearer—they must share common feelings, intentions, and beliefs in order for communication to be possible. She saw the same interactions in the written word that she observed in speech. In both kinds of texts, Win was interested in successful communication, how it worked, who could communicate effectively, and by what means: "All discourse," she wrote, "depends on the relationship between the participants." Thus, she argued, "speech act theory presents exciting possibilities for the linguistic analysis of written language, as well as some limitations."

Win quotes John Searle in her introduction: "The purpose of language is communication, the unit of human communication of language is the speech act, and a theory of language explains . . . how we get from guttural sound to sound with meaning, from the making of noises to the social fact of human communication." Two hundred pages later, she concludes, "Persuasion rests not on coercion or the imposing of one person's will on another; it depends finally on the establishment and recognition of relationships and the sharing of contextual experience. It is only within such shared relationships that persuasion is effected and communication is possible. Communication depends on an 'acting together' and a sharing of common 'concepts, images, ideas and attitudes.' Persuasion depends on men walking together, seeing, hearing, feeling, understanding the same world."

Now, I could tell you mistakes I made along the way. And one of them was, I came back and was so determined to run that composition program properly. But I should have worked on publishing my dissertation, because it was good! It sold a hundred copies from Ann Arbor, the microfilm place where they store dissertations. I did send it off with some variations to Indiana Press. They wanted to see more of it, but I never followed it up. That was a mistake! Putting my emphasis on the composition program instead of my publication was a big mistake. It took me a long time to put myself first, I guess.

Win told me many times over the years that she had made a mistake in prioritizing the composition program over getting her dissertation published. She would suffer the consequences of this when she was evaluated for her promotions in the years to come. If she had published her dissertation, it would have been the first solid entry on her list of book publications. Her topic was timely and would have garnered some respect from her colleagues in the English Department, especially if she had secured a university press. The work of John Austen and John Searle was growing more widely recognized. Speech act theory and text act theory were becoming concepts known to some in the literary world, and the study of rhetoric was gaining a foothold in speech departments as well as anthropology, sociology, and even English departments.

As is the custom, on the first pages of her dissertation Win thanked her graduate committee at Michigan for their guidance and support, but she also added a paragraph about the importance of the community of new friends she had made in graduate school: "No study can go forward without the kind of intellectual exchange that comes within a community of students. For the many hours of discussion and the excitement of mutual discovery, I am grateful to my fellow students." At Michigan, Win found common ground with other people, especially other women, who were there to learn, who possessed intellectual curiosity, and who wanted to write dissertations that offered something new to the academic world. Her family, too, found its way into her acknowledgments: "I want to thank my husband and family for their patience and continuing encouragement during this research," she wrote.

These words take on added poignancy when we remember everything that had transpired in Winifred Bryan Horner's life up to this point. It is 1975. Win is fifty-two, nearly fifty-three, years old. She stands in her small apartment, having packed the few belongings she has with her in Ann Arbor. She bids farewell to the quiet, the learning, the teachers and friends she has made, her beloved carrel in the library. After graduation, Win will drive herself home, remembering the day Beth drove with her to Michigan two years before. She is ready to greet Dave and David, happy to be going home again. She will return to Missouri to teach again, now with a PhD in hand. She does not know what awaits her there, but perhaps she has some inkling of the battles she will have to fight to secure her place among the faculty who never wanted her to get her degree in the first place. Win told me she *girded her loins* to face the music back home in the English Department.

7

Battling the Old Boys' Club

Anything I've ever done that was worth it, I started out scared.
You have to admit the possibility, even probability of failure if you're
going to do anything. You have to be selfish in order to do anything
like this.

—Win Horner, undated personal notes

THE NEXT TIME WIN AND I meet, I am eager to find out how she was
treated when she returned to the University of Missouri. We have hardly
sat down when I blurt out, "Win, were you treated better when you came
back to the department with a PhD?"

Win's short answer is a resounding "No." But her longer answer is
about how she received negative votes at every level in her bids for promotion and how she had to spend the next few years appealing those votes
and then arguing for equal pay. To understand just how tedious and painful this time was for Win, it might help to explain what the promotion
process looks like for most university professors. Then it will be evident
how easily injustices can occur and discrimination continue when secret
ballots are used and no one has to defend negative votes.

In general, a few rules apply to the process for tenure and promotions.
At the University of Missouri, as at many other universities throughout
the country, a newly hired professor generally comes to the university
with a PhD or another advanced degree and begins her career as an assistant professor (without tenure). This person has five or six years to teach,
do research, perform various administrative and committee duties, and

publish her work in peer-reviewed publications, including professional journals and books with recognized presses. Peer-reviewed publications are those that have been read and approved by scholars in the field before they are published. Articles must be original, well-written, and substantial in terms of offering new knowledge to the author's discipline. Having five or six years before a vote for tenure and/or promotion is necessary, as the process of doing research, writing articles, and actually having them appear in print often takes several years.

In a typical tenure and promotion review, the department reads all the scholarly materials produced by the candidate, considers assessments of her teaching expertise and success, and reviews grants written and received, as well as descriptions of administrative and committee work the candidate has done at the department, college, and university levels. In addition, the department chair collects five to ten letters from scholars at other universities that argue whether or not the candidate deserves to receive promotion and/or tenure based on her publications. All of this tells the department whether the candidate is a well-rounded faculty member, a well-published scholar, and a good university citizen. If all goes well, the department chair, or the chair of the Personnel Committee, will make a recommendation for tenure and promotion at the end of the "probationary period" (the first five or six years). In most departments, a discussion of the candidate's qualifications and efforts will be held without the candidate present, and a secret written ballot is taken. In most cases, the candidate must have the support of two-thirds of the voting members of the Personnel Committee (those in rank above the candidate) to be approved for tenure and promotion. The voting members of the department are not required to justify their votes.

After the vote, the candidate receives a letter from the chair, informing her of the outcome. If the candidate fails to get two-thirds of the vote, she may appeal to the department with a written document, followed by an oral appeal, after which a second vote will be taken. If this vote is positive, the candidate then proceeds for tenure and promotion at the college level (the colleges are Arts and Science, Law, Business, Agriculture, etc.), where the same procedure takes place. The process continues to a University Committee for the exact same scrutiny and vote(s). Then the entire file is delivered for evaluation by the chancellor of the university.

At every level, appeals are possible, and candidate files may proceed to the next level with or without positive votes, but in all cases the votes, letters, and appeals accompany the file all the way to the chancellor's desk. This process generally takes a full academic year. If a candidate fails to get a positive vote from the chancellor, she is released from employment by the university. If she receives a positive vote, she will generally be granted tenure and promotion to associate professor. This process is repeated in its entirety when a candidate later seeks the rank of full professor.

Win is ready today with a file folder of all the letters she had written to appeal the negative votes she received in her promotion process. When my recorder is turned on, I repeat my question. I already know the short answer—that the PhD did not ensure Win's immediate success at the university in terms of promotions and rank. What I do not know is just how long and why she had to battle against the negative votes and how hard-won was her eventual success. In many respects, the obstacles Win had to overcome were gendered and unexpected. She had completed her master's, worked hard for the composition program (doing the work of several administrators), had written successful grants, had completed her PhD, and had begun to publish in her field of rhetoric and composition, but to the department she was still not considered "one of them." I can hear the anger in her voice as she begins.

Oh, I was treated great by the university, but not by the department, because then I had the nerve to ask for a promotion. I did not stay in my place. I had already gotten tenure, but only as a sort of assistant professor. It wasn't very formal. So when I had the PhD, I came back from Michigan and asked to formalize my rank as assistant professor—that wasn't a problem, I got that right away. But then I wanted to be promoted to associate professor, and then to full professor. But oh, no, no, no! They were having none of that. The objections were laughable. One of them was that I hadn't been in rank long enough. I mean, I had been working there nearly twenty years, with tenure, but it was "too soon," they said. Anyway, eventually I got those promotions, all of them, but it took its toll on me. I had to fight every step of the way. All of that, really, it was really quite a big deal. I had to appeal every time. I appealed. I went up to the next level without their blessing, and I had a wonderful appeal, if I do say so myself. Which I have a copy of here; you can read it for yourself. It was really good.

Win looks through the file she brought to the table earlier.

I really worked on this, you know, on the language. I read it to the department, then I went to the bathroom, which was right in the next office. When I came out of the bathroom, James Cord said, "Fine presentation, Win. Fine." But I was still voted down! Can you believe that? I love to tell that story by ending it with, "I hadn't even gone to the bathroom when they voted me down! So I don't believe there was very much discussion!"

Win laughs, but I am troubled by this story. I ask her, "Approximately how many people were in the department voting on you at that point?"

I don't know—well, there were quite a few. At least ten or twelve. All of them men. All men! I think Mary was away or something at the time. Anyway, so when I came back with my PhD, I thought it would be smooth sailing. When I wanted to be considered for associate professor, you know, the next rank, they quickly voted that down, unanimously. So I appealed to the college committee, and then, you know how it goes, I had to appeal to the system level. At every level they turned me down because of that negative vote from the English Department, and I had to appeal—to the department, where they turned down my appeal, and then to the college committee for a vote, which was also negative, and then to the university committee. It's a very long, drawn-out process of votes. Same thing to go up for full professor. It took years! And then I was put on every damn committee at the university, after I got full professor, because there are no women full professors—well, damn few. But I'm getting ahead of my story!

At the college level, at Arts and Science, after I had been voted down by the department, including my appeal, I had to attend the meeting and do a verbal appeal as well as the written. The dean was sitting in the meeting with the college tenure committee, and I was sitting in as well. He asked the members of the committee, "Well, why was she turned down?" No one seemed to know the answer. And he said, "I can't imagine why," and he meant it. They had my file there with all the information about my dissertation and my work with the composition committee and the grants and all that. He thought I should have been approved for promotion. I think him saying that kind of squelched that, and I got the vote at the college level.

*Afterward, one of my colleagues said, "How can you live with the depart-
ment if you win it?" And I said, "No problem!" Can you imagine? He thought
I should be embarrassed or something or feel awkward in the department
if the next level approved my promotion. I would be happy to return to the
department having won my appeal. That was funny, that they thought I
might have a problem with that. Maybe it was them who would have a problem with that! That makes more sense.* We both laugh. *What did he expect
me to say? I said, "No problem!" If I won, I would definitely be around. And
I remember Bill Morgan—you knew Bill, he was sometimes my one supporter—said to me, "By God, Wini, you've got balls!"*

I am shocked. "Bill Morgan? Bill Morgan said that?" I am imagin-
ing the short, fussy man I had known. Win wipes away some tears from
laughing so hard.

*Anyway. It's been a great run. Actually, my story is less fun after my
promotions. You know, I think the fight was fun. It was fun because I won!*
There is a long pause as Win looks through her folders. *But it wasn't much
fun when it was happening. I had to fight for everything. Actually, it was exhausting and depressing. I have all my appeals here in these folders. I would
like you to read them. I think the language I used really points to why I continued to be turned down for promotions in a department that had known
me for over twenty years, yet had difficulty accepting me as one of the boys.
I spent so much time and energy on those damn appeals, it was ridiculous.
And trying to write them without exposing my anger and frustration was
really difficult. I had to use everything I had learned about rhetoric and
language, actually, in writing them. And I didn't hide what was going on. I
wanted the committees at the college and university level, even the chancellor, to really see what was going on. I had to prove, in a sense, that they were
discriminating against me largely because I was a woman, and because they
knew me so well as a subordinate that it was difficult to shift their thinking
about me to appreciate my PhD and what I was now doing and bringing to
the department at that time.*

*I don't remember when exactly I had to begin with the appeals, but in
1975, after I returned with my PhD, I finally became an assistant professor.
I held that rank for about five years. Then, in typical fashion, I went up for
associate professor, but I had to fight for that one. I finally got it in 1980.*

Four years later, after appeals at every level, I finally achieved full professor. That was in 1984, the year after you came to Missouri, actually. 1984. That was a battle, I'll tell you. That is quite a story. I hope you will read some of my appeals. I worked very hard on them. Some were nearly fifteen pages long. I had to describe everything I had written, every committee I served on, all the awards I had won for teaching and service, grants, and my publication record. And I had to write the appeals calmly, which was really hard for me to do. You will see how measured I tried to be. I knew they were voting me down because I was a woman and I did not fit their image of the perfect male colleague. Well, I was determined to win those battles, and I did.

But even after I won all the battles for my promotions, I had to fight, again, several times, for equitable salary increases. I always got the information about the increases other faculty in English were getting. It's actually in the public record, you know, and I noticed I never got my fair share. My salary increases never matched theirs, and I had to spend so much time and energy, again, arguing that my increases should be the same as everyone else's. It was exhausting. And I will tell you, which you will totally understand, by then I had outpublished all of the men in the department. They really were not scholars, most of them. That was so typical. I have heard it said that people dig in more when the stakes are high. In this case, I think they were threatened by the fact that I had gone off and gotten my PhD, written a dissertation, and had returned eager to pick up where I had left off. Here I was, ready to succeed! They had written something as a dissertation and got that published as their book, that's what most of them did, but they really did not continue to publish. But I did! I published all along and it really paid off. Eventually, it really paid off.

Working in the English Department, I discovered they were very, very nice to me as long as I kept my place, but when I tried to move into the department as a faculty member, get promotions, they didn't like that. In fact, they didn't like me! One time, I was at a national English meeting and we were at this dinner, some friends and colleagues together. And I invited one of my professors at Michigan to have dinner with us. It was several men from the English Department and this professor, and me—I was the only woman, of course. And we all had quite a bit to drink. At one point, my

MU colleague leaned over and said, "Win, I like you, but I don't like your notions." That was the word he used, "notions." He said, "I don't like your notions, but I like you."

And I said right back, "Roger, I don't like your notions, and I don't like you."

I remember that. I don't know if he remembered that conversation. We never discussed it, but my professor from Michigan remembered it. He laughed about it, repeating the line when he told the story later—"I don't like your notions, and I don't like you." He thought it was hysterical. But "notions," what a strange word to use. You know, women were "bright"— not intelligent—they were referred to as "bright." And they didn't have ideas, they had "notions." That's a sewing word. It's the little stuff you use, like pins, or, you know, funny ideas, "notions." Ideas that are not really good ideas, trivial. That really stuck with me.

I am not certain what I expected when I returned, triumphant, with a PhD in hand in language and linguistics. I was as legitimate as they come. I did it. Maybe I expected a red carpet, but actually I probably knew only the provost who had helped me would be terribly happy to have me return. The director of composition who had stayed on long enough for me to complete my degree and come back to do the work was happy, I am sure, to see me return—so I could get busy doing all the work he really did not want to do. In fact, it wasn't too long before they insisted I take on the directorship of the program, which eventually led to my prominence in the Writing Across the Curriculum program. But that's a another story.

Here, you might want to read these appeals and the letters I received when I was turned down. See if you think they are condescending. I thought they were.

With that, Win shoves several fat folders into my lap and waits while I read through some of the letters. I realize I will need to take these home and read them carefully, so I suggest to Win that we discuss the letters next time. She agrees.

We did, in fact, discuss all of the letters Win received in her bids for promotions in the English Department, as well as her carefully crafted appeals and responses. She read some of the letters out loud to me as we discussed them. Having gone through the same process in the very same department nearly thirty years later, I could definitely relate to her difficulties. In fact, many of the same men who had voted on Win were still in the department voting on me. We bonded over how we had been treated, the ways in which we were demeaned and discounted by many of the same colleagues. As Win shared her stories, I realized I had some to share with her as well. After my own tenure and promotion vote in the department, a colleague stopped me in the hallway to confide that the departmental voting committee "did not read any of your work, but we counted the pages." He patted me on the back as he departed, remarking, "Good job!" He was one of the same men who had disliked Win's "notions."

Understanding Win's frustrations when she returned to her "home" department after receiving her PhD at Michigan requires that we imagine what it must have been like for her to leave Ann Arbor and the academic life she so thoroughly enjoyed as a graduate student, and return to Columbia determined to find a new position for herself within the department she had left two years prior. With a newly minted PhD in language and linguistics, Win returned to the department no longer an embarrassment as a professor with "only" a master's degree. She had studied with some of the finest teachers and scholars at a highly ranked academic institution and had come back to teach and contribute to the scholarly life of the department. Win was aware that the support from the provost that enabled her to go to Michigan now required that she bring her new expertise to her job as director of the composition program, hopefully to locate ways to enhance writing at the university. Imagine the joy Win must have felt when she was directed to "enhance writing" at MU. Writing was her passion, and now she had the credentials to actually design writing programs at the university. She hit the ground running.

It took Win five years after her return to MU before she felt she had accomplished enough to make her bid to be promoted to associate professor. She had been active, doing everything that was expected of her, and she felt she was more than ready. Besides, Win had been a member of the department since 1961, which meant she had been teaching and managing the writing programs for more than twenty years. Perhaps she was confident as she polished her vita and prepared to meet the grueling demands of the promotion process.

Win submitted her file and waited patiently for the review and vote of her department. Before she received the official notification, Win was perplexed by the comments that were made to her in the hallways. Her colleagues went out of their way to tell her why they did, or did not, vote for her. Some mumbled that it was "just too soon." Others admitted that they just didn't know what Win "did." She must have expected the worst.

Indeed, the worst came soon enough. She received a cryptic letter from the chair of the department notifying her that her bid for promotion had been denied. He said, "I am glad senior members of the department had spoken with you," because he was "assured that they had given you the same 'reading' of the meeting" that he had. He gave no justification for the negative vote, but did indicate that the department felt Win's bid for promotion had come "too soon," given that she had only returned to MU five years prior. His letter took an upbeat turn as he encouraged her with the words, "Next year is a new year." The entire letter consisted of about six sentences.

Win's anger and frustration must have been palpable. She knew that the argument that she had made her case too early was a bogus one. Anyone reading her file carefully could track her years of service and conclude that her bid had not been early—that she had, in fact, been quite patient, given the circumstances. Further, Win knew just how much she had dedicated her life and energy to the composition program, having long done the work her senior colleagues refused to do. No doubt she turned to some of her dear friends, like the German professor with whom she had written successful grants. It is unlikely that she had any true friends in the department who would counsel her about an official appeal. But in true Win Horner fashion, she embarked upon a tortuous series of appeals that would take her far into the new year. Both Dave and her children recall how many nights Win spent in her damp basement office banging out appeals on her trusty old manual typewriter. Win remembers those nights as well. She told me of her grim resolve to *fight the bastards*. She had no models for her efforts; she had no mentors; she did not know the language needed for appeals; she did not even know why they had voted her down. She could only suspect the reasons and draw inferences from her colleagues' various comments to her about how the discussion had played out. She did the best she could to write a successful response to the negative votes her colleagues had cast in silent secrecy. But her first appeal failed. The department met, took another vote, and concluded again that Win should not be granted promotion at that time. They invited her to appeal to the college if she was "dissatisfied."

Win was most definitely dissatisfied. She asked that her file continue to the Arts and Science College review committee with the negative departmental vote, knowing full well that the vote would have a negative impact on the college review. Indeed it did, and she was faced once again with an official letter, this time from the college promotion and tenure committee, informing her that she had not received a positive vote in her bid for promotion. By now Win was prepared for what was coming. She was actually hopeful about appealing to the college committee because the professors on that committee were not her department colleagues who certainly had preexisting "notions" about her and her work, and so the playing field might have changed for the better. Win began to write her appeal to the college committee. This time she would be required not only to submit her written appeal but also to meet with the committee to discuss it. Win was encouraged. She knew she could be her own best advocate. She wore the same clothes she had worn for her dissertation defense in Ann Arbor. She was good to go, she told me. What follows is a portion of what she sent to the committee:

Gentlemen:

I am fully aware that one does not call eight persons from their breakfast and coffee on a cold winter morning without good reason. So, to begin with, I should like to go over with you the events that have brought us together this morning. I assure you that making this appeal has not been a snap decision and that I have not asked you here without a deep, and careful, attention to my case.

Since there are no clear-cut criteria for promotion or tenure in my department, and since I am the only person in the field of rhetoric and composition, I sought the advice of the senior person in my alternate field of linguistics. After looking carefully at my record he advised me to go for promotion and offered to nominate me. I then talked with our chair, and with several other senior members of the department who are conversant with my work. All of them, after a careful review of my vita, urged me to go ahead. They saw no reason why I should not get a promotion on the basis of my credentials. One person did comment that he had "absolutely no idea what I did." That was the first hint to me of the "Alice in Wonderland" world that I was getting into.

Win's appeal proceeded to inform the college committee that her chair had notified her that her bid for promotion had been turned down, but that he had offered little in the way of explanation. She summarized the chair's letter to her and responded to the argument that it was too early for her to apply for promotion with this: "Too soon" did not apply in my case, since the promotion was coming 21 years after my original appointment and 13 years after tenure." Furthermore, Win had other ammunition to support her appeal. She told the committee,

Although I did not initiate any discussions after the vote, several of the full professors spoke to me about it. The bulk of these official and quasi-official conversations dealt with what they characterized as the "real" unstated reasons that I was turned down. Here are some:

1. "They don't understand your field. They think only in terms of literary periods" [Rhetoric and Composition has no literary period].

2. "You know there are certain people who will never vote for you even if you write the great American novel."

3. "The more X talked in your favor, the more votes you lost."

4. "The fact that your vita was on computer didn't sit well."

It was also brought up that in the past, as Chair of Lower Division studies, I had made some hard but not always popular decisions and that this fact had worked against me.

I would hate to think that these kinds of petty considerations actually influenced votes, but the reality is that these ideas did indeed exist not just in my imagination but in the minds of my colleagues as well. They may have been unduly magnified by the fact that I never received an adequate academic reason that I considered valid for my having been turned down. The unstated "real" reasons given to me both formally and informally spoke only to political and personal issues within the department and had nothing to do with the quantity or quality of my work.

Everyone seemed to agree that I would get my promotion next year, not because my qualifications would change, but because, in fact, "the make-up of the committee would change. So and so would be back from leave, so and so would be a full professor next year, etc." In one of the discussions, it was suggested that I might request that my support letters be used again next year since they were so laudatory. My question was and is—If they are good enough for next year why aren't they good enough for this year? No one suggested to me that I needed to have another article accepted or that I needed to have a firm commitment on the book manuscript that is now out. In fact, my work was never mentioned. Finally, it all boiled down to one indisputable fact—as one of my colleagues put it: "Win, you just need to get a year older." (And I told him that that was something that I had been trying to avoid ever since my 39th birthday.)

Although I know it was not the intent, the reality of all these comments only reinforced my feeling that the decision was not an accountable act, and that finally I would have to go outside of the department for a fair evaluation of my work.

At this point in her appeal, Win begins the first of her arguments that women are treated unfairly and are judged harshly when their career paths do not compare favorably with those of their male colleagues:

Surely, to compare the time frame of my promotion to "other persons" seems to me to demonstrate a kind of tunnel vision and a lack of understanding or even awareness of the vast variety of career patterns. Many people, particularly women, do not fit the traditional career molds. To deny the possibility of the non-traditional career is to deny what is happening in the world today. To penalize those persons instead of encouraging them for hard won accomplishments seems a sad state indeed. I have been married for 39 years and have four grown children. In the last nine years I have started and completed a PhD from the University of Michigan, built a creditable publishing record, received a number of grants and awards, and gained national visibility. To deny my promotion on the basis of a conventional time frame seems senseless and unnecessary. Certainly, my case has no precedent in my department or, as far as I know, in the college.

As Win had recounted earlier, the dean was also in attendance at the meeting at which Win appeared in person to make her case, and his support for reversing the department's vote was crucial. Win was vindicated—she had won her appeal. At the age of fifty-eight, she became associate professor of English, but her battles were far from over. Three years later, following the publication of three coedited books, several published journal articles, and successful grants, to name only a few of her accomplishments, she was denied her bid for promotion to full professor by the department and the college. In similar fashion, she spent months on her pages-long appeals. Her appeals to the department failed to garner her a positive vote, but her appeal at the college level did win the vote, and her file proceeded to the chancellor's desk.

Her appeal to the college warrants a few excerpts here. She writes,

I do want to emphasize the two sentences in the Arts and Science guidelines document that concern the promotion from associate to full professor: "The differences between the two ranks are simply differences of maturity and degree. It need only be added that candidates for the full professorship are expected to demonstrate continuing growth in scholarship and teaching and to achieve greater recognition of this achievement both on this campus and nationally and internationally."

I think that I qualify as far as "maturity" is concerned—and not only the kind of maturity that engenders gray hairs, but maturity as a scholar, a teacher, and a full colleague. Also as far as "degree"—most of my published work has come after my promotion to associate professor. And, I am especially proud to report that in 1982, I received the University of Missouri Annual Alumnae Award for "outstanding contribution to the education of women."

Finally, I believe that my work evidences "continuing growth in scholarship and teaching," but such growth can only continue in an atmosphere of support and encouragement.

After months of agonizing waiting, Win was informed that the college committee had voted in favor of her promotion. This came via the chair of Win's department, who forwarded the short announcement that he had received from the college. He never spoke to Win in person or wrote to her about her struggles or about her subsequent success. Surely, receiving this final letter must have felt a bit anticlimactic to Win after all the worry, the measured arguments, the frustration:

Dear Chairman:
The Campus Promotion and Tenure Committee has approved our recommendation that:
Winifred Horner be promoted to [full] Professor
It would be appropriate for you to share this information with her, although she should be aware that the recommendations are still to be reviewed by the Provost, Chancellor, and the President.

Sincerely yours,
Interim Dean
Inter-Department Correspondence

Win was successful in getting her promotion to full professor, but now she had to begin the laborious task of fighting for equal pay. In so many ways, she found she was still not treated as a full-fledged faculty member. Although she was not eager to start new battles with her department, she felt it was important for her to challenge the discrimination she knew was evidenced each year in both her own salary and those of other women. A year following her promotion to full professor, she began another letter-writing campaign. In her letters to her department chair, she argued that her career path had been "non-traditional," that she had been a professor in the department for more than twenty years, and that she had directed the composition program and successfully initiated MU's highly regarded Campus Writing Program, which was being lauded by universities across the country. By now, Win was fed up with the behavior of her department; she was demanding justice. In one of the letters she enumerates her various struggles for promotions, a daunting task that would have discouraged someone with less grit. She concludes with these strong words:

> In all of these cases, I have been forced to fight for what has come quite easily to my colleagues. I regard this behavior on the part of the English Department as nothing short of harassment. All of these appeals have taken a considerable amount of time and emotional energy that could well have been spent on research and teaching. This destructive pattern is counter-productive both for myself and for the department.
>
> I apologize for the tardiness of this letter, but it is late for the simple reason that I feel an almost physical aversion to writing it. I have tried very hard not to dwell on past history, not to be bitter. I have tried to ignore the condescending and insulting attitude that some members in the department have toward my field of rhetoric/composition and toward women. I have tried to ignore these attitudes and to work positively and creatively for myself and for the department. It has not always been easy, and writing this letter brings to mind the frustration and anger that I try very hard to forget.

As she had done throughout her life, Win saved copies of all her letters, her appeals, and the responses she received from various administrators. She was eager to talk with me about her strategies for success, for getting her promotions, and for receiving equitable pay. Win definitely saw her fight as part of a larger struggle for women's equality, to ensure that those who came into the academy via a nontraditional path, or those who might have multiple responsibilities to juggle along with teaching, research, and committee work, would not have to face the same challenges that she had. She saw her own story as a model for those who might follow and wanted the female professors of the future to know that the women who had come before them had, in some way, tried to make their journey just a bit less strained and painful.

As you can see, arguing for my rights and raises became pretty much a full-time job for me. I spent so much damn time writing those appeals and letters. And in every single case, when I took the time to write down everything that should have been considered, the promotions and salary raises were awarded to me. But my point to the "higher-ups" was that my colleagues did not have to spend their time doing all this extra work. Their files were reviewed, and they were granted what was owed to them. I was the only one who had to spend all my time fretting over the rejections, the negative votes, the lack of attention to my career, and writing pages and pages of justification for what should have been my right. I was exhausted.

Once I became a full professor, I became a regular at the faculty meetings with Mary, and I thought, to hell with them. I began to speak up in meetings and argue for what I thought the department should prioritize. Pretty quickly I began to advocate moving the study of rhetoric out of the Speech Department and into the English Department, specifically to link it with composition. We already had the composition program, which focused on writing and teaching freshmen and sophomores how to write a composition. At other universities, the field of rhetoric and composition was gaining a foothold. This had become a sophisticated study of the intersections of rhetoric and writing, from Aristotle to more contemporary theorists. Now this field was more broad and included graduate seminars for the graduate students who could now major in rhetoric and composition within the English Departments all over the country. While literature was clearly an important part of an English degree, now students had choices beyond only literature. That was my idea. I worked for that, and eventually we had it—we had a major in rhetoric and composition, and eventually we began to hire new faculty in these areas. You knew several of them, right? Christine Ferris, Krista Ratcliffe, you knew them both. We had several really fine young professors who came to Missouri to teach in rhetoric and composition. We were right there on the cutting edge in this new area. But they didn't stay, because this department never really appreciated or knew what to do with rhetoric and composition as a field. And they always stuck the new people into the role of administrator of composition studies, meaning they were responsible for all the composition courses. This was a job no one really wanted to do. It sucked them dry, left no time for research, or innovative teaching, so they left.

The second thing I did at Missouri was, I think, equally important. But to tell that story, I must tell you I gained the support of the new Arts and

Science dean who came at that time. This is pretty wild. This is a fun story. I love to tell this story. Beth tells this story, too, when she tells stories about her mother. It just goes to show, you have to put yourself forward.

I think I told you that once I was finally promoted to full professor, I was on a lot of committees. I was always the token woman. They didn't have many women at that level. So, a few years later, I was on the committee to search for a new dean. And everybody thought I was very important, because I was with the English Department. Ha. Little did they know!

So we interviewed quite a few people for the job, some really good candidates, good people. Our favorite, the one we hired, was such a great guy. You knew him, didn't you? He was wonderful. I think he died rather young. When we were interviewing, he was in Michigan, not at the university, but at some other school. I went up there at a conference or something, and I asked the chair of the search committee if I could invite him out for dinner. I wanted to take him and his wife out and give him information about our school. She said that was fine, that I could go ahead and meet with him.

So I did that, and I got to know him a little bit before they came here. We did hire him. I liked him, and I liked his wife. And then they moved to Columbia.

The day they moved in, I took over a hamper of food—sandwiches and a carton of beer, you know, a six-pack of beer. I took it over and I said, "Welcome to Columbia."

"Oh, thank you so much." He was delighted.

Then he said, "Win, at some point I want you to tell me where I should get involved in the college. I want to know what you think is important."

Anyway, they were in the midst of moving, so they kept my hamper and I went home. I was thinking to ask Dave to pick up our hamper. But then I thought, are you out of your tree? Here is your chance. He wants to know what is important. Go talk to the new dean about writing!

I had recently learned about other Writing Across the Curriculum programs from conferences I was attending. I was big at going to conferences, and you should be too, you know—conferences in your discipline are really important. That's the very best thing you can do, go to conferences in your field. There I had heard people talk about the concept of "writing across the curriculum," and I liked it right away. I thought perhaps that would be the

very best way to teach writing, in each of the fields—add it to the curricu-
lum and teach the students how to write for biology journals, math, and
physics, et cetera. I thought it was a wonderful idea.

I waited a few days to let him settle into his new house, then I went back
to his house to pick up my hamper. This time I took a case of beer. Ha!

And I said, "Okay, I know what you should do."

He was definitely interested. He liked the beer, and we had a great after-
noon.

A few weeks later, he announced that he was going to appoint a commit-
tee to improve writing in arts and sciences, to develop new ways of concep-
tualizing writing across the curriculum. And I was to be the chair of this
committee. That's right!

I heard that three members of my department went over and talked to
him and said, "Win Horner should not be the chair of this committee. That's
a bad idea." But of course he didn't listen to them.

I love this story. I knew exactly where I wanted to go with this, and I was
ready. The first thing I had to do was find other really good people to be on
this committee. And we did, we had a wonderful committee. A lot of people
were interested in this. I remember one faculty person on the committee
was a dean in engineering. See, we got these really smart people from all
over the campus. The committee was campus-wide, not just arts and sci-
ences. We also had this guy from journalism. He's still around, I think. We
had a wonderful committee, because people were genuinely interested in
this. I knew exactly where I wanted to end up; I wanted us to develop a seri-
ous writing-across-the-curriculum plan.

But getting there was interesting. Another thing I had to do was to help
people realize the English Department did not really care about teaching
writing. Still don't! They were only interested in literature and only inter-
ested in writing if it was about literature. Of course, there were also the
creative writers, but that was different. None of them were interested in
teaching young engineers how to write like an engineer, how to write in
their field. We all learned together how differently journalism taught writ-
ing, for example.

Anyway, we did it. That committee laid the foundation for the University
of Missouri Writing Across the Curriculum program, and I was the first

director. *Eventually they got a search for a new director, but that was several years later when I was leaving for Texas Christian. And that's a different, a wonderful, story!*

Those are the two things I did at Missouri that I am really proud of—developing the rhetoric and composition major and initiating the Writing Across the Curriculum program. And I was credited with those two things, both at Missouri and beyond, at other universities. Because I went to conferences, people came to know me and I became fairly well known for the things I put in place at the university here.

Not only did I win the fight for my own promotions by appealing all the negative votes my file received at MU, I actually turned around and instituted several programs that gained attention from other schools. Pretty much, I did all that my last five years at Missouri before I was invited to Texas Christian University in 1985. Win looks up from her notes and smiles broadly at me. *And that is about when we met, isn't it? You came to the university in January of 1983 to interview for the folklore position in the department. We hired you, and you arrived as a new faculty member that fall, right? By the time you came you had Jessie with you. She was born before you got here. And that's a great story. Remember when you came to interview and I asked you how far along you were?*

Win has come full circle. I am remembering again the night I met her at the interview dinner when she knew I was pregnant, kept it quiet, and became my steadfast friend. Through her warm smiles and generous spirit, I could not see how difficult her career had been up to this point. I could only see a senior female professor, one who could hold her own in an English Department that still had only four women faculty in 1983 (I was the fourth). I was surprised and dismayed when Win told Mary and me that she was being "courted" by another university. I did not know Win's story then, so I could not totally understand her elation as she related to us how another highly respected university was interested in her. Perhaps only now can I understand how vindicated she must have felt when others recognized her talents and skills and considered them valuable, even exceptional, and were willing to pay her top dollar to move to Texas. Winifred Bryan Horner had never been courted like this before, and she absolutely could not stop smiling as she told me this part of her story.

8

--- ❧ ---

A Win for Texas

When I introduced myself, I didn't even think about what I was going to say, but I told them, "I am a feminist. You should know that going in." And this was Texas! . . . I'm rather amazed that I said that to my class.

—Win Horner, remembering her first class at TCU

AT FIRST, PERHAPS WE THOUGHT the attention Texas Christian University was giving to Win would not lead to anything substantial. Selfishly, Mary and I wanted our dear friend to stay in Missouri. But soon it was evident that the courting of Win Horner was sincere, and she began to ponder a move to Fort Worth. The job at TCU was not just a job at another university, she explained; it was an endowed chair position in writing and rhetoric, which meant a substantial salary and a great deal of prestige. For Win, it was her childhood dream come true. She would be a nationally known and honored writer, and she would teach writing to her own graduate students. And perhaps we would never quite understand just how glorious it was for Win to be offered this position after struggling so hard for so little in the department at Missouri.

Today I am eager to hear Win tell this part of her story. Although we were friends when she took the job and moved away, I had never heard the details of this momentous occasion. She is happy to tell me what the endowed chair in Texas meant for her.

I think people were really surprised when I was invited to Texas for the first endowed chair in rhetoric. It was the Lillian Radford Endowed Chair of

Rhetoric, and the first person to hold it was a woman—me! I remember at some point seeing a former Missouri colleague of mine at a national conference in Chicago who said to me, "Win, I think it's wonderful what you're doing, getting the PhD." He knew how difficult it had been for me at Missouri when I returned. But he would have been shocked, now, to know I'd been offered an endowed chair.

By 1985, I was sixty-two years old. I was getting tired of what I was doing in the English Department, and I was definitely tired of the English Department itself! I think I wanted some new challenges. It occurred to me that since Dave and I had gotten along so well with me at Michigan, I thought maybe I would look around to see what else was out there. Maybe I'll just go to some really nice place and get a job teaching freshman composition. So I started looking in the MLA job list when I could get hold of it. Usually that's difficult to do because all the graduate students are looking for jobs and they hog it!

But I started looking, and I saw this endowed chair position in rhetoric listed at TCU. Wow, I thought, an endowed chair—in rhetoric! Well, the graduate students could not apply for that! So I called a person I knew to see if he knew anything about the job. I wanted to ask whether or not they had an "inside person" already selected. That can happen, you know, even though they had to advertise the position. My friend assured me they did not have someone they had already tapped for the position.

He asked me, "Do you want to apply?"

And I told him, "Well, I kind of thought that I would. I was thinking about it."

He was delighted, which was really nice to hear. "Well, you apply, please do! I would really like you to apply for this job."

This was great. You know, looking for a job when you have a job is a lovely situation. Just lovely! So then the chair of the department at TCU called me. He told me he wanted to interview me at MLA—that's the major English literature and language conference, you know, the big conference. He came to hear a panel I was on with Walter Ong, who is really famous. You know him, don't you? That was a big deal. And it was great. The panel was really good—at least, I thought so.

Win looks at me over her glasses and laughs at herself.

Anyway, I interviewed with the chair at MLA. I couldn't believe it, he interviewed me sitting in the hall. I'll tell you, I was not impressed by that! But there you go. I learned later, he was a stickler for watching the budget, so he didn't really have a room for this. The interview was just him and me—the chair of the department, there to interview me. After I got home, I got a call and he said, "I would like to invite you to come and visit TCU." That's how I got my campus interview.

Of course, I said, "I would love to come and visit TCU." Again, it is really nice to interview when you do not need a job. I went to TCU, but in the meantime, I really checked out the school and the campus. The two things I wanted to check out turned out to be things that they liked about me. First I wanted to visit the library. I wanted to know more about the library. And then I wanted to meet with the graduate students. Alone. Other candidates might ask, "Well, what do you want to know about me?" But I went in and said, "I want to know about you. What do you think of this program?" That was a really good idea. They had a couple of things that they didn't like, but generally they liked the program. And they had ideas for improving it. I think they talked to me because I was interested in them, in their work.

I loved going to Texas. I did. The interview was fun. It was just fun. There was no pressure and I felt comfortable. I went out to dinner with people from the English Department, but also with people from around the campus. I remember that was fun too. And they were all so interested in me. Can you imagine that? I guess not. Ha! I remember the chair of the English Department ordered this sangria or something like that, some special kind of wimpy wine thing or something. Everybody around the table ordered it too. But when the waiter came to me, I said, "I'll have a scotch." They all kind of looked at me like—hmmm. I had scotch! Actually they treated me very well. And I liked the campus. It's about a month ahead of Columbia in terms of the weather, which was very nice. Michigan had been about a month behind. So in Texas in February, they had daffodils blooming. That was just lovely.

Anyway, I loved interviewing, had a great time, and I went home. I had barely gotten home, in fact, when the chair called me and said, "I would like to invite you to join us at TCU." That was my job offer for the endowed chair: "We would like to invite you to join us at TCU." Not "You're hired," or anything like that. Very formal: "We'd like you to join us." I loved it.

So then I had to find out what the salary was. He didn't even bother to tell me. Remember, this was 1985. Well, the endowed chair was fifty thousand dollars, which was more than anybody in the English Department at Missouri was getting at that time, by far! Anyone! That was a lot of money at that time. The position was "endowed" with that much money to pay the first chair, which was me.

Well, certainly, the salary was most definitely a plus. I drooled. Not so they could tell, but I certainly drooled. I didn't tell them I drooled—ha! Then the first thing I did before deciding was call up and find out what flights went between Columbia and Fort Worth. I did not want to be cut off from Dave and my family. And I knew Dave would never move with me. He was going to be here. He was going to be on his farm. And I would go down there, alone, if I took this job. And I remember Dave said, "If you don't take this position, Win, no one will ever take you seriously." He'd said that before—about the PhD. And he was right. And, as always, he encouraged me to go. You know, in addition to the salary, it came with a travel budget, and library budget, and a research assistant. I mean, it was a dream job!

Dave and I discussed it. And we agreed, I should go, and I should stay two years, a minimum of two years. It wouldn't be fair to them or me if I went for less time than that. I agreed, I'm going to try it for two years.

So, once again, Dave traveled with me to look for an apartment, in Fort Worth. This time I found a really nice apartment. By then I had made up my mind I was not going to be in a single room there like I had in Michigan. I was going to live well at fifty thousand. So I found a nice little apartment. It was very comfortable. It was not furnished. So, first thing, I bought a good bed, so when I got there I would have a bed. We knew I would be arriving a little late because I was giving a paper at Oxford University in England before I went to Fort Worth.

And they were all fine with that. They told me, "Well, that's okay, you can arrive a little late." They treated me like royalty! I guess that's how they treat endowed chairs. Big cheese! So I gave the paper at Oxford, and I saw my old buddies. And we left on the train from Oxford University at four in the morning. I remember the porter had to leave the key to the gate door under the mat. So we crept out at four in the morning, and we got this key, *unlocked the porter's gate, and we got out. There was supposed to be a taxi waiting for us, which, to our surprise, was actually there waiting for us. We got in the taxi and we drove down to the train. But I got sick. Up until then I was having a great time. Apparently it was something I ate. Anyway, I had to travel like that, sick, sick, sick. I arrived at TCU with a stomach upset. I got there, and I had a bed and an apartment. But that's all I had—a bed in that apartment. I remember I got there exhausted.*

But the very next day, I had to teach my very first graduate course—that day. Can you believe that? So I went in, and I was still green, you know, still sick. But I got along fine because I had them all introduce themselves. And that took a while. Then, when I introduced myself, I didn't even think about what I was going to say, but I told them, "I am a feminist. You should know that going in." And this was Texas! Where did that come from? I should look up that word, I should look up the term "feminist" to see when people actually began to use that word to identify themselves, when that came in to be used like that. It would be interesting to look in the Oxford English Dictionary *and see. That's something I always like to do—look up words in the* OED *and see their history. I'm rather amazed that I said that to my class.*

I do remember there were only women in my class. This was Texas, and they might have been shocked when I said that. But I thought, boy, they'd better find out right now. And that course went really well. You know, I never taught more than one course at a time at TCU. It was truly a dream job! And they were all graduate students. I was asked not to serve on too many graduate student committees, but that didn't work out. I ended up on all of them.

When I interviewed, I asked the provost, "What do you want the person in this chair position to do?" And he said, "I want you to put TCU on the map in rhetoric." And I really worked at that. I went to a lot of conferences, and I had to keep on giving lectures around the country. I developed the graduate program, and we got excellent students. And by golly, before I fin-ished, our graduate students did well. They got great jobs, and they are now teaching all over, teaching rhetoric and composition. We, all of us, put TCU on the map.

After a while, when I was feeling better, I went out and bought a chair and a lamp. Then I started looking for a couch and a table. And I bought a desk, but I bought it at Office Depot and it was in pieces. So Dave came up and put it together for me. That was fun.

I have to admit, that was great, being at TCU. Oh, man! At that university, I was hot shit!

Oh, that reminds me of a story I like to tell, about "hot shit." Before I got to TCU, I was in Oxford, right? And at that time, Beth would write to me every single day when she could. So, we were at this big, long table, you know, at Oxford, and the very proper porter came in with a letter for me. That was my letter from Beth when I was in Oxford, and the porter brought it in—"Here's a letter for you," or something like that. I was at this big, long table, you know, with the Oxford professors lined up in chairs along the wall. So when he brought in the letter for me, they all said, "Oh, read it to us." And I thought, oh, dear. You know Beth. I didn't always know what Beth might write. But I did it. I opened the letter, and I read, "Dear Mother, you are in Oxford and you have a new job at TCU, and you are indeed hot shit!" Beth was always getting me in trouble. Isn't that great? A great story.

The other thing they wanted me to do while I was the rhetoric chair at TCU was to publish. They wanted a scholarly endowed chair who published in rhetoric. So I applied for research grants. And I got them! I remembered how my friend Laverne and I had written grants together so many years ago at Missouri. She had taught me well. I told her all about it when I returned to Columbia. We'd have wine or martinis and I would tell her about TCU. She was so proud of me.

Compared to her, still at Missouri, I was truly lucky. They were very generous—the grants, I mean. I applied for an NEH research grant to go to study how rhetoric had been taught in Scotland. They would pay my way over there and per diem, you know, all my food and lodging while I was there. And for a full month, they paid for this wonderful research assistant to come over and help me. I was even sharing grants for research with my graduate students. I got a book out of that work. It was titled Nineteenth-Century Scottish Rhetoric: The American Connection. *And I also published lots of articles on that research, too. The important thing that I found in Scotland were these student notebooks that demonstrated how rhetoric had been taught in the colleges over there. It's a very interesting period, because they really did influence this country's politics. In England, only aristocrats were educated, but in Scotland, the thinking was that it was everybody's right to be educated. It was everybody's responsibility to see that everyone got an education. That was a whole different attitude about education. It was important when Scots came over here and were tutors in homes over here. They were very influential in our educational system and influenced the writing of the Constitution. They educated the soon-to-be politicians and the upper class in America. But then we adopted the idea that everyone should be educated, which was not true of England. That influence from Scotland was very, very strong.*

Okay, back to TCU. I remember telling the chair of my department at Missouri that I was interviewing for this job and the salary was fifty thousand dollars. And I remember his reaction. He was shocked! He was appalled. I remember the look on his face. And I thought, oh, this is fun! But I tell you what, down there, I knew I would be the big cheese, you know—a woman as an endowed chair. And I was! A big cheese. Man! When I went down there, it was like walking into heaven. And it was great! I mean, I would walk down the hall and people would say, "There's Dr. Horner." It was wonderful! I loved it. I was BWOC again. And for real this time. I was legit!

I wrote a lot when I was in Texas. I did my writing in my apartment, but I went in every day to my wonderful office. I was directing a lot of dissertations, I had ten or twelve dissertations at one time. I enjoyed working with the graduate students because I really loved that work, and they were good, really smart.

My time at TCU was great, and two years in Texas turned into twelve, even longer. I loved it. And Dave and I thrived. We did. We had fun when he would come down to visit. And I would often come home. With just the one scheduled class, I could often leave. Another really good thing about the job was I didn't have to give a final. So I would go home, I would come back to Missouri at the end of the semester, and I'd have the whole month of August off. I'd have a month at Christmas.

In those years, I learned how to teach a graduate seminar—how to lead a seminar, actually. I never lectured. I'm very much more inclined to ask questions. With my students, I really wanted to find out what they knew. I think my seminars were really good, but they really were not much work for me. I mean, they picked out their subject. Then they had to do a bibliography on it, which they gave to everybody in the class. And then they had to write a prospectus, then write a paper. They had to present the paper and what they learned. It was really great for them. Every class brings something different. I kept my comments and questions open-ended. You never close the conversation. You are a facilitator. I thought my job was to encourage them to read, to think, to learn, and to share with the others what they had learned in articulate ways. Then I really, really encouraged them to write. I expected them to write well. After all, we were the leaders in rhetoric and composition. We needed to model the kinds of writing the academy, the world actually, needed. And they were good writers. Most of them were excellent writers, and it pleased me no end to see their publications in print, to hold their books in my hands, to see them accept positions as professors all over the country. That was my legacy. My graduate students. And over time, they became some of my best friends. I loved going to conferences to see them, to hear what they were doing, to find out what was new in our field. I felt good about what I did at TCU—I did put it on the map. Together we created a new field, a new discipline, really, that combined the best of rhetoric and writing. I couldn't have been happier. Couldn't have been happier. I began to write more, too, and publish. That became the happiest time of my life.

Win actually never talked much about the specifics of her scholarly work and publications. She did mention her work on rhetoric in Scotland and the impact that research had on her development of the discipline of rhetoric and composition in the university. I think her book on Scotland is the only one of her books that she mentions in this entire account. To her credit, although she was not shy about saying how pleased she was to have been hired by TCU to occupy an endowed chair in rhetoric, she never bragged about her accomplishments, her many articles, or her nine books. She figured that those who needed to know, or who cared, would know her published work. Her intention for this memoir was to tell her life stories in terms of what mattered to her—the strength she got from her mother; the grounding that the summers at Water Oaks provided for her; the development of her relationship with David Horner; her marriage and the birth of her children; the miserable years she spent on the farm; the invitation to teach at the university; the ways she managed to shape her life differently by getting her MA and her PhD; her fight for recognition, rank, and a decent salary; and, finally, her becoming the most significant professor and scholar of rhetoric in the country.

Thirteen years after she arrived at TCU, she would be asked to retire. The university wanted to pass the endowed chair position on to a new scholar, and Win knew her time there was drawing to a close. Win was sad to leave Texas. She loved her job, her students, her colleagues, and her apartment. She was at the top of her game. She was the star at conferences. Her friends and former students were legion. As she packed up her lovely apartment in Fort Worth, she contemplated a life back in Missouri living with Dave again. She was nearly seventy-five years old. Her health was holding steady. She felt spry and capable, eager to meet whatever might lie ahead. She had ideas for books she wanted to write, and, perhaps most importantly, she was determined to write her own memoir. She and Dave moved to a smaller home on Tremont Circle, and Win set up her computer in her home office. She was ready to write, and without teaching or graduate students to advise, she would have the time to complete what she wanted to do. Win pondered the next stage of her life knowing she might never feel this complete, this satisfied, again.

It was late in December of 2013 when we paused our conversations for Christmas break. We both attended to family, celebrating the end of the year and anticipating a new one. With their adult children's help, Win and Dave had undertaken a huge move from their home on Tremont Circle, winnowing down their possessions to the few that might fit into an apartment at a local retirement facility, TigerPlace. Both of them loved how large their new apartment was, and they were eager to sit on the screened porch that came with it. Yet both of them, especially Win, also regretted the physical limitations that age was imposing on them.

Win and I made plans to meet again in January and continue her saga up to the present day. The way Win would shake her head, I knew her time back in Missouri was not particularly pleasing to her. She certainly enjoyed living with Dave again, and even enjoyed sharing her home with his *damn dogs*. And she loved seeing more of her children and her grandchildren. But I knew none of this was quite enough. I wondered what she would tell me when the new year arrived.

8

Reflections on a Life

I really think work—that is, doing the work you love—is the happiest you can be.

—Win Horner, on staying active and alive

TODAY IS WEDNESDAY, JANUARY 29, 2014. When I arrive, Win is coughing more than usual. Worried, I ask her about her health. She tells me a valve in her heart is failing, and, of course, her respiratory problems are not getting any better. She tells me a new prescription has helped some with the coughing, although at this moment that doesn't seem to be the case.

Win seems frustrated talking about her health and begins reading the notes she has written for herself for today's conversation. Some of what she tells me is a repeat of things she has already told me in our interviews. She seems to want to emphasize how important certain things have been in her life, and she makes reference to some of her favorite stories again. Mostly Win is in a reflective mood, wanting to talk about how we need to make good use of our time, but also insisting that sometimes we live too long. She will be ninety-two later this year, and she is not pleased that she did not continue her writing after she returned to Columbia from Texas.

I feel like today I have some confessing to do, or some clarification. There are stories I tell about my life. Some of them I have told many, many times.

Some are funny, some not so funny. At least I want to emphasize some of my favorite stories, and maybe clear up some things I have said about my life.

Now, my answer to the question of how I did it all includes when I went to TCU with an endowed chair. I remember a young reporter asking me, "How did you do it all? You have a long and happy marriage, four children, a PhD, a career, and an endowed chair. How did you do it all?" I've been asked that many times over the years, and generally I answer, "Well, Dave and I, we just did our own thing." But you know, that was actually a lie. If not a lie, then it was so small a truth, because we did not both just do our own thing! The truth is that for nearly twenty years, I followed Dave and did the traditional married "thing." I followed Dave in the military and after that onto the first of our farms. That was Dave's dream, not mine. I tried to be the good farm wife and mother, but I was so miserable I had to get off that farm and begin to do what I wanted to do. After that, I guess, to some degree we did do our own thing. But we always discussed whatever we were going to do, and I will say that once Dave knew how miserable I was, he did everything he could to help me. But it irks me now that I was so glib often with my answer to that question about how I did it all. I need to emphasize that for a very long time, I did not do my own thing. That came much later. It took me a long time to put myself first.

So then I got the opportunity to go to Texas as an endowed chair. I was sixty-two years old, when most people are thinking about retiring. And that's what I want to emphasize here, that you didn't have to do it all at the same time, but you do need to keep going. And if opportunities do not come along right away, you have to wait for them and you have to have energy to do them, and that's a physical thing. Some people have it, and some people don't. It's physical, but it's mental too. I had lots of energy, and I had my health—well, mostly I had good health.

All those years I was energized when I was at TCU. I loved teaching. I loved my graduate students. I loved going to conferences and giving lectures. I loved getting to know people in the field and networking, especially to help place my graduate students, who were very good and who were finishing their dissertations, ready to go on the job market. And that's where I did all of my writing, most of my published work. I wrote several books while I was at TCU and many of them are now in multiple editions, still being published. From there I did my lecturing, and most of my traveling. I was a keynote speaker at all the conferences. I was at the top of my game.

Another point I'd like to make is that I have had a long life. Because of that I have been able to do many things. I had a lot of energy and I had good health, mostly. I have had chronic respiratory problems, from years of smoking, but whatever ails us, most people live a good ten or fifteen years longer than our parents did. A lot of us have functioning good health, as I had. But there's a problem here, too, that needs to be pointed out. And that is, in fact, we are living too long. Medicine has improved to the point that we can be kept alive far longer than is good or necessary. This doesn't mean we should stop earlier—actually it means we should keep going as long as we can, especially as we realize that we will live much longer than we thought we might.

I retired in 1996 and returned to Columbia. That's a long time. That's more than fifteen years. And I haven't made good use of that time, after I came back. Little did I know that I would live so long. It is now 2014 and what have I done since I returned? Not much. I should have kept going. I should be writing, but I came home and expected, really, to decline and die. But I didn't. My health is one factor and just going to the computer to write has been another. I had to come back and adjust back to being a wife again, and a mother. I fret over my adult children. I should be over that by now. I mean, that is stupid, getting involved in their lives again. But this has been a stupid period of my life. I feel like I have let it become stupid.

I did not want to leave TCU. In a way I was actually forced into retirement. They could have extended my time there, but they had other people in mind for that endowed chair. There were other departments involved. They wanted to rotate different departments with new people. I can understand that. And Columbia is my home. I knew I needed to come home to Dave. We weren't getting any younger and Dave had had some heart problems. Well, eventually, we both did. So I came home.

It may sound odd to say, but we both enjoyed those years when I was in Texas. We did! People acted like I should be worried leaving Dave for so long and some thought he should be worried about me being alone in Texas. But we both enjoyed it. We were both doing what we loved at the time. Dave still wanted to be a farmer, and he would go to the farm every single day. He loved that. And I was happy in my apartment in Fort Worth, completely happy. And we had wonderful times down there. Dave would come down for the weekend, and we would have wonderful weekends together. And sometimes I would go to a conference, and he would come at the end of the conference, so we could enjoy whatever city the conference was in. We learned not to have him come during the conference, because you know how that goes. I was always so busy at conferences. Most of what happens at conferences happens at breakfast, lunch, and dinners. And he had no interest in that. I loved it all. I was in my element, and it was wonderful. Wonderful!

When I came back, we just decided it was time to live together full-time again. And that's what we did. It's not exactly true that I did nothing when I returned to Columbia. I taught in the adult learning program. I taught what I called "Life Writing"—that was also the title of one of my books. You attended some of those classes and recorded our sessions. Remember that? It was essentially memoir writing. I loved it, and the students loved it. I should have been writing my own memoirs then, too, but I wasn't. One of the reasons I loved it was that some of the people were really good writers; they just had never tried to write. And I loved it because you don't give grades. All I did was teach writing by pointing out what was good in their writing.

They loved reading each other's writing, and they gave each other good suggestions. It was an easy course to teach, really, and so enjoyable. It was interesting for everyone. There are two groups, two classes, that are still meeting. They read their writing and talk about their writing. I have always said that one measure of success, in writing, is that you must get people so they will write. Their writing will improve if they just write. It works that way for all of us.

I want to come back to that notion that you can't have it all at the same time. I think both the question and the answer are very gendered. In her book, Tina Fey makes a wonderful point in that she says she is often asked, "How do you do it all? Marriage, kids, career, movies, television, et cetera." She points out that they never ask her partner the same question. They never ask him, "How do you do it all?" But everybody asks her, "How do *you do it all?" But no one asks a man that. That's a gendered question, and I guess it's true. We have to get it all in different segments of our lives. The men can start at the beginning of their lives and go from there, but women often have to piece it together, achieving first one thing, then another.*

Win hands me two books I had brought to her several months ago. I hadn't realized she had read them.

I've read those two books you brought over for me to read. You wanted to talk about them. This one is Sheryl Sandberg's Lean In. *This other one is Debora Spar,* Wonder Women. *I'm glad you brought these books to me; you can take them back now. In some ways I could connect with both these authors. One is an academic, the other isn't. I read parts of both of them. Both of these authors admit you can't do it all. The author of* Lean In, *I like what she says about the "myth of doing it all"; I think she makes a wonderful point. She says, "You just learn not to do it all perfectly. You decide what you should do perfectly and then you just let the rest go a little bit."*

When I read that, I thought, well, that's what I should have done. You know, not trying to do the damn composition program perfectly, which the department did not care about in the end. They just wanted me to do the work. I worried about that too much, and I should have published my dissertation. That's what I should have done. Hindsight is great.

The other author says you can't do it all, and you shouldn't even try. I think she did try, but regrets it. She talks about the things she missed from her kids. I certainly didn't feel that way, because I devoted my whole damn life to my kids—I mean, to my marriage and my kids, at least for a while. Whenever I get into anything, I really get interested in it. I really put myself into those years, trying to make it work on the farm and having the four kids, all of it. I remember how I'd fantasized that it was going to be a breeze, that I was going to have all sorts of helpers, you know, servants, and I was going to run this wonderful life with children all around. I would look great in these flowing skirts and a grand hat, a hat with a velvet bow and ties. I told you about my image of me in a breeze on top of the hill with a film of gauzy stuff around my face. Ha! Of course, it wasn't that way at all. That image probably came from novels, 1850s novels, and from absolute ignorance.

I also told you what my father said about knowing you can pretty much tell what a person—a man, of course—was going to accomplish by the time he was thirty-five. I think I was thirty-five, and thinking about what he said sent me into a deep depression.

I'll tell you frankly what my problem is—I'm working on this, but now it's been so long since I've sat and typed, it's not happening. I used to type every day all day. I'm not doing it as well now. It's just riddled with errors. I think that's my problem, and I think it's purely physical. I'm working at it, but that is really distressing. When I write, when I start with a chapter, I have it pretty well organized. Then, when I type, I insert something. I think, oh, I shouldn't have said this or put this here, I should put it over here. It ends up being a disaster. So, when I get this back from you, what I'd like to do is just pretty much do that sort of thing, going through each section. It just infuriates me that the typing is that way, so difficult. I think it's temporary, but I don't know. You might say when I came back home I just ran out of steam. And that's not a good thing. I look back and it's a bad thing. Because I really think work—that is, doing the work you love—is the happiest you can be. I haven't been very happy lately because I haven't been writing.

You know, this place, this elder residence where we are living now, advertises with the motto "Aging in Place." Well, first of all, that's a rather absurd idea, sounds like running in place, going nowhere, doesn't it? What do they mean by "aging in place"? I think they mean, this is your last place to live. Actually they should call it "dying in place," but I guess that wouldn't be a very good advertising gimmick, do you?

Win laughs hard at her own joke and begins to choke. In time, she is able to talk again.

I've said this to you before. Coming here is like coming to a place to die. That is rather gruesome to think about. But the problem is, they are working so hard at keeping us all alive they are working against their own plan. We are living too long. People in our parents' generation did not live this long. They died in their seventies. That's when people died, or even their sixties. Now we are living well into our eighties and our nineties. We are living too long. The medical profession should begin to seriously think about this. If they keep us alive into our nineties and keep all the baby boomers alive into their nineties, there won't be any place to keep us all. What is the reasoning behind keeping us alive when our health is poor or our hearts are failing? This is a serious problem, don't you think?

I think it's a big problem.

Several times in the past year, Win had wanted to talk a bit about her mother's death, which had been a suicide. She had kept some notes about it during the time she was at Michigan, but she had not talked at length about how her mother's death had affected her. She did return to St. Louis for the funeral, but she did not talk, or write, very much about this event at that time. In some of her jottings on random pieces of paper in her Michigan files, I found these words: I have not dealt with my mother's death. I should. I should take some time and think about it. Sometimes when I walk around campus, I do think about her. She was a wonderful woman, a wonderful mother.

Win got her opportunity to process her mother's suicide and discuss some of her evolving thoughts about death with a group of close friends when she returned to Columbia. She and I belonged to a book club that had as its members several of our mutual friends, including three clergywomen, a psychologist, a massage therapist, Win, and me. This group had morphed over the years, adding people who came for a while then disappeared, and adding members when we suffered losses. We tended to read books about life and spirituality. We were not interested in books on religion per se, but works that explored moral choices, the friendships of women, and strategies for negotiating our family lives suited us just fine. Win was particularly uneasy with books about "the goddess" or goddesses in general, rolling her eyes when things got too "New Agey" for her. But then she wasn't very fond of "the god" either. Many of the books we read were about aging gracefully. In 1999, our group read Carolyn Heilbrun's book *The Last Gift of Time*, which led our group to a very serious discussion about death and suicide.

Win had a visceral reaction to Heilbrun's book, and particularly to the fact that after publishing this book on the importance of the last years of one's life, Heilbrun committed suicide. Like Win's mother, Heilbrun had told her family of her intention to end her life when she began to feel she might be easing into a dependent old age. She had first thought she would commit suicide at seventy, but when she got there and life was going along pretty fine, she decided to stick around for a while. At seventy-one, she published this book, and at seventy-seven she died by her own hand. At the age of eighty, Win wrote the following piece. For the first time since her mother's death she was finally able to deal with it.

MY TURN

Winifred Bryan Horner

The articles were short and the facts were bare. Carolyn Heilbrun, well-known feminist and Columbia University scholar, had committed suicide at the age of 77. Her son was quoted: "She always wanted to control her own destiny."

A series of conflicting emotions washed over me as I read: sadness, disappointment, loss and then deep anger. I didn't understand why I was reacting so strongly. Twenty-five years earlier my mother, with whom I had always been close, committed suicide and I had handled that well I thought. I felt no guilt—she had long supported euthanasia, and I knew how she dreaded illness and aging. Years later after the long dying of a good friend, I had even joined the Hemlock Society.

I hardly knew Heilbrun. The sadness especially surprised me. One year we were both featured speakers at a conference for chairs of University English departments and we were both early feminists. On that occasion I had gathered an informal group of women to discuss problems that they might have as women chairs of departments composed largely of men. We assembled in a large sunny general-purpose room. While we talked, several of the men, including my own boss, nervously circled our group. Carolyn turned to me and whispered, "They're not going to let you off the plantation again." Several years later I had occasion to write her about some professional matter. It was the beginning of the technology era, and in her response she said that the printing from my dot matrix printer reminded her of her grandmother's needlepoint. She had a keen eye and a way with words. My personal acquaintance with her rested on those two events.

But I knew Heilbrun best through her books, most of which I had read and some I had taught. In all of these she was a staunch supporter of women. I had read her last book, *The Last Gift of Time*, and just recently reread it. It spoke eloquently to me of the "gains that age might hold." I had read it earlier before my retirement, and I had been so busy living that I had not been particularly impressed. Twenty years later, as a different person, I had reread it and this time the words spoke to me. She speaks of being old at a time when she is "surer of what her life is about" with "less self doubt to conquer." Having considered at one time that life properly ended at sixty and that that milestone seemed the appropriate time to end the journey, she confesses that at seventy she looked back on "her sixties with pleasure astonishing." But as the three score years and ten approached, her doubts returned. "Quit while you're ahead was, and is, my motto," she wrote, and at the age of 79 [sic] she quit.

I could not understand my feeling of loss. Her books had long inspired me and I was disappointed that there would be no more. But the sadness was somehow, I realized, connected through some dark threads in my subconscious to the suicide of my mother. At the time of my mother's death, I was in the midst of pursuing my PhD at the University of Michigan. I was fifty years old and having my own struggles. I pushed my mother's death to the back of my mind. I thought I had handled it well, but I realized now that I hadn't handled it at all. Like Heilbrun, my mother was in her late seventies and in good health. She still walked several blocks to her health club where she swam each morning.

I thought then that she had so much more to give the world and her family. My work was easing up, and I looked forward to reconnecting with my mother. I was planning a trip that we might take together in the following year. I thought how proud she would be when I got my PhD, and I looked forward to having her at the graduation ceremonies. I felt a loss and a disappointment.

My mother, like Heilbrun, had long spoken of her plans to end her life at a time that she chose. She, too, spoke of taking control while she still could and not waiting until her body and the medical profession took over. She was not a deeply religious person, but she, like all of us, dreaded the long painful dying, not the death itself. But for me, I finally realized there was sadness, disappointment, and loss.

So why was I so angry at these two strong intelligent women? In a way I realized that they had just cancelled out the days they had left as worthless. Perhaps I was angry because I wanted Heilbrun to write another book. I wanted her to share her insights into living beyond the three score and ten. Perhaps I was angry because I wanted my mother to share the moment when I received my doctor's hood. She would have been so proud. I, like them, have now passed the allotted number of years. I, like all people in their late seventies and eighties, have aching joints and weaker muscles. I have to go to the bathroom more frequently these days, and I forget names of people and places. I breathe harder walking up hills, and my children rush to help me out of those low-slung car seats. I read more slowly because there are more real-life experiences to connect with, and I write more carefully because the words have to be drawn from a deeper well. And there are other issues between me and my doctor that don't bode well for the long haul.

But today, I value my family and friends with more understanding, less judgment, and more real love no matter where, no matter why. I still savor the return of the forsythia, the sound of the birds in the early morning, the wonderful smell after a spring rain, the reds and oranges of the turning leaves, the surprising blaze of an autumn sunset. I feel angry that my mother and Heilbrun did not value these things as I now value them in a new and more significant way. How could they leave all this glory! I feel angry that they felt that they had nothing left to give, that my life—my eighty years—have nothing left to offer to myself or anyone else. Each day is a gift that I shall use for myself and others. I'm in it for the haul—long or short. I too dread the slow dying, but I shall live out my life to the end. I love this life with all of its joys and sorrows, and dying is an integral part of that life—dying prepares me and my loved ones for the final act. I am not quitting. Today I have cancelled my subscription to the Hemlock Society.

END

As we near the end of Win Horner's life and her story, we might remember her diary entries from 1934 and '35, written when she was only twelve years old. As Win might say, "Have I told you about them? Have I told you that story? Well, either way, they bear repeating." Her entry on July 2, 1935, reveals the depth of young Win's thinking. Her words expose many of the issues she would take to her grave nearly a century later.

I'm beginning to feel the meaning of that old saying, "Life is complicated." It certainly is. Lately I've had some of the strangest feelings that I can't explain at all. I want to know more than I know now. I want to learn about the strange things beyond. I'm impatient, and it seems strange to live in a world where one knows no more than the life that you are living now. I'm uncertain whether you really live eternally, or if that's just religion. How can I have faith when I have no foundation to build my religion on? How can I, or why should I, believe history? . . . Scientists dig out theories and call them facts, and I am called upon to believe them and—shall I?

No, I will find out for myself. Is this narrow mindedness? I'm afraid so, but here I am wandering into unknown realms. I have made a surprising discovery today. There is no-one who has entire control of himself. Perhaps you can keep yourself from willful sin, but who is the person who can love God when there is no love in their heart? I find my entire life is governed and ruled by obstinate moods. The new moods I have experienced of late I can-not describe. They are mainly ones of uncertainty. I do not know whether to love the world or hate it, to be good or bad, and I usually lapse from this uncomfortable state into any other mood. I feel that if I could control this period I could control most of my pettish, stubborn feelings.

What are the moods? There is the Religious Mood, Mood of Indifference, Ambitous [sic] Mood, and Mood of Resignation.

Among these, the first and third are more desirable, while the forth [sic] tends to make an inferiority complex.

I don't know what mood I'm having right now. I think it's ambition.

This diary entry of a girl not yet in her teens is both astounding and prophetic. Win never really reconciled herself to any particular religious beliefs, although she found the church full of good people who became her lifelong friends. On the cusp of turning thirteen, young Win was facing her own childhood demons, rejecting indifference and resignation and consciously choosing ambition. The strength and drive that characterized Winifred Bryan's choice of ambition as a life goal has been evidenced in every page in this book. She wasn't modest about her abilities and achievements, and she wasn't shy about letting people know who she was and what she had accomplished. Not everyone liked what they saw, although few people could ever really dislike Win. They might dislike her ambition, her drive (her refusal to "stay in her place"), and her ideas (her "notions"), but most people who knew her recognized her exuberance for life, her generosity of spirit, and her unyielding sense of humor. Those traits can get a person just about anywhere they want to be. That was certainly the case for Winifred Bryan Horner.

*   *   *

When I left after our session on that Wednesday, January 29, I had no idea that was to be my last visit with Win. As I left, she told me she was relieved, feeling we had finished the task of getting her stories recorded. We were both pleased. I opened the screen door to go, but I heard her yell at my back, *Oh! Next time we're going to figure out the focus for this book and the title. Titles are very important, you know. That's what we both need to think about for next time—the focus and the title.* Smiling and happy, I heard the screen door slam behind me.

Before I left Win that day, I made certain we had scheduled another meeting for the following Wednesday to finish the details of her book. I promised I would give her all the transcriptions of her story, so that she could begin to shape her memoir as she pleased. She could hardly wait, she told me.

Tuesday night, my phone rang, late—too late for good news. Hearing Dave's voice, I somehow knew what he was going to say even before he spoke. Always precise with his words, but gentle in tone, he said, "Elaine, this is Dave Horner, and I want you to listen very carefully to what I am about to tell you."

There was a long pause.

"Are you there?"

I mumbled that I was listening.

"Win died this afternoon. I know you were coming over in the morning, so I wanted to be sure and call you."

Numb, I told him goodbye and thanks for calling. It seemed awkward to thank him, but I was grateful that he called me himself to tell me the news.

Not having been with Win when she died (and recognizing that that was not my place anyway), I was left with only a phone call and a sentence: "Win died this afternoon." I sat down and could not move for hours. How could Win just be gone? I felt acutely the vacuum in the space where she had existed for more than thirty years of my life, where she had existed for Dave for nearly ninety years, for her children all their lives, and for all those who knew and loved her for whatever time. I thought of the boy in Faulkner's masterpiece, *As I Lay Dying*, pondering the invisible line between life and death after losing his mother. Only a breath, the boy thought, separates the "is" from the "was." A breath. Breath was life to Win, and for years she recognized that tenuous connection between the body and the breath. I thought about what she had told me, that she did not want to die from lack of breath, nor did she wish for a "long dying." I hoped her going was easy.

At the "Celebration of Win's Life," a memorial service held on March 29, 2014, in Columbia, memories of Win were shared by many people who had known and loved her. Dave, still in shock that she was gone, told about first meeting Win when they were both still children, and how she had impressed him even then. "What struck me," he said, "what riveted me about that kid splashing in the river a long time ago, was a spark, a spirit, an energy, a determination that I had never encountered, and I was intrigued. If Win were here, absolutely no one would have as good a time as she would. She would visit with each person, inquire as to what was going on in her or his life, have a word of encouragement, and she would feel really bad when the meeting was over if she learned that she failed to see someone that was here." In a few short statements, the man who knew her best summed up so many key aspects of Win's life—her determination and can-do attitude, her care for everyone, and her spirit.

A few months after Win died, I heard her daughter, Beth, tell the following story during a performance of stories about her mother. This story highlights another key aspect of Win's personality and how she touched those who knew and loved her. Win and Beth were attending a national conference where Win was being honored by a distinguished panel of scholars and former students. Win wanted to go, but thought perhaps her health wasn't quite good enough for her to attend alone. She invited Beth to go with her. Beth was delighted and went proudly to see her mother honored by those in her field. Beth told the story this way:

I walked into Mom's hotel room to accompany her to the conference session titled "Honoring the Vision of Winifred Bryan Horner." She was sitting on the bed, professionally dressed as always, staring out the large picture window overlooking San Francisco, but not really seeming to be taking in the view. At first it didn't seem to me that she knew I was there—until she turned and matter-of-factly stated, "You know, Beth, I'm not afraid to die."

Being in a "Hey, we are honoring Mom today" frame of mind rather than a "Let's talk mortality" frame of mind, I was caught off guard and didn't quite know how to respond. So I walked around the bed and hugged her. We hugged for longer than usual. Then, knowing that Mom is not overly comfortable with tears or emotions, or hugs for that matter, I smiled and said, "Mom, I'm so glad that you're not afraid to die. However, could you hold off on that for about two hours—until we go downstairs to that roomful of people who are waiting to honor your vision?" We both laughed and she replied, "If you insist."

She did hold off "on that" for the next five years.

In January of this year, my father and I took my mom to have an echocardiogram, a heart test that uses sound waves to produce moving images of the heart. Mom and I went into the echocardiogram room. She got suited up in the appropriate gown and into the bed next to the monitor. Immediately, she got irritated at the technician when told, "You have to take out your hearing aids." So she sat up in bed and, pointing her finger back and forth to the technician and to me, sternly said, "Okay, but no talking, you two. No talking. I don't want to miss anything."

I knew that she was serious when she said that she didn't want to miss anything. When she lay down, I couldn't see her face, only the various wires stretching from her body to the machine. So I simply said, "'Okay. I promise not to talk."

I sat there at the end of the bed and, because I was not to talk, began attending to business on my smartphone. I was deep in texting, e-mailing, business mode, when I heard a beep. Looking up, but with my thumbs still poised on my phone screen, I stared. There on the monitor was my mother's heart . . . my mother's heart . . . beating. I remained still as the enormity of that moving image sank in. That's the first sound I had ever heard. That's the heart beating when she indicated in her high school yearbook that her life's ambition was to be happy and to realize it. That's the heart my father fell in love with more than eighty years ago. That's the heart that beat for nine babies, five of whom never made it into this world, four of whom did and were raised by that heart. That's the heart that beat for grandchildren and for a great-grandchild soon to be born. That's the heart that beat for hundreds of students—undergraduate students, graduate students, grand-graduate students. My mother's heart.

Silently, I lifted up my phone, opened the camera app, and clicked on "video"—so that I would always have my mother's heart with me.

Win's husband and children, her grandchildren, and her friends recognized all the aspects of Win's "heart" that made her special. She was a people person, as Dave would say. Recently he asked me if I'd ever seen Win "work a room." I had, of course, and it was always instructive to watch her mingle. She could talk to anyone, and would somehow manage to make each person feel special. Next time she saw you, she would ask again about your work and how you were getting along with it. Win genuinely cared about people and she sincerely wanted to know about our work, our thoughts, our successes. She was everyone's cheerleader. Beth was trying to make a video of Win's generosity of spirit. Her thumping heart was her zest for life, the connection she made with other people.

Following Win's death, Dave and their children decided to place a marker for Win in the Columbia cemetery. In this place of tranquility, Dave stipulated that Win's marker would bear this message to the future: "Win Horner, to her successors: 'EMBRACE LIFE.'" Win's family and friends gathered to enjoy a picnic near her grave. They had brought a folding table and chairs, a tablecloth, food, and wine. They chatted with each other, and communed with Win, then poured some scotch on her tombstone before they left. We all feel Win's absence, yet her heart and her spirit bind us together. Each of us will keep finding ways to keep her memory alive and to acknowledge the importance of her life among us.

After her death I felt more strongly than ever that Win's book, her memoir, needed to be published. I had the completed transcriptions of her life story. I had boxes and boxes of her letters and documents. I had access to hundreds of photographs of her. So I began to organize the materials and outline the book. When the semester ended and I had more time to devote to this work, I began in earnest to piece it together. It is hard to believe that three years have passed since she died. Teaching and working with my graduate students often interfered with my writing time, but I had learned from Win to enjoy my students and our work together as special and valuable, never regretting the time I spent with them. At times my family interrupted the work, but always in good and important ways: Madison, Luke, Chloe, and Olivia were born and added so much to our family.

There were also other interruptions. In 2015, I became gravely ill and spent several weeks in the ICU, two of them in a coma. After rehab I was able to go home and, once again, think about Win's book. In many ways, it was extremely helpful to have her book waiting for me. The doctors were concerned about how my brain would function following my collapse, but Win would have been pleased to see me struggle to open my computer, determined to complete her book. Without a doubt, Win's stubborn determination and can-do spirit guided me every day to continue my work on her memoir.

Win Horner's presence in my life helped shape my career in too many ways to enumerate. What I needed, and got, from her was what she was able to give to me in generous proportions—support for my work, respect for my training, enthusiasm for my successes, mentoring for the battles I had to fight in the academy. And consistent love and friendship. What I gained from my relationship with Win was confidence, self-esteem, bravery, persistence, faith in my abilities and my work, and a sense of humor—all built into conversations about things that mattered to us as women, as academics, as wives and mothers, and as friends.

I also became a feminist during the years that Win and Mary Lago were "radicalized." We moved into that territory together, braced against a system that did not appreciate or support us, that put up barriers that we could only overcome through the strength of our collective spirits. What wonders could happen over a good glass of wine, intellectual conversation, and dear friendships between women who were bucking the system, claiming their place at the university, and sharing their losses and wins together. I never found it odd that my companions on my academic journey were two women a generation older than I was. They were the crones, the wise women, fortunately stationed near me for guidance, love, and support. They were angels on my path. They are both gone now, but their spirits still guide me every single day. All the time I think, what would Win and Mary say about this? How would they respond, retort, examine whatever I am facing? The best thing I can imagine is that they would somehow respond in a way that would make me laugh. And truly, laughter and camaraderie are the best medicine for life's difficulties. Not laughter that dismisses the situation or undermines the seriousness of the conflict, but laughter that clears our brains, opens up new spaces for healing, and helps us understand better what really matters and what doesn't.

As I finish this book, I recognize that I also learned from Win how to craft experience into a story, something that assisted me tremendously in fashioning this work. I learned from Win how to hone a good story, hopefully to give it a good punchline. She taught me how to set the scene, include the things people actually said, describe their expressions, and share the climax and outcome of what happened. Learning to tell a good story enables us to examine things from a different perspective. Over the years, when we would meet, we would order our wine (or martinis) and one of us might say, "Oh my god, you won't believe what [fill in the blank] did on Tuesday." This was not gossip. The important thing was not actually what so-and-so did or said on Tuesday. This was not about that person, in fact; it was about *who was telling the story*. What mattered was how we told it, how we outlined the characters, depicted the scene, recounted the dialogue (in different voices the listener might recognize), and ended on a note that recognized the emotional significance of the event but also illustrated how we had moved beyond the actual incident into analysis, evaluation, and renewal. In fact this can be described as "healing through storytelling." And Win Horner taught me that. Without question, that was Win's gift to us all. Name it, examine it, craft a story about it, laugh, and move on. Such an approach to life served her well, kept her going, and enabled her to enjoy the wins with exuberance and joy, and to leave the losses behind.

My belief in the importance of sharing Win Horner's story has guided me to complete this book. While many of the obstacles Win faced as a woman in the academic world may have been resolved, many issues remain difficult for women in our country. In 2016, we saw the first woman candidate selected by a major political party run for president in the United States. Women all over the country felt proud and emboldened by this push against the glass ceiling. But the female candidate did not win the election, and suddenly women are faced with the reality that many of the policies and laws they have fought to get in place to protect women's rights are threatened. Even in 2017, it is not a given that women in this country who are equally trained will be hired equally or paid the same wages as men. As in Win's case, too many avenues for promotion and stability in our careers are hindered by secret ballots, where voting committee members can reject candidates who are women or mothers, or whose skin is a different color. Win's battles may be all of our battles, on larger or smaller scales, depending upon our circumstances. We learn from the stories of our female models how best to conduct ourselves, how to fight, how to resist complacency, how to word our appeals for justice. Reading the story of the liberation of Winifred Bryan Horner provides all of us with information, with strategies, with evidence of the power of grit and determination when the stakes are high. The result is our collective empowerment. Win managed to "have it all," which to her meant having a successful career doing what she loved, while keeping her family and her marriage secure. We might strive to find ways to protect all that we hold dear as we push for our own freedom and liberation from expected norms and expectations. If Win knew you, she would ask, *How's it going?* And she would expect a thoughtful answer, one that suggested that you knew the importance of standing up for yourself and what you wanted from life.

There is no easy way to finish this book of Win Horner's stories and her life, but it seems appropriate to include one last story. One day, back when Win and Dave were living on the farm, maybe around 1958, the oldest of their children, her namesake, Win, asked questions about death over breakfast—questions that Win felt she had perhaps not answered very well at the time. Later, in an attempt to provide a clearer answer, Win wove her daughter's questions into a story about the children playing on the farm. Without a doubt, Win wanted to live. But even though she loved living, we know from her conversations with Beth that Win was not actually bothered by the thought of death itself. In that regard, I'm thinking she should have the last word:

The children played in the yard all morning and about eleven o'clock decided to go down to the field where Dave was plowing. By then, Beth had lost her mittens, Richard had unbuttoned the one button he had left on his jacket, and Win's tattered coat seemed to hang by one final thread. As they went through the gate, they stopped for a minute, took off their coats, and hung them over the fence. Then they ran down the road laughing, calling to each other, shouting.

As I watched them go, I thought that surely death is as easy as this. Walking through the gate into warm sunlight and another springtime, leaving behind the worn-out coat that the spirit has outgrown.

Winifred Bryan Horner, Vita and Bibliography

EDUCATION

PhD, University of Michigan, Ann Arbor, 1975, English Language, Literature, and Linguistics
MA, University of Missouri, Columbia, 1961, English
AB, Washington University, St. Louis, MO, 1939, Major: English

PROFESSIONAL EXPERIENCE

English Department, Texas Christian University, 1985–1996

Ida and Cecil Green Distinguished Tutor, Radford Chair of Rhetoric and Composition, and Professor of English

English Department, University of Missouri, Columbia, 1961–1985

Professor of English, 1983
Chair, Lower Division Studies, and Director of Composition Program, 1974–1980

BOOKS

Gaillet, Lynée Lewis, with Winifred Bryan Horner, eds. *The Present State of Scholarship in the History of Rhetoric: A Twenty-First Century Guide.* 3rd ed. Columbia: University of Missouri Press, 2010.
Hodges, John C., Robert Keith Miller, Winifred Bryan Horner, and Suzanne Strobeck Webb. *Hodges' Harbrace Handbook.* 14th ed. Fort Worth, TX: Harcourt College, 2001.

Horner, Winifred Bryan. *Life Writing.* Upper Saddle River, NJ: Prentice Hall, 1997.

Horner, Winifred Bryan, and Michael Leff, eds. *Rhetoric and Pedagogy: Its History, Philosophy, and Practice; Essays in Honor of James J. Murphy.* Mahwah, NJ: Lawrence Erlbaum, 1995.

Horner, Winifred Bryan. *Nineteenth-Century Scottish Rhetoric: The American Connection.* Carbondale: Southern Illinois University Press, 1993.

Horner, Winifred Bryan. *The Present State of Scholarship in Historical and Contemporary Rhetoric.* Rev. ed. Columbia: University of Missouri Press, 1990.

Horner, Winifred Bryan. *Rhetoric in the Classical Tradition.* New York: St. Martin's, 1988.

Horner, Winifred Bryan, ed. *Composition and Literature: Bridging the Gap.* Chicago: University of Chicago Press, 1983.

Horner, Winifred Bryan. *Historical Rhetoric: An Annotated Bibliography of Selected Sources in English.* Boston: G. K. Hall, 1980.

SELECTED ARTICLES AND BOOK CHAPTERS

Horner, Winifred Bryan. "The Changing Culture of Rhetorical Studies." *Rhetoric Review* 20, nos. 1/2 (2001): 5–9.

Horner, Winifred Bryan. Introduction to *Rhetorical Memory and Delivery: Classical Concepts for Contemporary Composition and Communication,* edited by John Frederick Reynolds, ix–xii. Mahwah, NJ: Lawrence Erlbaum, 1993.

Horner, Winifred Bryan. "The Scottish-American Connection and the Emergence of Belletristic Composition." In *Composition in Context: Essays in Honor of Donald C. Stewart,* edited by W. Ross Winterowd and Vincent Gillespie, 28–45. Carbondale: Southern Illinois University Press, 1991.

Ferreira-Buckley, Linda, and Winifred Bryan Horner. "Writing Instruction in Great Britain: The Eighteenth and Nineteenth Centuries." In *A Short History of Writing Instruction: From Ancient Greece to Twentieth-Century America,* edited by James J. Murphy, 121–149. Davis, CA: Hermagoras, 1990.

Horner, Winifred Bryan. "Nineteenth-Century Rhetoric at the Universities of Aberdeen and St. Andrews with an Annotated Bibliography of Archival Materials." *Rhetoric Society Quarterly* 20 (Summer 1990): 173–186.

Horner, Winifred Bryan. "The Roots of Writing Instruction: Eighteenth- and Nineteenth-Century Britain." *Rhetoric Review* 7 (Spring 1990): 322–345.

Horner, Winifred Bryan. "Nineteenth-Century Scottish Rhetoric: The Missing Link between Classical and Modern." In *Discourse Studies in Honor of James L. Kinneavy*, edited by Rosalind J. Gabin, 41–62. Potomac, MD: Scripta Humanistica, 1989.

Horner, Winifred Bryan. "Rhetoric in the Liberal Arts: Nineteenth-Century Scottish Universities." In *The Rhetorical Tradition and Modern Writing*, edited by James J. Murphy, 85–95. New York: Modern Language Association, 1983.

Horner, Winifred Bryan. "Speech-Act Theory and Writing." *Forum: A Newsletter of the English Composition Board* 3 (Fall 1981): 9–11.

Horner, Winifred Bryan. "I'm Fed Up with Family Togetherness," *Ladies Home Journal*, October 1958.

Horner, Winifred Bryan. "How Long Can We Stay on the Farm?" *Saturday Evening Post*, April 14, 1956.

PUBLICATIONS IN HONOR OF WINIFRED BRYAN HORNER

"Tributes to Winifred Bryan Horner (1922–2014)." *Peitho: The Journal of the Coalition of Women Scholars in the History of Rhetoric and Composition* 16, no. 2 (Spring/Summer 2014): 114–145.

Eble, Michelle F., and Lynée Lewis Gaillet, eds. *Stories of Mentoring: Theory and Praxis*. Anderson, SC: Parlor, 2008.

Enos, Theresa, ed. *Learning from the Histories of Rhetoric: Essays in Honor of Winifred Bryan Horner*. Carbondale: Southern Illinois University Press, 1993.

ACKNOWLEDGMENTS

No words of gratitude can ever express how much I owe to Win Horner's family in the writing of this book. They understood from the beginning that this was Win's project, not mine, but they were generous in their critique of how I put it together. I want to thank Win's husband, Dave Horner, daughter Win Grace, and daughter Beth Horner for reading every word of this manuscript, sometimes in multiple versions, and giving me thoughtful feedback. At times they were concerned when Win got the facts wrong or played fast and loose with chronology. I did not always agree to change things they thought Win got wrong, but in the end, they all agreed that we should basically leave Win's words alone, that she would have wanted it that way. Importantly, I thank them all for leaving the final decisions up to me.

Over the years, my husband and I got to know both Win and Dave, a gentle soul who is still our close friend. Win's daughter Beth, who lives in Chicago, spent hours placing her mother's folders in labeled brown envelopes that she then filed in large boxes, carefully dated and stacked in the closets of the apartment where Win and Dave moved in 2012. Those boxes made their way from Dave's closets to my home study, as did stacks of Water Oaks journals, travel diaries, and scrapbooks created by Win during all the years of the family adventures. Beth made sure I was able to peruse these chronicles, many of which I had not seen before, and she tracked down many photos before the book was done. I was also fortunate to be able to have conversations with Win's eldest daughter, Win, who lives in Columbia and read the draft of the book, and with her older son, Richard, when he visited here with Dave. "She was one of a kind," they all told me on different occasions—both a tribute and, perhaps, a caution. I have tried to listen carefully and not provide a halo for Win that did not actually fit her head.

The most important gift anyone can give a writer is to read her work and give her good, honest feedback. In addition to thanking the Horner family for this, I also thank the women in our book group—Moray Loring Kiehl, Kim Ryan, Colette Schaef, Betty Acree, Coletta Eichenberger, and Gertrude Lindiner-Stawski—who read the completed manuscript draft and talked with me about what worked and what needed more attention. Win was a member of our book group, so these women knew her when she was at her most serious (as when we were discussing death and suicide) and when she was at her most mischievous (as when she might pointedly recount a particular incident that rubbed her the wrong way, especially regarding politics related to women's rights, Planned Parenthood, or discrimination). She brought her true self in all its delightful permutations to the book group, regaling us with her stories and making jokes about her bad habit of keeping two or three different calendars, which, rather than keeping her more organized, of course hindered her ability to keep her dates straight.

I also want to thank Kate (earlier referred to as Kathy) Loring, Win's friend from her Michigan years in graduate school. Kate read portions of the manuscript and talked with me about their friendship, which flourished in spite of the fact that Win was thirty years older than she. Her perspective on Win as a fifty-year-old graduate student was particularly helpful to me and helped us become closer as Kate's own mother, Moray, was dying.

I want to thank my former PhD student Darcy Holtgrave for driving to Win's apartment week after week in 2013 and early 2014 with her video camera and audio recorder. Quietly and professionally, she set up the equipment and sat listening while Win and I talked. Occasionally Win would turn to acknowledge Darcy and ask her a question or say something to make her laugh. No matter where she was, Win never forgot who was in the room.

I thank my transcriptionist, Teresa Bergen, who patiently transcribed every word of my interviews and conversations with Win. In a world of hypermedia, I could place the interviews in my Dropbox and Teresa, working in Oregon, would retrieve then, transcribe them, and send the transcriptions to me via email. Her help was invaluable to this project.

I need to thank the executive assistant in the English Department at MU, Sharon Black, who has graciously assisted me in many of my endeavors over the years. For this book, she and her work-study students retyped many of Win's farm stories and other materials that I had located in her boxes but that were too old and brittle to be scanned. Their work helped me flesh out this book in significant ways. Sharon also served as my most careful final reader, making sure the manuscript was ready for the press.

I thank Gary Dunham and Janice Frisch at Indiana University Press for encouraging me to submit this manuscript. The manuscript I sent to them was improved immeasurably by Janice's sensitive editing skills. I truly appreciate all the time and energy she devoted to this book; every edit she suggested served to make it so much better. Two celebrated folklorists, Jane Beck and Patricia Sawin, took the time to read my work as outside readers and provide suggestions for improvement. More than anything, I am gratified that the readers were able to understand the scope of this enterprise, see the value in Win's story for future readers, and laugh out loud at her humorous anecdotes.

Finally, I thank my husband, Sandy Rikoon, for his encouragement and support for my work. He reminds me to live well and do what makes me happy. Once, rather recently, when I was feeling guilty about staying holed up in my study working on this book rather than helping him in the garden, Sandy quietly assured me, "It's not a contest." Which pretty much sums it up. He knows I'd rather be writing than almost anything else, something I most definitely had in common with Win Horner.

In 1991, Win Horner established the Winifred Horner Fellowship for single parent graduate students in English at the University of Missouri. Proceeds from the sale of this book will be contributed to this fellowship in Win's name.

Win Horner and Elaine J. Lawless, Conley House, University of Missouri, 2010. *Photograph from the author's collection.*

ELAINE J. LAWLESS is Curators' Distinguished Professor Emerita of English and Folklore Studies, Women's and Gender Studies, and Religious Studies at the University of Missouri, where she first met Win Horner in 1983. Lawless is author of eight scholarly books, most recently *Women Escaping Violence: Empowerment through Narrative* (2001), *Troubling Violence: A Performance Project,* with M. Heather Carver (2009), and *When They Blew the Levee: Politics, Race, and Community in Pinhook, Missouri,* with D. Todd Lawrence (2018). She served as general editor of the *Journal of American Folklore* for six years (2000–2006) and was elected president of the American Folklore Society in 2006. She is the recipient of the Missouri Governor's Award for Excellence in Teaching (2012) and both the Kenneth Goldstein Award for Lifetime Academic Leadership (2007) and the Lifetime Scholarly Achievement Award (2015) from the American Folklore Society, as well as many other awards for both teaching and scholarship.

CPSIA information can be obtained
at www.ICGtesting.com
Printed in the USA
LVOW06s2140081217
559124LV00047B/1108/P

9 780253 032355